Social W
P. O. Box 70,645
East Tennessee State University
Johnson City, TN 37614-0645

REACHING HIGH-RISK FAMILIES

Intensive Family Preservation in Human Services

MODERN APPLICATIONS OF SOCIAL WORK

An Aldine de Gruyter Series of Texts and Monographs

Series Editor

James K. Whittaker

Ralph E. Anderson and Irl Carter, **Human Behavior in the Social Environment: A Social Systems Approach** (Fourth Edition)

Richard P. Barth and Marianne Berry, **Adoption and Disruption: Rates, Risks, and Responses**

Larry K. Brendtro and Arlin E. Ness, **Re-Educating Troubled Youth: Environments for Teaching and Treatment**

Kathleen Ell and Helen Northen, **Families and Health Care: Psychosocial Practice**

James Garbarino, **Children and Families in the Social Environment**

James Garbarino, Patrick E. Brookhouser, Karen J. Authier, and Associates, **Special Children—Special Risks: The Maltreatment of Children with Disabilities**

James Garbarino, Cynthia J. Schellenbach, Janet Sebes, and Associates, **Troubled Youth, Troubled Families: Understanding Families At-Risk for Adolescent Maltreatment**

Anthony M. Graziano and Kevin C. Mooney, **Children and Behavior Therapy**

Roberta R. Greene, **Social Work with the Aged and Their Families**

Robert M. Moroney, **Shared Responsibility: Families and Social Policy**

Norman A. Polansky, **Integrated Ego Psychology**

Steven P. Schinke (ed.), **Behavioral Methods in Social Welfare**

George Thorman, **Helping Troubled Families: A Social Work Perspective**

Albert E. Trieschman, James K. Whittaker, and Larry K. Brendtro, **The Other 23 Hours: Child-Care Work with Emotionally Disturbed Children in a Therapeutic Milieu**

Harry H. Vorrath and Larry K. Brendtro, **Positive Peer Culture** (Second Edition)

Heather B. Weiss and Francine Jacobs (eds.), **Evaluating Family Programs**

James K. Whittaker and James Garbarino, **Social Support Networks: Informal Helping in the Human Services**

James K. Whittaker, Jill Kinney, Elizabeth M. Tracy, and Charlotte Booth (eds.), **Reaching High-Risk Families: Intensive Family Preservation in Human Services**

James K. Whittaker and Elizabeth M. Tracy, **Social Treatment, Second Edition: An Introduction to Interpersonal Helping in Social Work Practice**

REACHING HIGH-RISK FAMILIES

Intensive Family Preservation
in Human Services

Edited by

James K. Whittaker, Jill Kinney,
Elizabeth M. Tracy, and Charlotte Booth

Aldine de Gruyter
New York

About the Editors

James K. Whittaker is Professor of Social Work and Director of the Social Work Ph.D. Program at the University of Washington.

Jill Kinney is Executive Director, Behavioral Sciences Institute, Federal Way, Washington.

Elizabeth M. Tracy is Assistant Professor, Mandel School of Applied Social Sciences, Case Western Reserve University.

Charlotte Booth is Associate Director, Behavioral Sciences Institute, Federal Way, Washington.

Copyright © 1990 by Walter de Gruyter, Inc., New York

All rights reserved. No part of this publication may be reproduced or transmitted in any form or by any means, electronic or mechanical, including photocopy, recording, or any information storage and retrieval system, without prior permission in writing from the publisher.

ALDINE DE GRUYTER
A Division of Walter de Gruyter, Inc., New York
200 Saw Mill River Road
Hawthorne, New York 10532

Library of Congress Cataloging-in-Publication Data

Reaching high-risk families: intensive family preservation in human
    services/James K. Whittaker . . . [et al.].
        p.   cm.—(Modern applications of social work)
    Includes bibliographical references.
    ISBN 0-202-36057-1.—ISBN 0-202-36058-X (pbk.)
    1. Family social work—United States.   I. Whittaker, James K.
II. Series.
HV699.R38   1990
362.82′8′0973—dc20   89-18008
                                                                                          CIP

Manufactured in the United States of America
10 9 8 7 6 5 4 3 2 1

CONTENTS

Contents

Chapter 9

Creating Social Change: "Mission-Oriented" Research and Entrepreneurship
Mark Fraser and Shirley Leavitt

Chapter 10

Intensive Family Preservation Services: Broadening the Vision for Prevention
J. David Hawkins and Richard F. Catalano

LIST OF CONTRIBUTORS

Richard Barth
School of Social Welfare
University of California
Berkeley, CA 94720

Betty Blythe
School of Social Work
University of Pittsburgh
2206 Cathedral of Learning
Pittsburgh, PA 14260

Charlotte Booth
Associate Director
Behavioral Sciences Institute
1717 South 341 Place
Federal Way, WA 98003

Richard F. Catalano
School of Social Work
University of Washington
4101 15th Avenue N.E. JH-30
Seattle, WA 98195

Elizabeth Cole, Consultant
Children's Services Consultants
286 Thompson Mill Road
New Hope, PA 18938

Mark W. Fraser
Graduate School of Social Work
University of Utah
Salt Lake City, UT 84112

David Haapala, Executive Director
Behavioral Sciences Institute
Ninth Avenue Center, Bldg. A
34004 9th Ave. S. Suite 8
Federal Way, WA 98003

J. David Hawkins
School of Social Work
University of Washington
4101 15th Avenue N.E. JH-30
Seattle, WA 98003

Jill Kinney, Executive Director
Behavioral Sciences Institute
Ninth Avenue Center, Bldg. A
34004 9th Ave. S. Suite 8
Federal Way, WA 98003

Shelley Leavitt
Director of Training
Behavioral Sciences Institute
1717 South 341 Place
Federal Way, WA 98003

Anthony N. Maluccio
School of Social Work
University of Connecticut
1798 Asylum Avenue
West Hartford, CT 06117-2698

Brenda McGowan
School of Social Work
Columbia University
McVicar, 622 West 113th Street
New York, NY 10025

Douglas Nelson, Deputy Director
Center for the Study of Social Work
1250 Eye Street N.W. Suite 503
Washington, DC 20005

Peter Pecora
Graduate School of Social Work
University of Utah
Salt Lake City, UT 84112

Eliazabeth Tracy
Mandel School of Applied Social
   Sciences
Case Western Reserve University
2035 Abington Road
Cleveland, OH 44106

James K. Whittaker, Director
Social Welfare Ph.D. Program
School of Social Work
University of Washington
4101 15th Avenue N.E. JH-30
Seattle, WA 98195

Foreword

The helping professions are, by definition, designed to deal with human problems. Pain, depression, skill deficits, and innumerable other human feelings and attitudes are the stuff of everyday work for helpers. Yet for certain populations or human circumstances, we often respond to problems in manners shaped more by tradition or habit than is helpful. Sometimes we create our own limits to success because of a perceived image of "professional" behavior or role. At other times one, or sometimes many, organizational constraints impinge on our ability to be truly responsive to the problems we face.

Once in a while a fundamentally different approach appears that holds promise of filling a gap in services or meeting a typically neglected or poorly served population in ways that challenge conventional practice wisdom. One ought to be skeptical of such proposals, for many are made and few are proven. But how should one respond when such an approach holds up to observations and evaluations that seem to meet or exceed the norm for such assessments of effectiveness? How then should those whose lives are committed to research or teaching react to and confront unusual and apparently effective models of practice that challenge accepted principles?

In my opinion, Homebuilders is such an approach. It is time-limited while most are open-ended. Services are short-term and home based, not long-term and office based. Homebuilders crosses the traditional barriers of hard and soft services. These contrasts and other related issues are further explored and expanded upon in the following chapters.

Reaching High-Risk Families is the result of one effort to come to terms with the implications of such a strikingly different approach to services for social work teaching and research. It may encourage examination of ways to incorporate these developments into methods courses, research, administration, policy, and other aspects of professional thinking and teaching. At their most ambitious, the information and insights presented here may initiate a fundamental revision in the manner in which we approach children and families in the social service, mental health and juvenile justice fields. These principles have already led to a multidisciplinary and multi-sector collaboration to address service needs free (or at least freer than usual) of the inherited definitions and boundaries which often are exaggerated in the human services field.

Each contributor to this volume acknowledges the unfinished nature of this inquiry, yet it is a good beginning. The Homebuilders model, while well into its adolescence, continues to develop, adapt, and mature while remaining remarkably true to its origins and core convictions.

Reaching High-Risk Families should provoke and challenge; I hope it will inspire and encourage. It is not only timely, but a welcome addition to the discourse on social work education and practice.

Peter W. Forsythe
New York, NY

Introduction to the Volume

Social work as a profession has long been concerned with strategies for effectively helping the multiproblem family: from Mary Richmond's (1917) careful delineation of familial and environmental assessment, through the pioneering work of the St. Paul Project (Birt, 1956) with high risk families, to the conceptual synthesis offered recently by Hartman and Laird (1983) on the contours and boundaries of family centered social work practice. While differing in theoretical orientation, contributors to this volume share a common belief in the value of examining exemplary practice models as a guide to good professional education.

This work was supported by a grant from the Edna McConnell Clark Foundation. An earlier draft of this volume *(Improving Practice Technology for Work with High Risk Families: Lessons from the Homebuilders Social Work Education Project*, 1988) was printed for limited distribution by the Center for Social Welfare Research, University of Washington, School of Social Work.

Happily, the rapid emergence of intensive family preservation services designed to prevent unnecessary out of home placement, and the equally rapid ascendancy of the Homebuilders model as perhaps the best known and most clearly articulated model of family preservation practice, afforded a group of social work educators, staff and consultants the unique opportunity to address some critical questions:

- To what extent does the Homebuilders model of aiding families contain implications for the content of practice methods curricula in graduate professional education?
- To what extent does the Homebuilders model present challenges to the teaching of research and, in particular, clinical practice evaluation?
- Are there organizational and administrative features inherent in the Homebuilders agency structure that might have implications for administration courses?
- What is the theoretical and empirical base for Homebuilders, and other intensive family preservation services?

- What is the policy context for intensive family preservation services generally, and how ought we to *think* of such family centered
  services—e.g., where do they fit on the continuum? What are their
  limits and potential?

We were clear at the outset that we were not viewing a fully developed
model, nor did we begin with the presumption that the Homebuilders approach defined the family work task in human services. We *were* intrigued,
however, (and continue to be) at the wealth of practical information on family assessment, engagement and intervention contained in the Homebuilders
model. Whether our discussion focused on treatment, organization, or evaluation, Homebuilders provided a useful point of reference grounded in the
experience of current practice. Whatever our different conclusions on this or
that aspect of the Homebuilders model, we unanimously agree on the value
of "studying" a whole cloth, practice approach, *as it is presently practiced:*
including treatment technique, organization/administration, knowledge base
and evaluation. A definite motivation for this volume is the belief that these
areas of practice and knowledge are all too often compartmentalized in
professional curricula in such a way that students learn about the individual
"trees," but rarely glimpse the "forest."

The results of our effort are limited by individual perspective and group
design. We neither asked for nor received a pledge of faith in Homebuilders;
varying amounts of skepticism remain about the model itself and about the
broader field of family preservation services. Similarly, we did not impose
a common template on all chapters—one which, for example, might have
taken us back to the class, field and curricular implications for each topic.
The resultant chapters are thus varied in scope and depth, but we hope
stimulating and useful. Each of the chapters could profitably find a place in
conventional human service education courses. Still, much of the work of
teasing out the *specifics* of curriculum development remains to be done.

Our primary focus is on the social work discipline and, in particular,
on implications for professional social work education. We believe there is
much practical information in the chapters to follow that has implications
across disciplines. We are also mindful of the fact that specific implications
for such sister disciplines as clinical and community psychology, counseling, community health nursing, and others remain to be developed. We hope
the insights contained in *Reaching High-Risk Families* will serve as a stimulus to further discussion in those disciplines. Effective and humane family
preservation services are not the province of a single discipline. Similarly, we
recognize that while much of our discussion focuses on applications in the
child welfare system, the concept of family preservation has considerable
implications for other social service areas as well: mental health, juvenile
justice, maternal and child health, and developmental disabilities. In fact,

it was instructive to us as educators and researchers to note the extent to which Homebuilders has successfully adapted their approach to work within each of these systems. We believe a critical task for child and family policy and practice is to discover the relatively compartmentalized interventive approaches that exist in each of these service streams, and examine their applications to other client problems and service sectors. The same case can be made for technology and knowledge transfer across the life span. For example, successful programs to keep the frail elderly in their own homes may have something to offer Homebuilders—and vice versa. Stated simply: How do the "good ideas" get from one sector of service, from one client population to another?

In addressing this last point of knowledge and technology transfer, we identify a critical gap in the existing chain of professional education—agency-based training and development of model service programs. Nowhere in human services education do we find the equivalent of centers for applied technology that so often exist between professional schools of engineering and key sectors of industry, like micro-computers or aerospace. Similarly, and as noted earlier, we have few analogues where model service programs themselves—in all their complexity—*become* the core case material for professional education. We believe that programs like Homebuilders, the Prenatal Early Infancy Project (Olds et al., 1986) and other similar model efforts should represent for graduate education in the human services what Microsoft and Apple Computers represent for any first rate school of engineering or business administration. We are convinced of the need for new mechanisms to join the university's traditional mission of knowledge development and dissemination with the agency's historic mandate of service and training. Hopefully, this book will provide some further stimulus to that discussion.

We realize that our focus in this volume is limited to one particular segment of the service continuum. From a policy perspective, this may seem less than satisfactory in light of the need for similar in-depth study of more basic primary preventive approaches and traditional service areas such as regular and specialized foster family care, specialized adoption, school-based intervention, and residential and day treatment. We view these and other services as necessary, but not sufficient components of an overall continuum of child, youth, and family services. Moreover, in a political arena where competition is often fierce for scant resources, we are mindful of the criticism of some thoughtful analysts that an over emphasis on short-term, goal-oriented service designed to prevent unnecessary placement may divert attention from the need for more universally available general social services for families, and may result in government's being satisfied with a "minimalist" approach to family service (Kahn, 1988).

While misplaced concreteness and political expedience are ever present dangers in any discussion involving family policy, they should not retard program experimentation, expansion, and critical discussion of the strengths, limits, and critical components of family preservation services. If for no other purpose, this discussion should serve to re-evaluate the basic presumption of the traditional child welfare system that based it's services on "child rescue" through out-of-home placement rather than on family maintenance and support. Even if, as Wald (1988) suggests, we are going "too fast" in the expansion of family preservation practice, the field and ultimately families themselves will benefit from thorough and sustained debate (based on empirical evidence rather than what is *presumed* to be more intensiveness in service) on what it takes to prevent family disruption, how such services are best designed and delivered, and what the benefits/costs are of such an approach. We join with those who criticize the over-enthusiasm for family-based services—particularly when such services are loosely defined and lacking in focus and intensity—and endorse efforts to link family preservation practice to an argument for a much broader, comprehensive and less categorical approach to social services for all families, in particular those where children are at-risk for a range of adverse developmental outcomes. We hope the issues raised in the chapters to follow will provide a stimulus to further inquiry.

The chapter by Whittaker and Tracy enumerates the common characteristics of family preservation services and develops some preliminary implications for professional education. Nelson's chapter treats in more detail the *meaning* of family preservation and its implications for services. The chapter by Kinney, Haapala, Booth and Leavitt traces the history and development of the Homebuilders model and provides a skeletal overview of the basic features of the program. McGowan elaborates the policy context for Homebuilders and related family preservation services. Barth examines the knowledge foundations of family preservation services in a chapter most clearly related to human behavior and social environment content and conventional approaches to family therapy instruction. Maluccio develops the implications of intensive family preservation services for the teaching of direct practice skills and knowledge. At the meso-level, Pecora examines some of the administrative practices and organizational requisites of the Homebuilders model and identifies challenges for the teaching of administration and planning. Blythe explores the challenge and potential of a Homebuilders type service for measuring practice effectiveness, with clear implications for a clinical research sequence. Fraser and Leavitt examine the philosophical/motivational base of Homebuilders as an agency and explore implications for innovation and model development in family and child practice. Finally, Hawkins and Catalano locate Homebuilders in the spectrum of preventive services and identify linkages between primary prevention and family preservation services.

Our discussion has raised the issue of the fundamental relationship between a broad based professional curriculum and a more narrowly focused training strategy: what is (or ought to be) the relationship between the two? Where does one begin and the other end? In many ways, Homebuilders (as an exemplar of model programs) doesn't neatly fit into existing graduate curricula. The components of this model—e.g., treatment, evaluation, organization—operate in an integrated manner. In graduate professional education these components are often taught separately, and frequently without reference to actual programs. We hope that the chapters to follow will stimulate thinking about ways in which "whole cloth" programs can become more of a focal point for professional courses and sequences.

The concept and development of this volume benefitted from an all too rare event in professional education: sustained, lively and critical discussion among research-scholars and practitioner-administrators from a model service program. Numerous staff members participated in selected presentations and greatly enhanced the quality of discussion. These included, in addition to the four senior staff participants in the seminar: Peg Marckworth, Colleen Cline, Deborah Perman, Jack Chambers, Sue McCarthy and Mary White. The present and former deans of the School of Social Work at the University of Washington—Nancy Hooyman and Scott Briar—provided unwavering support for the project from start to finish and encouraged in numerous ways the closer articulation of the worlds of research, practice and teaching. From the Clark Foundation, President Peter Bell and Vice President Peter Forsythe provided early encouragement and sustained support for the seminar discussion. Susan Notkin made valuable contributions along the way and Stephanie Busby was extraordinarily helpful in arranging our New York City meeting. Sharon Christiansen and Claire Frost of Social Work Continuing Education performed admirably in arranging all of the logistics of our meetings and providing an atmosphere conducive to critical discussion. Mary Grembowski provided high quality typing support, and Virginia Senechal deserves special thanks for her sharp critical eye and considerable patience and skill in editing the final manuscript in a very compressed period of time. Our publisher, Trev Leger, was a source of support and encouragement from the beginning. Finally, we are in debt to all practitioners who work with families at risk of disruption—in particular, the many therapists whose clinical skill, imagination, creativity and endurance continue to shape and re-form the "Homebuilders" model. Their collected practice wisdom provided depth and background to all our discussions. We are in their debt.

James K. Whittaker
Seattle, WA

References

Kahn, A. J. (1988). *Societal change and social work: The next decade.* Paper prepared for Plenary Session, 90th Anniversary Celebration, Columbia University School of Social Work.

Olds, D. L., Henderson, C. R., Chamberlin, R., and Tatelbaum, R. (1986). Preventing child abuse and neglect: A randomized trial of nurse home visitation. *Pediatrics, 78,* 65–78.

Wald, M. (1988). Family preservation: Are we moving too fast? *Public Welfare, 3,* 33–38.

Chapter 1

Family Preservation Services and Education for Social Work Practice: Stimulus and Response

James K. Whittaker and Elizabeth M. Tracy

Rationale for Family Preservation Services

Families with children at risk for out-of-home placement have long been a concern in the child welfare field. Traditionally, parents of children at risk for placement were viewed more as part of the problem, rather than as part of the solution. Out-of-home placement was seen as a substitute for an inadequate family. Few attempts were made to include parents in the decision making process prior to placement, or in the treatment process during placement (Whittaker, 1979). As a result of a renewed emphasis on "permanency," however, child welfare services have experienced a shift from an overriding emphasis on child placement to a focus on family support (Stehno, 1986). This shift has affected the entire continuum of child welfare services. Placement and in-home services need no longer be viewed as mutually exclusive (Small and Whittaker, 1979).

In its broadest sense, permanency planning refers to activities undertaken to ensure continuity of care for children, whether that be action to keep families together, to reunite families, or to find permanent homes for children (Maluccio, Fein, and Olmstead, 1986). Strengthening the family's knowledge, skills, and resources for parenting has become a critical concern. A variety of services designed to strengthen families and to prevent out-of-home placement have emerged. In addition, supportive family services are increasingly recognized as elements in the aftercare service plan following placement (Whittaker and Maluccio, 1988). A still small but increasing number of residential programs incorporate services to families as part of

1

preplacement and after care, as well as during the placement process. Over-all, there is increased commitment to families of children in placement, as well as those at risk of placement.

Definition and Components of Intensive Family Preservation Services

Intensive family preservation services (IFPS), as discussed in this volume, are characterized by highly intensive services, delivered generally in the client's home, for a relatively brief period of time. Family preservation services are closely related to "family-centered social services" (Hutchinson, 1983; Bryce and Lloyd, 1981; Lloyd and Bryce, 1984) in philosophy and rationale, but generally provide more intensive services to families over a shorter time period. The primary goals of IFPS are (1) to protect children, (2) to maintain and strengthen family bonds, (3) to stabilize the crisis situation, (4) to increase the family's skills and competencies, and (5) to facilitate the family's use of a variety of formal and informal helping resources. Typically, IFPS focus on the current situation; the intent is not to "cure" the family. The time-limited nature of these services sets upper limits on what outcomes can reasonably be expected, but the intensity of service, coupled with referral at the point of imminent risk of placement, produces a situation capable of dramatic change.

While there is no clear consensus on the exact nature of family preservation services and wide variation in how such services are delivered—or even by what name they should be called—such services are increasingly popular in child welfare. The National Resource Center on Family-Based Services, in Iowa City, currently lists over 200 such programs; by comparison, the first directory in 1982 listed only 20 programs. Over 60 separate programs are administered by state and county agencies, and a number of states have passed home-based legislation and are developing statewide programs. Still, many communities have limited preventive services.

Family preservation services differ along a number of dimensions: staffing patterns, auspices (public/private), target population, client eligibility, intensity of service, and components of service. Pecora, Fraser, Haapala, and Bartlome (1987) have identified key dimensions in the areas of treatment technique and services, program structure, and program outcomes, which can be used to compare and contrast different IFPS programs. These dimensions are helpful in making comparisons among different programs and in identifying key components of IFPS. The primary focus of this volume is the Homebuilders model, which is described more fully by Kinney et al. (this volume, Chapter 3), and which represents one end of the continuum of intensity and brevity of services.

Notwithstanding the differences among programs, there are a number of shared characteristics and features. Some reflect the nature of services delivered, while others reflect staff attitudes and values which are distinctive to this type of service. Elements common to both Homebuilders and other family preservation services programs include:

- Only families at risk of imminent placement are accepted.
- Services are crisis-oriented. Families are seen as soon as possible after referral is made.
- Staff are accessible, maintaining flexible hours 7 days a week. For example, Homebuilders give out their home phone numbers to families.
- Intake and assessment processes ensure that no child is left in danger.
- Although problems of individuals may be addressed, the focus is on the family as a unit, rather than on parents or children as problematic individuals.
- Workers see families in the families' homes, making frequent visits convenient to each family's schedule. Many services are also provided in school and neighborhood settings.
- The service approach combines teaching skills to family members, helping the family obtain necessary resources and services, and counseling based on an understanding of how each family functions as a unit.
- Services are generally based on identified family needs rather than strict eligibility categories.
- Each worker carries a small caseload at any given time. A limited number of programs make use of teams. Homebuilders work individually with team back up but have caseloads of only two families at a time.
- Programs limit the length of involvement with the family to a short period, typically between 1 and 5 months. Homebuilders typically work with a family over a 4- to 6-week period.

In short, the service delivery features of intensive preservation programs are designed to engage families in service (even those families who have "failed" in other counseling attempts), to keep them in service intensively for a time-limited period, and to increase the likelihood that they will benefit from service. IFPS provide a combination of services designed to deal with crisis situations, to enhance family functioning, to meet both concrete and clinical service needs, and to decrease the family's isolation. Most IFPS work from family strengths and include use of extended family, community, and neighborhood resources (Lloyd and Bryce, 1984). These services make maximum use of a variety of worker tasks and roles—counselor, parent trainer, advocate, consultant, and resource broker.

Conceptual Framework

While the notion of providing support to parents is not necessarily new (Sinanoglu and Maluccio, 1981), a number of emerging trends within child welfare services are congruent with and have added to the impetus for family preservation services. The development, expansion, and future of family preservation programs take on more meaning when viewed in the broader context of child welfare service systems.

Theoretical Perspectives

The child's need for continuity and stability, and the need to protect the parent–child bond from unnecessary state intervention have been recurring themes (Goldstein, Freud, and Solnit, 1973). The significance of the biological tie to the child's identity (Laird, 1979), and the impact of separation on parent and child (Jenkins, 1981) are also important theoretical factors. Family integrity and the primacy of the parent–child attachment are among the strongest values in American society. Family preservation programs are congruent with this perspective since the primary purpose of these services is to avert unnecessary placement and to enable the child to remain at home safely.

Another theoretical perspective related to family preservation programs is the shift within human development research from a personalistic to an ecological perspective (Bronfenbrenner, 1979; Garbarino, 1982), which looks to the environment as both the source of and solution to children's and families' problems. This view considers both client's competencies and clients' environments (Whittaker, Schinke, and Gilchrist, 1986). The implications of this perspective are: (1) view the family as the unit of service, (2) increase parental skills and competencies, and (3) remove or reduce obstacles that interfere with coping (Maluccio, Fein, and Olmstead, 1986). This perspective is also congruent with the goals and methods of family preservation programs.

Child Welfare Reforms

Growing dissatisfaction with out-of-home placement, particularly foster care, has led to the search for alternatives and major policy shifts in legislation. During the 1960s and 1970s, the most frequent criticisms of the placement process within child welfare services included: (1) children were often removed from homes more frequently than necessary and often by default, due to the lack of alternatives; (2) children from minority, poor, and single parents were greatly overrepresented in foster care; (3) children were often placed in unstable and unnecessarily restrictive settings; and (4) little effort was made to keep biological parents involved, or to facilitate reunification of children and parents (Knitzer, Allan, and McGowan, 1978; Maas and Engler, 1959; Shyne and Schroeder, 1978). Fiscal policies favored out-of-home placement as opposed to preventive or supportive services. In many cases, biological families had continuing needs for services and supports even after the child's return home (Fein, Maluccio, Hamilton, and Ward, 1983; Barth and Berry, 1987). The underlying hypothesis for family preservation services is that many more children could remain with their families if services were provided earlier and more intensively.

The passage of PL 96-272, The Adoption Assistance and Child Welfare Act of 1980, added new impetus to family preservation services. PL 96-272 requires that "reasonable efforts" be made to prevent family disruption, to reunite families where separation has been necessary, and to enable children to be placed in alternative permanent settings failing reunification. While the standards for "reasonable efforts" are not agreed upon, family preservation programs are increasingly included in the range of prevention and reunification services to be made available to families (National Center for Youth Law, 1987).

Economic Factors

Rising costs of substitute care have led to the search for less expensive alternatives. The National Resource Center on Family-Based Services (1983) estimates that the total program cost for home based intervention does not exceed the cost of one foster care placement. While per diem costs of IFPS appear higher than traditional casework methods, cost savings per child are dramatic and are multiplied even further when more than one child in a family is prevented from entering out-of-home care. Individual programs, such as Homebuilders in Washington State, and Oregon's Intensive Family Services, report savings of approximately $2500 or more (depending on the type of placement) for every child kept out of placement for three months.

As Magura (1981) points out, the basis for determining cost effectiveness is the subject of considerable debate and controversy. Estimates of cost savings are often based on variable factors, such as how many children would have entered care, for how long, and in what types of placements. Few studies make these assumptions clear, and when they do, they often assume the worst scenario—that all children served would have entered the most expensive placement. It is also important to calculate length and intensity of services, costs of ancillary services, and costs of initiating family preservation services, which requires staff development and training, particularly as part of large publicly funded agencies. Cost-effectiveness analysis, which describes program costs as well as outcome effects, has been suggested as a viable way to measure the costs and benefits of prevention programs (Armstrong, 1982). A rigorous cost/benefit analysis of IFPS remains to be done.

Service Effectiveness

Initial results of early projects, such as the St. Paul Family Centered Program, increased enthusiasm for home-based preventive intervention (Maybanks and Bryce, 1979; Bryce and Lloyd, 1981). Early permanency planning projects also increased confidence in our ability to create and maintain permanent homes for children (e.g., Oregon Project and Alameda Project). It is estimated that nationally between 70 to 90% of children who receive home-based care services are enabled to remain home (National Resource Center on Family-Based Services, 1983). Individual family preservation programs, such as Homebuilders, Oregon's Intensive Family Service, Utah's Family Preservation Program, and Florida's Crisis Counseling Program, report even higher rates.

Initial enthusiasm with service effectiveness has been tempered somewhat; reviews of intensive home based interventions find relatively few studies with statistically significant differences in placement rates for those served by these programs (Frankel, 1987; Magura, 1981; Stein, 1985). There have been few controlled studies. Without the use of control or comparison groups, it is difficult to determine the true effectiveness of the program. There are a number of methodological problems in comparing evaluations of family preservation programs, including (1) the lack of clear, consistent intake, and eligibility standards, (2) poor specification of the services delivered or the integrity of the services delivered over time, (3) nonstandard outcome measures, and (4) a lack of long-term follow-up data and data analysis methods which are necessary for an examination of the relative effectiveness of various program components. There is a need for more rigorous studies of service outcomes of family preservation programs.

A fuller discussion of program evaluation methodology will be presented in subsequent chapters. Evaluation issues are under general discussion in the field, and figure prominently for those administrators, legislators, and practitioners in the field. For example, the California legislature was sufficiently confident in the success of IFPS services to mandate that in-home service programs must demonstrate a success rate of 75% in avoiding out-of-home placement 6 months after intervention, with increased success rates in subsequent years.

In summary, family preservation services appear to be congruent with a number of emerging trends in child welfare services: the desire for permanent homes for children; the use of least restrictive settings; the ecological perspective; foster care reform; and cost containment. In addition, the legal mandate for prevention services favors interest in and development of home-based services in the years to come.

Implications for Social Work Education

The service components and service delivery features of family preservation services hold a number of implications for the training and education of social work and other human service practitioners. The IFPS worker must be skillful in adapting and applying a broad range of theoretical knowledge gained in the classroom into a field based work setting. The following knowledge base and competencies appear requisite to this form of practice:

- A knowledge of the person-in-environment perspective and an understanding of the family as a unit;
- An ability to combine concrete and clinical services and to assess and intervene with formal as well as informal helping resources;
- An ability to assess and utilize family strengths, to engage families actively in helping efforts, and to establish clear goals with families;
- An ability to communicate and cooperate with a variety of service providers;
- Knowledge of how and when to teach parenting skills, life skills, communication skills, etc. to families;
- An ability to offer services that are compatible with cultural traditions and established cultural help seeking patterns;
- An understanding of the importance of evaluating clinical work—from single case studies to full scale rigorous program evaluation;
- Knowledge and skill in crisis intervention.

Future Trends/Issues in Family Preservation Services

A number of issues remain unresolved concerning intensive family preservation services and these will likely occupy researchers, practitioners, and administrators in the immediate future:

Defining Success

The criterion question is far from resolved in professional debate. Should simple absence of placement 60 or 90 days following termination of service be considered an adequate measure of success? Some considerable evidence is accumulating that intensive family based service may simply be post- poning placement and/or that children from at-risk families who remain at home may be subject to continued abuse at a rate higher than if they were placed (Jones, 1985; Wald, Carlsmith and Leiderman, 1988; Barth and Berry, 1987).

There is a need to consider outcomes other than placement status, to include more standardized measures of family and child functioning in a variety of settings, and to better understand which families can benefit from which family preservation services.

On the issue of placement per se, some studies have used more liberal criteria for success (e.g., percentage of *potential* placement days used) to discriminate between long-term out-of-home care and short-term shelter, or crisis care (AuClaire and Schwartz, 1986). More fundamentally, the "placement avoidance" criteria assumes out-of-home placement is always a negative outcome. Are there instances where service intensity (for example, brief placement in a drug or alcohol program for an adolescent) might count as a success rather than failure for intensive family based services? Studies such as that recently completed by Fraser, Pecora, and Haapala (1988) will hopefully provide the field with a broader range of potential criteria measures for intensive family preservation services.

Quality Control

Considerable diversity of program and language exists in the field of family based services. Ultimately, questions of caseload size, length and intensity of intervention, and training should lend themselves to empirical analysis of planned variations. For the short term, however, given the increasing interest in family-based services (of all kinds), one needs to exercise extreme caution in aggregating results across studies of programs. The issue of quality control is paramount since the primary reason most states and jurisdictions are interested in family preservation services is in response to the "reasonable efforts" provision of current federal legislation. A critical issue for programs like Homebuilders is the extent to which their approach to family helping is portable and can easily be adapted to a variety of cultural and geographic conditions. At this point, the danger is high that intensive family preservation services can come to mean so many different things that its saliency will be lost. This and related concerns propelled us to examine Homebuilders, as an exemplary model with well specified program elements, rather than the field of family based services in general.

Place in the Continuum

Should intensive family preservation services be seen as a discrete service in the overall continuum or as one manifestation of a more general approach to family helping which has application far beyond prevention of imminent out of home placement? For example, the Homebuilders service model has been applied with adoptive families facing disruptions. It may be that reunification programs that seek to return the child from out-of-home care to the biological parents may also benefit from the service features and components of IFPS. Elements of family preservation programs may find a place in aftercare as well as prevention services.

Another point of expansion for IFPS may be to client populations other than children and families. At present, IFPS serve children and youth from child welfare, mental health, juvenile corrections, and developmental disabilities service streams. IFPS may also be applicable to families stressed by the caregiving demands of adult children with chronic physical, mental, or emotional problems, and to families providing home care for older adults.

Organizational Requisites

Our brief exploration of the Homebuilders model impressed upon us the importance of organizational factors in effective family preservation services. We suspect that the relative importance attached to things like low caseload size (two families per worker), well specified preservice and in-service training, case evaluation, and peer consultation and supervision have a great deal to do with Homebuilders' successful replication, perhaps even more so than the particular treatment techniques involved. This raises an interesting question for professional education: whether the teaching of direct practice should be separate from the teaching of administrative and organization development, which raises the more fundamental issue of how graduate professional curricula ought to relate to model service programs. We hope this volume is a stimulus to further discussion on both of these issues.

References

Armstrong, K. A. (1982). Economic analysis of a child abuse and neglect treatment program. *Child Welfare, 62,* 3–13.

AuClaire, P., and Schwartz, I. (1986). *An evaluation of intensive home-based services for adolescents and their families as an alternative to out-of-home placement.* Minneapolis, Minnesota: Hubert H. Humphrey Institute for Public Affairs.

Barth, R. P., and Berry, M. (1987). Outcomes of child welfare services under permanency planning. *Social Service Review, 61,* 71-90.

Birt, C. (1956). Family-centered project of St. Paul. *Social Work, 1,* 41-47.

Bronfenbrenner, U. (1979). *The ecology of human development.* Cambridge: Harvard University Press.

Bryce, M., and Lloyd, J. C. (Eds.). (1981). *Treating families in the home: An alternative to placement.* Springfield, Il: Charles C. Thomas.

Fein, E., Maluccio, A. N., Hamilton, V. J., and Ward, D. E. (1983). After foster care: Outcomes of permanency planning for children. *Child Welfare, 62,* 485-558.

Frankel, H. (1987). Family-centered, home-based services in child protection: A review of the research. *Social Service Review, 62,* 137-157.

Fraser, M. W., Pecora, P. J., and Haapala, D. A. (1988). *Families in crisis: Findings from the Family-Based Intensive Treatment Research Project.* Salt Lake City: University of Utah, Graduate School of Social Work, Social Research Institute; and Federal Way, WA: Behavioral Sciences Institute.

Garbarino, J. (1982). *Children and families in the social environment.* New York: Aldine.

Goldstein, J., Freud, A., and Solnit, A. (1973). *Beyond the best interests of the child.* New York: Free Press.

Hartman, A., and Laird, J. (1983). *Family-centered social work practice.* New York: Free Press.

Hutchinson, J. (1983). *Family-centered social services: A model for child welfare agencies.* Iowa City: University of Iowa, National Resource Center for Family Based Services.

Jenkins, S. (1981). The tie that bonds. *In* A. Maluccio and P. A. Sinanoglu (Eds.), *The challenge of partnership: Working with parents of children in foster care,* pp. 39-51. New York: Child Welfare League of America.

Jones, M. A. (1985). *A second chance for families—five years later: Follow up of a program to prevent foster care.* New York: Child Welfare League of America.

Knitzer, J., Allen, M. L., and McGowan, B. G. (1978). *Children without homes.* Washington, DC: Children's Defense Fund.

Laird, J. (1979). An ecological approach to child welfare: Issues of family identity and continuity. *In* C. B. Germain (Ed.), *Social work practice: People and environments,* pp. 174-209. New York: Columbia University Press.

Lloyd, J. C., and Bryce, M. E. (1984). *Placement prevention and family reunification: A handbook for the family-centered service practitioner.* Iowa City: University of Iowa, National Resource Center for Family Based Services.

Magura, S. (1981). Are services to prevent foster care effective? *Children and Youth Services Review, 3,* 193-212.

Maas, H. S., and Engler, R. E., Jr. (1959). *Children in need of parents.* New York: Columbia University Press.

Maluccio, A. N., Fein, E., and Olmstead, K. A. (1986). *Permanency planning for children: Concepts and methods.* New York: Tavistock.

Maybanks, S., and Bryce, M. (1979). *Home based services for children and families: Policy, practice, and research.* Springfield, IL: Charles C. Thomas.

National Center for Youth Law. (1987). *Making reasonable efforts: Steps for keeping families together.* Available from National Center for Youth Law, 1663 Mission Street, San Francisco, CA 94103.

National Resource Center on Family-Based Services. (1983). *Family-centered social services: A model for child welfare agencies.* Iowa City: University of Iowa.

Pecora, P. J., Fraser, M. W., and Haapala, D. (1987). *Defining family preservation services: Three intensive home-based treatment programs.* Salt Lake City: University of Utah.

Richmond, M. (1917). *Social diagnosis.* New York: Russell Sage Foundation.

Shyne, A. W., and Schroeder, A. G. (1978). *National study of social services to children and their families.* Washington, DC: U. S. Department of Health, Education and Welfare (Publication No. OHDS 78-30150).

Sinanoglu, P. A., and Maluccio, A. N. (1981). *Parents of children in placement: Perspectives and programs.* New York: Child Welfare League of America.

Small, R., and Whittaker, J. K. (1979). Residential group care and home-based care: Towards a continuity of family service. *In* S. Maybanks and M. Bryce, *Home based services for children and families,* pp. 77-91. Springfield, IL: Charles C. Thomas.

Stehno, S. M. (1986). Family-centered child welfare services: New life for a historic idea. *Child Welfare, 65,* 231-240.

Stein, T. J. (1985). Projects to prevent out-of-home placement. *Children and Youth Services Review, 7,* 109-121.

Wald, M. S., Carlsmith, J. M., and Leiderman, P. H. (1988). *Protecting abused and neglected children.* Stanford: Stanford University.

Whittaker, J. K. (1979). *Caring for troubled children: Residential treatment in a community context.* San Francisco: Jossey-Bass.

Whittaker, J. K., and Maluccio, A. N. (1988). Understanding the families of children in foster and residential care. *In* E. W. Nunnally, C. S. Chilman, and F. M. Cox (Eds), *Troubled Relationships: Families in trouble series Volume 3* (pp 192-205). Beverley Hills, CA: Sage.

Whittaker, J. K., Schinke, S. P., and Gilchrist, L. D. (1986). The ecological paradigm in child, youth and family services: Implications for policy and practice. *Social Service Review, December,* 483-503.

Chapter 2

Recognizing and Realizing
the Potential of "Family Preservation"

Douglas Nelson

American child welfare systems are fast becoming captive to a continuing crisis. The steady increase in the occurrence, recognition, and reporting of abuse, neglect, and intrafamily conflict is in many jurisdictions threatening to overwhelm the public sector's capacity to protect children from unacceptable deprivation and harm. In more than a few states, reports of abuse and neglect are failing to receive the prompt and uniform investigations that current law requires. When investigations do occur, the assessment of risk is too often hasty, incomplete, and sometimes tragically mistaken. The mistakes, moreover, range from inadequate recognition of real danger, in some cases, to unwarranted intrusion, in others.

Equally alarming is the deteriorating quality of the responses to substantiated problems. In many places, increasing admissions to placement are outstripping the available supply of appropriate out-of-home resources. Overcrowding of group care facilities, assignment of children to unnecessarily restrictive placements, the temporary warehousing of youngsters awaiting placement, and reliance on sometimes overextended or insufficiently trained foster families are symptomatic of the current crisis. Even in those instances where placement is not recommended, the extent of public intervention has frequently declined to unsystematic referrals, sporadic monitoring and unwarranted hope that all will be well.

The crisis in child welfare is not newly arrived. Its origins lie in three national trends that have been apparent for some time. The first is a wholly desirable heightening of societal expectations and standards for acceptable family functioning. Since the 1960s, states have steadily broadened the definition of child abuse and neglect, clarified and expanded the mandates for reporting suspected violations, and increased public sensitivity to the symptoms and signs of child endangerment.

13

At the same time, the nation has been producing growing numbers of families who—by virtue of poverty, discrimination, family structure, and other factors—are at increased risk of being ill equipped to meet their parental obligations. Dramatic growth in teenage birth rates, in single-parent families, in the percentage of child rearing households living below the poverty line, and in families with two working parents—all these factors— combined with declining informal and extended family supports available to young parents, have conspired to compromise the resilience and coping capacity of an ever larger pool of at-risk families.

The third contributor to the crisis lies in the overall failure of public child welfare policy and practice to respond to the fundamental changes noted above. Over the past 40 years, public policy has scrupulously confined a state's authority to intervene on behalf of children to those circumstances in which a family has demonstrably failed to meet accepted social standards for parental performance. As those standards have increased and the functional capacity of many families has declined, the inevitable demand on a still largely reactive and remedial child welfare system has steadily exceeded its capacity to keep pace. Without a basic reorientation in public policy toward families, the current cultural, economic, and demographic trends appear certain to prolong this continuing child welfare crisis indefinitely into the future.

Against this backdrop, a small but growing number of child welfare practitioners and policy reform advocates have argued that at least part of the child welfare crisis could be addressed through a systematic expansion of a programmatic intervention known as family preservation. In essence, family preservation refers to the provision of intensive professional assistance to families in crisis for the purpose of restoring adequate family functioning and thereby averting the need for the removal of children. Its principal components include: active aid in the solution of practical problems that contribute to family stress; instruction in parenting skills and in the resolution of intrafamily conflict; on-site monitoring of family members at risk; and development of on-going linkages with formal and informal support systems for participating families.

This emerging concept of family preservation can be traced to a number of historical forerunners, but its clearest and most direct antecedent lies in the work of Homebuilders of Tacoma, Washington, begun in the mid-1970s. The founders and staff of Homebuilders not only pioneered and refined what remains one of the central models of family preservation, but they also played a key role in promoting and disseminating the concept as a potentially powerful means of placement prevention.

By the late 1970s, family preservation services were being offered by a dozen or so private family service agencies across the country. The viability of the concept was advanced not only by the continuing advocacy of its practitioners, but also by its relevance to two other broader currents in the child welfare world. The first was the increasing acceptance of a family-centered approach to the diagnosis and treatment of behavioral dysfunction in children and adults—an approach that family preservation seemed to illustrate concretely and persuasively. The second was family preservation's obvious relevance to the growing national concern over the unnecessary and excessive placement of children away from their families—a concern that contributed powerfully to the passage of Public Law 96-272 in 1980.

Among those who recognized the potential of family preservation to contribute to the goals and values of P.L. 96-272, none has been more influential than the Edna McConnell Clark Foundation. Since 1983, the Clark Foundation's Children's Program has devoted its staff, prestige, and the bulk of its grant resources to promoting the use of family preservation interventions as a primary response to the needs of families in crisis. To that end, the Clark Foundation has provided seed money to initiate new family preservation programs under both private and public auspices in several states. It has subsidized the dissemination of materials that describe the core elements of family preservation as well as evidence of the intervention's program effectiveness and cost efficiency. Clark money has also enabled leading family preservation practitioners to train new line and supervisory staff who are getting into the field. More recently, Clark has undertaken to create a national network of varied technical assistants who specialize in helping states and communities acquire the programmatic, legal, and fiscal expertise needed to expand their family preservation service capability.

But the Clark Foundation role has gone beyond promoting program replication. It has also been a key actor in defining the concept itself. Under Clark's leadership, the term "family preservation" has come to mean short-term, face-to-face support and therapy services provided in the homes of families who are at immediate risk of separation. The governing objective is to enable families to reach a level of functioning that eliminates the need for removal.

Due in part to Clark's efforts, services of this general kind have grown steadily throughout the 1980s. At present, over 50 private agencies and units of public systems are offering "family preservation" programs in about 15 of the 50 states. It is estimated that as many as 5000 families will receive such services this year.

The foremost question raised by this history is whether an alternative intervention that touches some 5000 families can realistically be seen as a "lever" to help reform a child welfare system that now removes more than a quarter million children from their families each year. As noted above, an increasing number of family preservation advocates believe that it can. They contend that a large-scale expansion of targeted family preservation services could alleviate some of the current crisis in child welfare services;

they believe it could begin to realign and reorient public responses to the needs of at-risk children; and some even see in it the potential for a radical redefinition of the state's obligation to families.

The balance of this chapter is devoted to an assessment of this change potential. The first section examines the extent to which the development of a family preservation capacity can alter the basic locus of a state's response to at-risk children. A second section explores the implications of the basic form and content of family preservation programs for broader social service practice and for the organization and financing of family service delivery. Each part includes a brief review of the paramount strategic issues that will determine the extent to which the potential implications of family preservation can in fact be realized.

The Implications of Family Preservation as Placement Prevention

Any significance that adheres to family preservation ultimately depends on whether it can do what it says: that is, can it really preserve families who would otherwise be temporarily or permanently separated?

The experience to date warrants confidence in addressing this pivotal question. The records of Homebuilders, the longest running family preservation model, suggest that between 80 and 95% of the families they serve remain intact 1 year after their intervention. Independent assessments of the referral patterns and case histories of Homebuilder clients further suggest that the overwhelming majority of these families were at genuine risk and would have experienced separation without the assistance provided. Comparable evidence of the efficacy of intensive, short-term family intervention has also been gathered as part of the on-going evaluation of Hennepin County, Minnesota's pilot project with families of at-risk adolescents. Findings to date indicate a substantial reduction in both admissions to and duration of placement among families served, when compared to a control group of comparable families not receiving the intervention.

Testimony, anecdotal evidence, and self-reporting from other family preservation programs tend to reinforce the above findings on the efficacy of intensive, in-home interventions in avoiding probable placements. The evidence, of course, is not yet either broad-based or definitive. Nevertheless, it appears sufficient to support the reasonable inference that family preservation, where properly executed, can prevent or at least defer the placement of children in *a significant percentage* of the families which are now being separated.

This, in and of itself, is important. If nothing else, it suggests that, in principle at least, there may be a public policy alternative to the timing and location in which child welfare systems now characteristically respond to the protection and support needs of severely at-risk children and their families. Noting that a policy alternative is possible, however, is not the same as demonstrating that it is practical. To establish the potential policy relevance of an expanded family preservation capacity, a case must also be made for both its affordability and replicability.

With regard to the first of these criteria, public affordability, the available data relating to family preservation is encouraging. Almost all existing family preservation programs assert that the average cost of their intensive interventions is substantially less than the *average* cost of placements in the same jurisdictions. Homebuilders, for example, calculates the average cost of the placements prevented through their intervention as ranging from $3,600 to $19,000 per child, while the cost of providing intensive family services averages between $2,600 and $4,000 per family. Even if one assumes that Homebuilder-type programs will succeed in preventing placement in only 60% of the families served (a rate below Homebuilders' experience), the intervention would appear to "save" more than it costs.

Some optimistic advocates of family preservation have generalized such calculations into a very expansive estimate of the cost efficiency of a systemwide commitment to intensive placement prevention. By asserting that well-designed intensive services can avert the need for placement in a large percentage of all the families at-risk of separation *and* by pointing to family preservation's alleged capacity to prevent not only the immediate placement risk, but also subsequent placements of siblings, these advocates are prepared to argue that a systemic investment in family preservation is likely to reduce dramatically what otherwise would be the total future public costs of providing child welfare services.

Such ambitious claims, whether warranted or not, may actually exceed what is necessary and prudent for establishing the fiscal practicality of expanding family preservation services. In fact, overpromising may run the risk of creating inordinate expectations that subsequent evidence will fail to fulfill. Given the presumed benefits of protecting children *while preserving families,* it is sufficient to assert that the costs of enlarging a family preservation capacity are likely to be at least partially offset by the costs avoided through some measure of placement prevention. Inference from existing data, albeit limited, would appear to allow that assertion as a responsible claim.

If, upon further investigation, this claim proves to be valid, it constitutes one of the most important reasons for seeing family preservation as a politically viable component in a reformed system of services to children. In essence, the existing fiscal analysis suggests that the development and expansion of family preservation services can largely be achieved through *self-financing* even over the short term. Unlike most preventive investments in health care and human services (where prospective cost avoidance is difficult to calculate and may take many years to realize), the savings implicit in family preservation would appear to be achievable through fairly short-term cost substitutions. It is probable, in other words, that new expenditures for services that succeed in avoiding placement for a significant fraction of families served are likely to be "repaid" through savings that accrue within a relatively brief period of time.

The political and advocacy implications of this conclusion are fairly clear. In principle at least, it means that effective family preservation can be built and paid for with little net increase in what otherwise would be a state's longer run expenditures for child welfare. Put more meaningfully, it suggests that the substantive benefits that expanded family preservation can bring to children and parents are benefits that can be purchased with a limited increase in tax expenditures in the near term, and perhaps even with tax savings over the long run.

While these direct cost implications are the most obvious and politically relevant, they may not be the only ones. Over time, an enlarged family preservation capacity may prove capable not only of avoiding those costs associated with the particular placements it prevents, but also of making more affordable the *price* of the placements it cannot prevent.

It is already apparent that, in many jurisdictions, the demand for out-of-home resources is exceeding the supply. Shortages of family foster homes, group care facilities, shelter resources, residential treatment slots, and beds in child caring institutions are affecting child welfare systems in a growing number of states. The consequent market reality is that in many places out-of-home care for children has become a sellers' market. Foster care payment increases, proposals to "professionalize" foster care, and escalating per diem rates for group and institutional care illustrate what promises to be a long-term price inflation as states seek to buy enough resources to meet the demand represented by growing numbers of children in their custody. In many instances, of course, these pressures reflect legitimate needs to assure quality out-of-home care and treatment. However, to the extent that future costs will be inflated purely by supply shortages, family preservation could have an important moderating effect simply by reducing the size of the demand. Over the long term, the savings to taxpayers of these real (albeit hard-to-estimate) costs could be very large indeed.

This longer term fiscal implication of family preservation may have an even more significant analog on the programmatic side. The child welfare benefits of family preservation are most often (and understandably) envisioned in terms of the children whose removal is prevented. But family preservation may also enable an improvement in the care and welfare of children in placement. By virtue of its ability to reduce the number and incidence of removals, a strong family preservation capacity could materially lessen the pressure on a state's available out-of-home resources. This, in turn, ought to increase a child welfare system's probability of sustaining a true continuum of care, of making prompter and more appropriate placements, of finding placement settings closer to home, and of assuring better supervision and treatment of those children in its care. In short, a commitment to family preservation contains within it at least some potential to alleviate the crisis that currently afflicts child welfare's response to the needs of children in placement.

The foregoing fiscal arguments are probably sufficient to support optimism about the cost-effectiveness of family preservation, but they do not yet add up to an incontrovertible and compelling case. To reach that level of persuasiveness, the cost implications of family preservation have to be far more thoroughly documented and more broadly tested. For too long, legislative and policy advocacy on behalf of family preservation has ridden on limited and often anecdotal evidence of its ability to substitute for placement at comparable or lower costs. Present and developing family preservation efforts need to be subjected to evaluations that are sufficiently rigorous to establish the true costs of intensive services, the actual probability of placement without intervention for families served, the precise outcomes achieved for these families, and responsible estimates of avoided costs. The findings from such studies, in turn, need to be packaged and disseminated in a manner that allows their widespread use for political advocacy, program design, and specific budget and fiscal planning.

Closely related to these evaluation needs is a somewhat more complicated strategic issue. As most advocates for family preservation recognize, the probability of enlisting a genuine political commitment to a systemwide intensive intervention capacity is greatly increased if it can be shown to be self-financing—that is, funded through the reinvestment of avoided costs. To the extent that advocates intend to rely on this fiscal strategy, however, they must also be prepared to exercise considerable discipline over the targeting and application of family preservation services.

Care, first of all, must be taken to reserve family preservation services for families at real and imminent risk of placement. It may even be strategically appropriate to further target interventions to that subset of at-risk families for whom family preservation is most likely to be efficacious. Second, continual efforts have to be made to balance a high enough service intensity to achieve adequate family functioning with a sufficiently compressed duration to assure strategically defensible per case costs.

From many perspectives these recommended constraints have and will continue to appear problematic. As is described in the next section, there are many service elements and features of family preservation practice that have beneficial application outside the context of placement prevention. Consequently, there have been and will always be strong temptations to extend the intervention to families who can benefit from it, but who are not at real risk of dissolution. Similar temptations will exist to extend the period of intense intervention with at-risk families past the point of restored functional capacity to some more ambitious level of family performance.

These are powerful temptations, but succumbing to them in the design and delivery of family preservation services represents a basic compromise of at least the fiscal grounds for expanding the program itself. The simplest strategic significance of family preservation is that it represents a technically practical and politically possible intervention that is capable of moving child welfare systems measurably away from their current reliance on placement while, at the same time, doing so within existing resource realities.

Demonstrating that family preservation is affordable and even cost-effective, however, constitutes only part of the case that has to be made for its practicality. It must also be shown that the intervention can be successfully expanded in the real world context of available knowledge, skills, manpower, and service delivery technology. Put another way, if effective family preservation entails exceptional talents that only a few prospective workers can acquire or if it involves a level of commitment beyond that which most professionals can be expected to sustain, then family preservation may never prove expandable beyond small-scale pilots staffed by peculiarly skilled practitioners. On the other hand, if the characteristics that really make family preservation work are replicable—that is, they are skills that can be learned or delivery features that can be created in varied settings, then the prospect of expanding family preservation into an integral part of the child welfare system becomes a highly practical one.

Which of these characterizations most accurately describes family preservation is difficult to establish. The problem is that the best of the existing programs are carried out by exceptional people—by pioneering professionals who are highly motivated, inordinately innovative, and particularly skilled in the diagnostic and therapeutic techniques they employ. Were the presence of such people judged to be indispensable to family preservation's effectiveness, then it might be fair to conclude it has already neared its optimum application.

There is, of course, an alternative perspective. Without denigrating the value of personal talent, the power of particular therapeutic strategies, or the importance of good staff training, it can plausibly be argued that it is the objective design, structure, and delivery features of family preservation which, in the end, make it effective. It is, in other words, the fast response, the in-home presence, the high intensity, the low caseloads, the family-centered approach, the broad case worker responsibility, the availability of "hard services" resources, the deliberately brief duration, and the express goal of preserving the family, that singly or collectively enable workers to help families in crisis avert the need for child placement.

Common sense, as well as years of family practice experience, tell us that these elements have to make a difference. We know that many instances of child abuse are the product of temporary crises that could be managed without endangerment through the timely help or even the mere presence of another person. We know that family dysfunction is sometimes rooted in extreme social isolation that could be alleviated by face-to-face interaction in the short run and help with building some social linkages over the longer term. We know that more than a few children are removed from their families for want of a month's rent or food or heat that a bit of emergency money or referral to entitlement programs might satisfy. Finally, we know that certain family problems which resist resolution when treated in isolation or as individual disorders, can be adequately addressed if they are approached in the context of the entire family and its interrelationships.

None of the foregoing is intended to minimize the complexity of the causes of family problems or to oversimplify the challenges to effective family preservation. In many instances, family problems—whether they be rooted in persistent economic disadvantage, addiction, or severe behavioral disorders—will not yield to even the best service interventions. Nonetheless, it is essential that we demystify what in many cases does enable family preservation to work. The prompt response, low caseloads, the presence in the home, and the charge to deal with the whole array of presenting problems—these are elements of a model that can be replicated in any committed state or substate jurisdiction. They also encompass abilities and skills that available professionals can acquire and sustain through appropriate training and organizational support.

In summary, in order to promote a broader appreciation of the practicality of expanding family preservation, we need clearer and more concrete descriptions of the *replicable* elements of the existing successful models. Detailed descriptions of successful family preservation cases, for example, would assist advocates not only in communicating what family preservation is, but also in persuading skeptical audiences that such a capacity can be realistically created where it now does not exist.

Most of the previous discussion is centered on establishing the affordability and practicality of preserving a significant number of families who, under the current child welfare system, would be separated. From certain perspectives, advancing those arguments would seem to add up to a compelling case for system-change. The short- and long-run cost avoidance, the real ability to expand effective placement prevention, and the positive impact on the state's role as custodian would all appear to make political commitments to family preservation almost automatic.

The difficult truth, however, may be otherwise. At the heart of the issue of institutionalizing family preservation is not merely the question of whether it can be done, but also the graver question of whether it ought to be done.

To advocates of family preservation the answer may seem self-evident. But to many others, including social service professionals, politicians, and much of the public, it is not. Everyone, to be sure, is appreciative of the values and benefits of families for children, and thus they are supportive of policies that preserve families. However, for many, this commitment quickly crumbles when extended to fragmented, stressed, chemically dependent, profoundly poor, neglectful, conflict-ridden or abusive families—that is, precisely the kind of families that family preservation exists to support. In these contexts, the benefits and meaning of family remain difficult for many individuals to identify with or even envision. In contrast, the evidence or image of a child's deprivation in these environments is unmistakable and concrete. It is not surprising, then, that when confronted with what appears a choice between the survival of an abstraction (i.e., "family") and the safety or nurture of a real child, it is the latter that seems the paramount goal.

This is, of course, an incomplete perception. The human value and benefit of family continuity to the children of even the most vulnerable families remain, more often than not, real and immensely important. Children who are enabled to remain safely with their families are the beneficiaries of an individually-varying range of psychological and developmental advantages—such priceless and immeasurable things as continuity in identity, a sense of belonging and place, the special relations rooted in parent–child bonding, the security of membership, and the assurance of conforming to social norms. Even these words, however, fail to convey the intensely personal experience and meaning they are intended to describe.

Equally relevant, and perhaps less elusive, are the still underrecognized human costs of family separation. No matter how compelling the reason, children who are removed from their family can be expected to suffer. The known and predictable hardships include dislocation, fear of the unknown, guilt, diminished self-esteem, stigmatization, loss of identity, and exposure to risks from caretakers who have no familial obligations. The adverse consequences for parents and siblings are identifiable as well—loss, humiliation, demoralization, and a vulnerability to even greater incapacity in the future.

To a surprising degree, the human benefits of family preservation and the human costs of child placement have gone unarticulated. Admittedly, they are difficult to capture and may be even harder to communicate. Nevertheless, succeeding in doing so is critical for realizing the reform potential of family preservation. In essence, securing the advantages of family continuity and averting the hardships of separation constitute the ultimate moral significance of family preservation for at-risk children. Unless and until those advantages and hardships are understood and felt by a broader public, the commitment to family preservation, however cost effective and expandable, will be a limited one.

The Implication of Family Preservation for More Effective Service Delivery to Families

The arguments exist—fiscal, practical and moral—for a broad public policy commitment to family preservation as a systemwide vehicle for placement prevention. Were those arguments to be more fully developed and advanced, the resulting expansion in family preservation services could materially alter the locus, timing, and character of current child welfare responses to at-risk children, and they could do so within the foreseeable future. At a minimum, a commitment to institutionalize family preservation—to making it an entitlement for at-risk families—would yield a system less reliant on placement, less reactive and more affirmatively committed to families as the context for securing the safety and welfare of vulnerable children.

The fact that family preservation could prevent significant numbers of current child placements is what gives the intervention its *strategic* importance. This is what makes it an "entry point" or lever for system change. In the end, however, the significance of family preservation may actually go far beyond its strategic role. That is, it may not only be what it does, but how it does it that gives family preservation its full social policy potential. Stated simply, the reasons that family preservation works—the design and practice characteristics that make it effective—may well prove to have very powerful implications for a whole range of fundamental human service delivery issues.

As briefly noted in earlier sections, several elements set existing models of family preservation services apart from most other forms of service provision to families and children. To begin with, family preservation tends to be a genuinely family-centered intervention. While most conventional services have been oriented toward the identification and resolution of individual needs and problems through implementation of individualized service and treatment plans, the assessment of needs undertaken by family preservation workers deliberately extends not only to the problems and strengths of all family members, but also analyzes how the behavioral interaction of individual members limits or contributes to effective family functioning. The difference is not just formal; it is substantive. Family preservation practitioners believe that many forms of individual behavioral dysfunction have their origin in or at least are expressed through familial relationships. Consequently, therapeutic and teaching interventions are designed to promote more positive and mutually supportive family relationships; in this way, altered family interaction becomes not only an end in itself, but a therapeutic vehicle to address individual problems and needs. Putting all of this more simply, the family is *the focus* of family preservation services and the overarching "treatment" goal is enhanced family performance.

A second distinguishing characteristic of family preservation services is their delivery in the home—or more generally in the real life environment of the family. Unlike most office-bound, counseling and treatment models, family preservation personnel work in the home and at times when their involvement is most needed or most likely to be effective. This means staff are involved with families when and where crises occur, day or night, and if required, continuously over an extended period of time.

In part, of course, the intensive in-home, flexible character of family preservation is a practical necessity. Family preservation is a form of crisis intervention frequently triggered by the potential endangerment of a family member. Accordingly, prompt responsiveness and on-site presence are often essential ways of assuring the mitigation of risk to children or others, until family functioning is restored. Even more basically, being in the home assures contact with those in need—a feature that does not occur when clients have to be relied on to make and fulfill appointments at distant locations.

The in-home locus of family preservation, however, reflects more than practical considerations; it also derives from a more general theory of practice. Family preservation practitioners believe that in the home they can best understand the context, pattern, and nature of the problems that underlie family dysfunction. Moreover, it is in the actual setting of family stresses that a worker can most effectively propose and promote problem solving techniques and the altered behavior patterns that are likely to alleviate those stresses. Finally, working with family members in their real world environment is believed to enable the professional to recognize and thus to help families utilize informal and community support systems that will contribute to their successful functioning in the future. Indeed, assisting families to access these appropriate supports is seen as one of the critical strategies in *sustaining* the improved family performance that is begun during the time-limited crisis intervention.

A third distinctive characteristic feature of most family preservation models is their broadly generic or multi-problem orientation. In this regard, family preservation services are unlike most human service delivery systems, which are organized and financed around particular clusters or categories of problems: income needs, drug abuse, mental health, housing, protective supervision, acute health care, delinquency, and so on. Instead of assuming such a targeted orientation, family preservation programs are predicated on the assumption that a multiplicity of interacting and different problems most frequently disable family functioning. Accordingly, family preservation workers are deliberately charged with a responsibility for recognizing and responding to a range of presenting needs. This often means that workers are directly involved in practical problem-solving (e.g., transportation, emergency income, home management), simultaneous with their counseling and instructional assistance to address inappropriate behaviors or intrafamily conflicts. Family preservation staff also help families use more specialized resources, say health care or alcohol treatment, and they try to link them with on-going programs like Medicaid or job training where these are needed to create or maintain adequate family performance. This integrated approach to problem-solving is seen by many as critical to family preservation's effectiveness in quickly, but durably, upgrading family capacity to care for children.

A final distinguishing design element of family preservation lies in the nature and duration of its worker-family relationships. On the one hand, the intensity of family preservation workers' involvement with family members, their presence in the home, and their readiness to be involved in the whole range of presenting problems create a professional–client relationship far more personal than that achieved by conventional nonintensive services offered by a changing cast of office-bound specialists. At the same time, however, this intimate involvement is consistently guided by the reality of short service duration—a feature that reinforces an emphasis on increasing the family's capacity to function independently.

These two characteristics—a highly intensive interaction, yet one of short duration—tend to produce a model of family service delivery that can best be described as an enabling strategy—an investment in residual family strengths and capacities. As such, it contrasts with a competing and perhaps prevailing model of family service practice, one which presumes chronic decision-making deficits and seeks to offer access to continuing compensatory or formal therapeutic assistance from outside the family. From the perspective of family preservation practitioners this conventional orientation not only underestimates the problem-solving capacity present in even seriously dysfunctioning families, but it also inadvertently encourages a deepened dependency and vulnerability to future crises. Family preservation advocates point to the durable behavioral improvement in many of the families served with intensive services as evidence of the efficiency and realism of their "empowerment" model.

Considered collectively, these four principles—family centeredness; in-home intensive services; a generic and integrated response to multiple problems; and time-limited service duration—constitute the content characteristics that define family preservation practice. What gives these practice principles a special persuasiveness is their demonstrated effectiveness and efficiency in achieving desired outcomes with some of the most challenging of human service client populations. The families targeted for family preservation interventions are usually in extreme crisis. Many have endured a long history of problems as well as multiple prior episodes of service or treatment from human service agencies. The fact that family preservation interventions are frequently able to succeed in enabling such families to regain and maintain an adequate level of functioning lends powerful credibility to the methods and practices they employ.

Also contributing to the appeal found in the practice principles of family preservation are the implicit social values they affirm. Respect for individual and family potential and the aspiration for client independence and self-sufficiency are viewed by the supporters of family preservation as healthy alternatives to the patronizing and dependency prolonging approaches that continue to characterize much of the social welfare culture.

Taken together, this positive value orientation and the evidence of practical efficacy suggest that the practice principles of family preservation have applicability in a far wider array of service interactions with families. Perhaps the most obvious opportunity for extension is in the application of the family preservation model to families at risk of child removal due to delinquency or mental health treatment needs. While these presenting problems differ in character from the abuse and neglect that now triggers most family preservation interventions, the frequent presence of similar underlying needs such as improving a family's behavior management, communication, conflict resolution or "survival" skills implies that many juvenile justice and residential treatment placements could be averted through access to timely and intensive in-home services.

Elements of the family preservation model, however, would also seem to have significant relevance for noncrisis situations. The principles of intensive service and family-centeredness, for example, might well enable prompter and more successful reunification efforts than are now typically achieved by services in which those responsible for the care of placed children have little regular involvement or responsibility for the progress of the families from which those children were removed.

Even more broadly, family preservation principles would appear to have implications for child protective services in general. The majority of child abuse and neglect cases, in which the level of risk does not warrant placement, are now commonly relegated to a service response consisting of little more than sporadic monitoring, some counseling sessions, and referrals to specialized help from other sources. According to its critics, this typical protective service response frequently fails to assess the underlying problems that generate family stress and often even ignores the presence of individuals (e.g., fathers or other adult males) who may be most responsible for the conflict and neglect initially reported. In light of this, it would seem that some increased reliance on a more family-centered assessment of needs, combined with a more integrated plan for addressing the range of contributing problems, would at a minimum produce better risk assessment and more purposeful case management of service plans for many protective service families.

Perhaps most significant of all is the relevance of family preservation's generalist approach as a potential guiding principle for all family services. It is already fairly well understood that families who demonstrate a need for a particular kind of help also often experience other related but separate problems. Serious drug abuse in an adult family member, for example, commonly correlates with a heightened probability of family conflict, inadequate parental supervision, and adjustment problems in children. Similarly, families headed by a single teenaged mother display a higher likelihood of having parenting education and early childhood health care needs as well as a need for income support.

In today's human service context, however, there is rarely a single agency or even an entry point in the system that is organized or financed to assume responsibility for helping resolve the multiple and interactive problems of such families. Drug treatment programs may address the addiction problems of a family member, but the household's related needs for income security or improved parental supervision are outside the treatment counselor's jurisdiction. Welfare offices can determine a teenage parent's eligibility for AFDC, but they are not equipped or expected to assess or address the need for nutrition education, parenting support, or alcohol treatment. These remain the responsibilities of other parts of the system.

The irony here is that often a placement-threatening crisis must occur before such multineed families encounter an individual professional who seeks to address the range of factors that undermine adequate family functioning. And even that occurs only in those exceptional places where a true family preservation capacity has been established. Some alternative to this pattern seems compelling. The answer probably does not lie in the wholesale extension of intensive in-home services to precrisis situations, but it does seem appropriate to borrow the breadth of the family preservation worker's responsibility as a standard for the redesign of intake points, needs assessment, service planning, and case management that someday ought to be more routinely available to families in need.

The use of the practice insights gained from successful family preservation programs as a guide for broader child welfare and family service reforms seems persuasive in principle. Nevertheless, for such insights to become a practical force in service system change, several developmental activities have to be undertaken. First of all, the practice components that comprise and contribute to the efficacy of family preservation need to be more systematically documented and analyzed. Much of what is widely known about family preservation practice comes from self-characterizations by its practitioners. These reports have to be supplemented by more objective studies of actual practice content and patterns and by systematic evaluation of how the elements of family preservation, singly or in combination, contribute to successful client outcomes. Such findings would establish a far richer and more credible knowledge base for the extension of family preservation principles into the wider arenas of service organization and delivery to families.

Equally important for capitalizing on the practice implications of existing family preservation models is the development of a more institutionalized training capability. As family preservation advocates repeatedly attest, the success of the intervention is ultimately dependent on competent practitioners. Family preservation workers, to be effective, have to understand and know how to use the design features of their service model. They have to have the kind of training that enables them to recognize and accurately analyze a wide variety of individual and family problems. They have to possess interpersonal and communication skills sufficient to instill trust and comprehension on the part of client family members. Also required is some mastery of appropriate behavioral or psychodynamic approaches, as well as a working familiarity with the specialized and other community resources that may need to be brought to bear on particular family problems.

Right now the acquisition of these skills occurs primarily through transfers (on the job) between experienced staff and new recruits of the existing family preservation programs. With the exception of the training unit within the Homebuilders program and perhaps a few other organizations, there is virtually no institutional training capacity in the country tailored to promote more broadly the practice strategies implicit in family preservation programs. Orientation to the intervention itself and specialized training in its component practice skills remains largely absent in standard social work curricula.

In order for family preservation itself to be systemically expanded and for its practice principles to be introduced into other services to families, a far larger and more accessible training capacity has to be created. In the short run, this may mean the development of more specialized training providers, but in the long term, it requires incorporation of new content into the curricula of the social work schools that will prepare many of the future's child welfare and family service workers.

While the need for a more accessible training capability constitutes a substantial developmental barrier to expanding the practices and values implicit in family preservation, it is by no means the only, or even the most challenging obstacle. Far more complicated and difficult are the changes that have to occur in the structuring, organization, and financing of existing child welfare and family services, if they are ever to accommodate the effective practice principles of family preservation.

Perhaps the most readily apparent illustration of the barriers to change is in the existing job structures of most frontline family service and child welfare workers. It is clear, for example, that the customary size of worker caseloads, combined with their office-bound work routine, preclude any real opportunities for the in-home locus and flexible intensity of contact that appear indispensable to family preservation's effectiveness. Realigning caseloads and job structures are thus obvious prerequisites for any wider application of these practices.

This, it should be emphasized, is no simple task, especially within public service settings where resource constraints, established employee contracts, traditions of uniformity, and conventional measures of worker accountability add up to strong reinforcements for the status quo. For these reasons, the promotion of family preservation programs under public sector auspices may have a significance far beyond the immediate services provided. Insofar as such pilot efforts can demonstrate new and acceptable ways of assuring worker rights, adequate supervision, and the efficiency of reduced caseloads, they point the way toward accommodating more effective service practices in the public sector's far larger noncrisis involvement with client families.

Job restructuring, however, is but one of the systemic changes involved in a wider reliance on the practice principles demonstrated by family preservation. A substantial movement toward a truly family-centered approach to the needs of children and parents or a commitment to genuinely integrated and empowering responses to the circumstances of multiproblem families carries with it even more basic reform implications for existing service organization and financing.

At the heart of these implications is a challenge to the categorical character of current human service funding and delivery. Family preservation works, in some measure, because its workers assume responsibility for the range of problems that may threaten family capacity and because they have the training and resources to respond to multiple and often changing needs. Application of that model to family services generally would inescapably entail more comprehensive methods of need assessment and new vehicles for service coordination and continuity. At a minimum, it points to the long-sought but rarely achieved consolidation of intake and assessment for families in need of assistance. Also, it suggests the value of a truly generic case management capacity—one which can empower a single professional or team to marshal resources on behalf of a family across categorical systems and over time. To enable such an authoritative and responsive case management system, of course, further implies the decategorization of service resources, that is, the elimination of those categorical eligibility and authorization requirements that currently prevent timely and coordinated delivery of multisystem responses to multineed families.

In their most stringent formulation, family preservation practices probably require thorough reorganization of the service system. Many states now have a bureau, division, or department nominally responsible for the coordinated delivery of what are called "family services." In reality, however, the jurisdiction of state and local "family service" units encompasses only a fragment of the resources and services that are relevant to enabling an at-risk family to more adequately provide for the care, welfare, and development of its children. "Family service" agencies typically have no responsibility or authority over income support resources, public health services, housing, mental health services, or delinquency programs, despite the fact that the need for one or more of these supports is often at the bottom of a family's referral to "family services." If the response of family preservation to families in crisis constitutes a micromodel of an appropriate response to the support requirements of vulnerable families at all stages of need, then it surely points to a far broader organizational and resource jurisdiction than "family service" agencies currently possess.

Conclusion

In many ways, family preservation (as defined in this paper) appears a peculiar vehicle for the potentially radical reforms it is said to imply. Family preservation, after all, is a very specialized programmatic intervention. Its appeal to date has been grounded not on ideological or reformist arguments, but on its potential as a cost efficient and practical screen against unnecessary placement. Even its most ardent advocates stress the necessity, not of extending family preservation's reach, but of continuing to target the small fraction of families at greatest risk of imminent dissolution.

Paradoxically, however, it is this very practical and narrow focus that may make family preservation an entry point to longer term system change. By demonstrating, without need of vastly expanded resources or a grand new public policy consensus, the ability to efficiently alter outcomes for what are seen as the most vulnerable of children and families, family preservation inevitably calls policy attention both to its own distinctive service design principles and to the contrasting characteristics and inefficiencies of the larger delivery systems that surround it. Herein lies the subtle, but ultimate significance of family preservation.

Chapter 3

The Homebuilders Model

Jill Kinney, David Haapala,
Charlotte Booth, and Shelley Leavitt

Homebuilders is an intensive in-home family crisis intervention and education program designed to prevent the unnecessary out-of-home placement of
children in state funded foster care, group care, psychiatric hospitals or corrections institutions. The families, who are referred by state workers, have
one or more children in imminent danger of placement. The presenting problems may include child abuse, neglect, other family violence, status offenses,
delinquency, developmental disabilities and mental illness of either children
or parents. Families' problems rarely fall into these neat categories. One
family, for example, might involve a very depressed mother with a history
of suicide attempts, a teenage daughter who is not attending school and may
be prostituting on the side, and an infant who is failing to thrive.

Once they are accepted into the program, these families are provided with
intensive services. Therapists are on call 24 hours a day, 7 days a week for
a 4-month period to help defuse the precipitating crisis and, further, to teach
families new skills that will help to prevent the crisis from recurring. Almost
all of the work we do with families takes place in the homes, neighborhoods
and schools of our clients. We may work on housecleaning with a mother
at home or see the teenage son at the local McDonald's and go with him to
school to help assess what is making it so punishing for him and how the
setting could be made more rewarding.

Workers serve only two families at a time. They provide these families,
as needed, with a wide range of services, including helping with basic needs
such as food, shelter, and clothing, and counseling regarding emotions and
relationships.

Begun in 1974, by 1987 Homebuilders had seen 3497 cases. Three
months after termination, 97% had avoided placement in state funded foster
care, group care, or psychiatric institutions. Twelve month follow-up data
available after September 1982 showed that placement had been averted

in 88% of the cases. Service catchment areas include both urban and rural settings. Homebuilders programs operate in four Washington State Counties—King, Pierce, Snohomish and Spokane. Since 1987, Homebuilders has also had a program in the Bronx, New York City. Together, the 5 sites serve over 550 clients each year. We also provide a good deal of training to other agencies wishing to begin family preservation programs. We have provided some type of training or consultation in every state and to groups within 8 countries. In the first quarter of 1987, we responded to 152 requests for information, provided training or consultation to 32 groups, and gave presentations at conferences or other meetings. Table 3.1 shows how the agency has grown over time.

Program Philosophy

Why Avert Placement?

   Homebuilders is built upon several beliefs and values we hold about providing services to families. The most fundamental is that, in most cases, it is best for children to grow up with their natural families. There are many benefits for the child, the family, and the community when families remain intact and problems are solved within the context of the family rather than through placement. In almost all families emotions are incredibly strong and intertwined emotions so that they cannot be severed without great pain. Even where these emotions are mixed and interactions are sometimes painful, there are usually parallel feelings of connectedness, concern, yearning, hope, and love that can blossom as family members learn new ways of coping with their problems and differences. In one case in Tacoma, for example, a teenage girl had nothing but bad things to say about her mother, most of them unprintable. When the girl earned money by doing her chores, however, she spent two hours at the local shopping mall searching for a gift for her mother, a special kind of jelly beans that her mom really liked.
   It is best for most families to learn to handle their own problems rather than continually relying on the state to rescue them when things get rough. Family preservation services reinforce tenacity, hard work, commitment and duty; they discourage avoidance, dependence, and hopelessness.
   In the Homebuilders Program, families learn new behaviors in the environment where they will need to use them. In the majority of cases, parents can learn to set limits, control their emotions, and provide for their children's basic needs. Children learn to assess their own goals and to control their behavior in ways that lead to more reward and less punishment. Homebuilders is not a cure-all. It does not produce perfect families. When service is ter-

Table 3.1. Development of the Homebuilders Programs

1974	Project begins in Tacoma, Washington, with four therapists, under the auspices of Catholic Community Services. Serves children from any referral source as long as imminence of placement is documented. Success rate during the first year is 92% 3 months after termination.
1976	Project expands by three therapists with funds from U.S. Department of Health, Education and Welfare, Administration for Children, Youth and Families. Referrals from the Pierce County Juvenile Court involve tracking of overflow cases to see if placement occurs. Success rate 12 months after intake is 73%. 73% of comparison cases are placed.
1977	Homebuilders Training Division begins providing training to other organizations as well as Homebuilders staff.
1978	Project expands to Seattle, Washington. Initial success rate 3 months after termination is 100%.
1979	Washington State Legislature funds mental health project to see if referrals from the Pierce County Office of Involuntary Commitment can be prevented from entering Western State Psychiatric Hospital. Success rate is 80%. One hundred percent of cases that were not seen because the program was full were placed!
1980	Washington State Department of Social and Health Services funds pilot project to prevent placement of developmentally disabled children in more restrictive settings. Success rate 3 months after termination is 87%.
1982	Homebuilders create their own new parent organization, Behavioral Sciences Institute.
1983	Washington State DSHS expands program to Spokane County. First year success rate at 3 months after termination is 92%.
1984	Washington State DSHS expands program to Snohomish County. First year success rate at 12 months after termination is 96%.
1986	Administration for Children, Youths and Families funds joint project between Behavioral Sciences Institute and Medina Children's Services to test model with adoptive families with special needs children. 3 month success rate is 86%.
1987	New York City Human Resources Administration and the Edna McConnell Clark Foundation fund program in the Bronx, New York. First year success rate is 87%, 3 months after termination.
1988	Washington State DSHS expands program to Kitsap and Whitman Counties.

minated, however, most families are in better shape than they were at the point of referral, and family members are able to make it together.

Children who are separated from their families can miss out on significant portions of family history which makes it difficult for them to ever regain their original firm sense of belonging and continuity. It makes a difference when families are not together for a birthday and for Christmas. It is difficult to regain original strong bonding when there are fewer and fewer shared milestones. Moreover, when family members participate in solving their problems together, individual family members are less likely to feel rejected, inadequate, or like failures, and are less likely to use blaming, separating and giving up as ways to solve problems. Children in placement may feel envious of siblings remaining at home. Children in group care may use other troubled children as role models. Children in any placement may be labeled as deviant by their peers, or feel torn loyalties between natural and foster parents or group home staff. Children in placement are also apt to suffer the effects of frequent caseworker turnover and frequent moves from one living situation to another. For some, there are no real reference people, no one to count on. This discontinuity can make it hard for them to establish an identity, to feel like they are important, or to plan for the future.

Along with the belief in the importance of the family as the foundation of the program, several other important values, attitudes and beliefs also influence the strategies of the model.

First, experience has led us to conclude that *one cannot easily determine which types of families are "hopeless," and which will benefit from intervention.* For example, in one of our first cases in Tacoma, in a multiracial family, a mother had had a serious fight with her husband. He had grabbed her keys and run out and started to drive away in her truck. She had run after him and reached in through the window to try to turn off the key. He had rolled the window up on her arm and dragged her for three blocks. She had been in the hospital for a week and was now home trying to recuperate. She could barely move one side of her body and was unable to keep her job. She had no money and no food. Her car didn't work. Her 14-year-old son had dropped out of school. She had seen him trying to strangle her 6-year-old son. During the second session we found out that the 16-year-old daughter was pregnant.

Just hearing about this, we felt overwhelmed and discouraged. How could all of this ever get resolved? We sat down with the mother at her kitchen table and she wrote down all the different problems and then all the different alternatives for coping with them. Then we all worked on the pros and cons of each alternative. We found a mechanic training program that would fix her car for free. We found a food bank. She got emergency public assistance. Her employer agreed to rehire her when she became physically able to work. The daughter decided to have an abortion. The teenage boy got into an alternative school program. The mother learned better parenting techniques for managing her younger son and he stopped doing the things that triggered the older son's attacks. As the older boy did better in school, he felt less frustrated.

We still hear from this family every once in a while. Ten years after the intervention, the older kids had graduated from high school and were married and working. The younger ones were doing fine. The mother was trying to refer a friend who was having trouble to Homebuilders. During our first week of involvement with this family it would have been difficult for us to believe things could have worked out so well.

Now, after 13 years of experience, the only group we are reluctant to serve are parents who are so addicted to hard drugs that their entire lives are focused on obtaining them and in surviving in very dangerous drug cultures. We feel it is too dangerous to leave children in situations where addicts are climbing up fire escapes, breaking into each others' apartments, selling each others' food, and threatening each other with butcher knives when payments are not available.

Aside from this population, and even after numerous computer analyses of the relationship of success to various client characteristics, we cannot predict ahead of time which families will not benefit from the services. Sometimes referrals will involve discouraging case histories, documented failure of many previous services, and alarming presenting problems. Many have been seen by psychiatrists and others who "should know" if a family is hopeless or not. Some have diagnoses like "schizophrenia" or "manic depressive psychosis." Although workers are often concerned about these referrals, we now believe that, except where the potential for violence leaves family members at too much risk, all families deserve a chance to learn to resolve their problems together. Families who have previously had parenting classes, family therapy, police intervention, and out-of-home placement (and remain troubled) are still capable of learning to resolve their problems. At the same time, a family whose initial complaint is that the teenage daughter only soaps her hair once when she washes it, may end up having the daughter placed outside the home.

It Is Our Job to Instill Hope. Most families seen in intensive home programs have good reasons for not wanting to try very hard anymore. Most have been through numerous programs and been assigned a succession of workers and have experienced very little success. A large proportion of our families have a plaintive refrain during our first session, "But I've had counseling, and it didn't work." The task, then, is to help them see that Homebuilders is not just counseling, and that there are many, many alternatives left to try before we're willing to believe their problems are hopeless. In the past, failure has been built upon failure. Is it any wonder that the families come to additional services out of resignation rather than optimism? They have little reason to believe that another try will succeed where all else has failed.

We can best instill hope by minimizing barriers to change, making it easy for them to see us, talk to us, like us, and understand what we are trying to do. We can also help them, and ourselves, by defining realistic goals and by continually working on our own creativity, enthusiasm and optimism.

Clients are Our Colleagues. We do not think that there are two types of people, healthy and sick: one group who can manage on their own and another group that probably will never be able to do so. *Everyone* needs help sometimes. The power for change rests within the client. It is the worker's job to help clear away barriers for change so that the clients' power may be better utilized. Almost all of the families we see want to get along with each other, to be respected and liked, to feel they belong, to make it in society, and to make it on their own. They want to grow and become more competent in running their lives. We can't help but be moved as we listen to a third generation welfare mother talk about how she yearns for "just one" of her six children to graduate from high school, to "get out of here, somewhere safe and clean." It is very important that we listen to these people and believe in their budding hopes as well as their good reasons for thinking some of our ideas are nonsense. They have more information about their own lives than we, with all our professional insight, will ever have. They also have information about potential constraints and resources which can make our wonderful ideas and interventions sink or swim.

If we believe clients have valuable information and viewpoints, and treat them as colleagues, they sense our respect. They also are more likely to treat us with the same respect and tact that we show to them. When workers treat family members with dignity, it sets a foundation for pleasantness and cooperation during the entire intervention. Even when a worker initially has bad feelings about a client, if the worker behaves respectfully, the client is more likely to respond in a similar way, making it easier for the therapist to like the client.

It is relatively easy to hold these beliefs about respect and liking with articulate, cooperative middle class clients who come to offices and talk politely about their problems. It is more challenging to hold them with people who smell bad, go after each other with butcher knives, leave fingernail tracks in their kids' faces, and swear at counselors. We believe it is imperative to be as nonjudgmental as possible when hearing clients' stories. Who wants to tell somebody something if they will be ridiculed or put down or punished for it? On the other hand, how can we possibly help people if we don't know what's really going on with them? Almost always, when we really understand, it is not hard to feel compassion. It's when we jump to conclusions and close ourselves to the complexities of people's lives that it is most difficult to refrain from judging and blaming. We try hard to maintain the position that inside every frantic, overwhelmed, unpleasant client, there is a decent person struggling to get out.

People are Doing the Best They Can Do. With the information, energy, and resources any of us has at any one point in time, most of us are doing the best we can. Rarely do we hurt others out of sheer spite. Often, abuse is a side effect of our personal struggles to manage to get through our days. When we are frustrated, hurt, and confused, we are likely to lash out at whatever or whomever is closest at hand. All of us can relate to snapping at our spouses after a hard day's work. It's not difficult to imagine a distraught mother—after a day of cleaning up after six little kids, having an extended family member take the last box of oatmeal, having mice eat part of the mattress, and discovering bug bites all over her legs—slapping the child who tugs at her skirt and whines for comfort or candy or a better life.

Even in the worst presenting situations, Homebuilders workers often observe that family members care a great deal for one another. Although they may hurt each other terribly, people usually do what they do with reasonable intentions. We believe that people usually hurt each other out of lack of information regarding skills such as anger management, and wrong information such as believing severe punishment is necessary in parenting. In many situations a mistake, such as an overly harsh word, triggers a protective retaliative gesture, which starts a destructive chain. Most of us can remember ourselves as teenagers. Our mothers would ask where we were going and we would say, "Nowhere." She would feel shut out and say, "You have to tell me." We would feel rebellious and say "Mind your own business." She would feel angry and say "You can't go." Some of us would go to our rooms. Others of us would run out the door, slamming it. A few of us might have ended in a physical tussle with our mothers. One thing leads to another. In some families fairly innocuous comments can snowball into serious physical fights. These same families can usually learn to break the chain at low levels of emotion.

By striving toward a more compassionate view of the problems of the families with which we work we are less likely to be caught up in the blaming that is common in families experiencing pain. We are less confused and frightened. Calming people down will be easier because we will be capable of hearing family members' cues about how hard they are trying and how much they care about each other. For example, when we listen, we can usually hear a mother's fear for her daughter's well being, behind her anger, as she discusses her daughter's running away.

We Can do Harm as Well as Good; We Must be Careful.   Our potential to help families makes it possible for us to hurt them as well. With sophisticated technologies come certain dangers, and we must be careful not to hurt our clients by prescribing treatments that can end up making their situations worse. Knowing that certain techniques "should" work may encourage some therapists to inflict them rigidly on clients. Manipulating, strategizing against, or tricking clients can reinforce client feelings of impotence and confusion. If workers set expectations too high, clients feel overwhelmed. If we ask clients to do things the clients may not want to do, such as talking in detail about their childhood or sharing good feelings about one another when they're angry, clients feel frustrated. If we blame clients for being resistant, the clients may feel guilty, increasing their feelings of inadequacy. If we tell clients that they don't understand their own family problems or how the problems might be solved, family members feel less strength and self-esteem than before they were "helped."

Too frequently, in our role as therapists, we feel we have to do something. Often, however, we do not know what to do. We may recommend unnecessary placement, or side with the "scapegoat," or teach assertiveness training to a mom we can not really support, or stir up marital issues we will not be around to help resolve. We believe we cannot ethically avoid the responsibility that comes with the power we hold. If we believe we can help people change for the better, we must also admit that we can help them change for the worse. We must be careful.

Since we can do harm, our actions had best be scrutinized carefully to ensure against the measure of our authority. We can tell if we are being helpful or destructive by objectively describing how the family's situation was when we began and by keeping track of whether things are getting better or worse for our clients during our involvement. We owe it to the clients to be able to tell them what we are doing (helping them learn new ways of coping with their problems,) and why we are doing it (because we believe most families are happiest when they work things out together, rather than placing their children outside the home). We also owe it to them to state that they will have to give a substantial amount of time and effort in order to gain a happier family life. We owe it to the clients to listen to their responses both during and after the intervention so our methods can be as helpful and comfortable for them as possible. A final core belief to the approach is that we need to provide the same supports for staff that we provide for clients. Supervisors and administrators must be available 24 hours a day, seven days a week. We need to listen to staff and respond to their concerns. We also have to provide them with the skills that they will need to do the Homebuilders job and live a reasonable life. We see training as a key, ongoing support for all staff. A list of training modules delivered to all therapists is shown in Table 3.2.

Table 3.2. Homebuilders Line Staff Training Modules

1. **Introduction**
    The history of the Homebuilders program, a description of Homebuilders' clients, and information on cost and treatment effectiveness. An introduction to crisis intervention and a discussion of "headset" for training.

2. **Strategies of the Homebuilders Model**
    The strategies, characteristics, and guiding beliefs of the Homebuilders model.

3. **Stress Management for Therapists**
    Strategies therapists and others can use to maintain their physical and emotional well-being; the use of cognitive restructuring in stress management.

4. **Defusing, Engaging, and Confronting Clients**
    The use of active listening and other skills to defuse and engage clients. Trainees participate in exercises and behavioral rehearsals to practice these skills.

5. **Assessment of the Potential for Violent Behavior**
    The major issues surrounding the prediction of violent and dangerous behavior and ideas for improving therapists' skills in assessing the potential for violence in families.

6. **Structuring before Visits**
    Strategies for structuring the family's situation to prevent violence from occurring prior to a visit. Participants practice specific structuring techniques in behavior rehearsal situations.

7. **Assessment and Goal Setting**
    The Homebuilders method of assessing families and developing intervention goals; the use of active listening to obtain information; and techniques for prioritizing problems and developing realistic goals.

8. **Structuring during Visits**
    The use of cognitive, environmental, and interpersonal strategies for structuring the situation to prevent violence during a visit to a family's home.

9. **Structuring between Visits**
    Environmental and behavioral strategies for structuring the family's situation to prevent violence and other harmful actions from occurring between therapists' visits.

10. **Teaching Skills to Families**
    Three methods of teaching skills to families—direct instruction, modeling, and using consequences—and the use of additional aids to enhance the teaching process.

11. **Teaching Families Behavior Management Skills**
    The design and use of behavioral intervention strategies to encourage desirable behaviors and discourage problem behaviors; specific behavior management skills to teach families, including the use of contingent consequences, behavior charts, motivation systems, and contracts; methods for tailoring the intervention to the family and helping families implement behavioral interventions.

Table 3.2.   (continued)

12. **Teaching Communication Skills**
Methods for teaching families the basic communication skills—active listening and using "I" messages.

13. **Teaching Families Cognitive Intervention Skills**
Methods for helping clients recognize that their cognitions (their self-talk) can elicit feelings and behavior and how they can examine and change their cognitions.

14. **When Progress Isn't Occurring**
Some issues to examine when the intervention is not progressing and when a therapist feels "stuck."

15. **Teaching Assertive Skills to Families**
Use of territorial model of assertiveness; how to teach clients to recognize levels of irritation, to respond with assertive behaviors, and to decide when to be assertive.

16. **Anger Management with Families**
The use of cognitive and behavioral interventions in anger management and specific ideas for working with angry or assaultive clients.

17. **Depression and Suicide**
Strategies for intervening with depressed clients.

18. **Multiple Impact Therapy** (MacGregor *et al.,* 1964)
A structured multiple therapist intervention technique, used when a therapist is feeling stuck and when communication within the family is weak.

19. **Teaching Families Problem Solving Skills**
Basic problem solving methods therapists can teach to parents and children; how therapists can help clients to use these problem solving skills in their daily lives.

20. **Teaching Interactions**
The use of the teaching interaction, a direct and positive approach for teaching skills and correcting behavior, and how to teach it to parents; the use of preventive teaching and corrective teaching; dealing with ongoing behavior. Participants practice these skills in behavior rehearsal situations.

21. **Termination Issues**
Guidelines for the termination of intensive, in-home services and for the extension of services: the process of termination; the use of networking; and referrals to ongoing services.

Basic Components of the Model

The beliefs, attitudes and values heretofore explained have influenced the important components of the Homebuilders service delivery model. All are related to each other as well as to the program philosophy. We believe their interaction makes the approach more powerful than if any of the components was to be used separately.

Therapist Availability

As stated, if there are few barriers to receiving services, families are better able to use their existing motivation to change. It is also helpful to utilize their pain to work toward change; therefore the worker must be available to the family at those times when the members are hurting the most. For these reasons, a number of strategies are used to make services easy for the families to access.

Workers are available to clients whenever the families feel that their services can be helpful. Schedules are defined by client need rather than by worker or program convenience. For example, if a family is having the most trouble at 6:30 A.M., when their children must be made ready for early classes, that may be the best time for the therapist to be in the family's home, even though it is probably not the hour she would have chosen for the start of her workday.

By making therapists available at the convenience of the clients, we increase the chances that all family members will be willing to participate in the intervention. Moreover, clients in pain are highly motivated to change and try new ways of coping. It is more difficult for them to say they do not need help when one of the family is sobbing, or the children only have T-shirts and the temperature has suddenly dropped to 20 degrees. When therapists are involved during this highly emotional time and are available when needed, clients are more likely to trust them with a large amount of information. A personal bonding occurs between client and therapist that greatly facilitates further cooperation.

When clients are first accepted into the program, based on certain criteria and on worker availability, a face-to-face meeting takes place within 24 hours. Thereafter, therapists are on consistent call to the client families, available to be in the client home immediately or within a few hours, if a new crisis arises. All clients are given the home phone numbers of their therapist, their therapist's supervisor, and program administrative staff. Because we strongly believe in the advantage of continuity of care, however, the primary worker is expected to let the client know where he or she can be reached, especially during periods when the family seems most fragile. If, by some rare chance, all these staff members are unavailable when needed, clients are able to call a beeper number where a project therapist is always on call.

We have heard concerns expressed that this availability and flexibility might foster dependence. Homebuilders workers, however, feel that the client would not be calling unless something was wrong, and if that is the case, resolving the issue is part of the therapist's job. Loneliness, lack of skills in using resources, or in controlling emotions are all seen as very valid problems, deserving of the therapist's time and effort when the client feels ready to address them. The majority of clients are extremely thoughtful about phoning their therapists. Those who do make frequent calls may need to know there really is someone around whom they can trust; only then will they find the courage to try some new coping behaviors. Most clients are very impressive in their desires and abilities to work through close helping relationships into self sufficiency.

We are, however, continually concerned about making clients dependent instead of strong. We try wherever possible to encourage them to make decisions about every aspect of the service delivery and their lives. We might attempt to summarize their problems for them, but rapidly we begin asking, "Which is most important to you to work on? Here are some alternatives that we might try. Which one makes the most sense to you?" As soon as possible, we want them to be working on their problems themselves. We might go with them to get food at a food bank, to support them and model interactions with the agency, but the goal from the beginning is to teach them how to do it on their own, not to have us do it for them.

Flexible Scheduling

Workers have a flexible schedule, with only two families at a time, allowing them to give clients as much time as needed. We will stay long enough during the defusion stage of the intervention to be sure clients are calm and can be left alone. After the initial visit, appointments are scheduled as often as needed, at times most convenient to the client, including weekends, evenings, and holidays.

A typical case might require 4 hours the first day, 3 hours the second day, telephone contact the third day, 4 hours the fourth day, 3 hours every other day for about a week, and 3 hours three or four times a week for the remaining weeks. Often, there will be one or two additional 4-hour emergency sessions within this period. It is possible, however, for several staff members to work together on especially difficult cases. There have been a few cases in which teams have spent up to 60 hours a week on site. These have usually been cases with a very high potential for violence, where we felt harm might befall one or more family members if there were no outsiders present. In one case in Seattle, 8- and 10-year-old boys had pinched and punched their mother until her body was covered with bruises. The boys overturned furniture and tore out the stuffing. When she tried to set limits on them by putting them in their rooms, they climbed out their windows onto the roof and threatened to jump off. With this family, therapists took shifts so that someone would be there to back up the mother during every waking hour until the situation got under control. In this case, for one boy, it never did. He was placed in a group home. His brother remained at home and the rest of the family settled down. About a year after termination with this family we saw that the boy who was placed had been kidnapped from the group home. Often, if a case requires shifts of workers, we are not able to help them to the degree we would like. As time goes on, we are less likely to try these superhuman efforts for a very long period of time. It is very difficult for workers and the chances of success are not great. Where necessary, workers can spend the night if either parents or children are worried someone will say or do something harmful before morning. Usually, however, it is possible to bring the situation under control without such extensive measures.

Location of Services

Although the bulk of Homebuilders interventions occur in the clients' homes, therapists go where the problems are surfacing—frequently schools, community centers, and teenage hangouts. Although some teenagers are embarrassed to be seen with their therapists, some Homebuilders staff are young and attractive enough to be viewed as status symbols. Teenage clients feel important and involve their friends with their therapist. This can be very beneficial. If we can influence a whole peer group, our client is much more likely to retain progress he or she has made. Sometimes it is helpful for family members to be seen individually, but there is no privacy available at home. A good deal of counseling takes place in restaurants which are often a treat for harried parents. McDonald's therapy can be very beneficial. It is amazing how many teenagers still prize the little toys that come in Happy Meals. It is amazing how many parents prize a little time in peace with a sympathetic adult. Therapists notice that many withdrawn teenagers will talk while they are being driven somewhere. A car or a park may be a better place than an office or even a home to do therapy with a child or teenager. In the Bronx, there are few children who won't suddenly look a therapist right in the face if a visit to the Bronx Zoo is a possibility.

It is possible to reach a much wider range of clients and it is possible to reach much more seriously disturbed clients by seeing them on their turf. In times of crisis, many families are too disorganized to get themselves scheduled for and transported to office visits. In addition, many have had past unsuccessful social services and feel ambivalent about trying again, so that any barriers to service delivery may discourage them completely. No-shows, drop-outs, and cancellations are very rare if services are brought to the client.

Workers are able to make much more accurate assessments because they can see processes in action. They can observe family members using new behaviors, revise plans as needed, and provide support until clients experience success. We can be there when a mother first attempts to put her three year old in his room for time out. We can, with her, hear him tear the drapes down. We can support her in taking the drapes out and closing the door again. We can, literally, if necessary, hold the mother's hand while the child yells. We can model and encourage her in welcoming him back when he calms down. We can have a cup of hot tea with her and congratulate her when it's over. Clients know that the therapists have directly witnessed and experienced their family's problems, instead of just hearing about them and possibly making incorrect assumptions about what happens. It increases a therapist's credibility if a mother knows the therapist experienced a rat running across her foot in the family's apartment, or heard the language a teenage girl used to curse out her father when he asked what time she would return.

Ultimately, families need to be able to use new skills at home. If they learn them in the office, it is often difficult to carry the knowledge to a new situation. Many new behaviors never transfer to the environment where they are really needed. Families can hear about rewarding good behavior, but it is very difficult to understand all the little behaviors involved by just hearing about them. When they watch a therapist praise a child for accepting "no," it becomes much clearer. When the therapist is on the spot coaching them on how to reinforce the child next time, they begin to feel confident they might be able to pull it off. Usually, generalization or transfer of learning is greatly facilitated if all services are provided in the natural environment of the client. Therapists can model skills in the situation where they will be needed.

When intervention takes place in the home, it is more likely that all family members will participate. It is more convenient for them. They get a chance to observe for themselves that no one is being blamed or pushed around. Even if some family members don't participate directly—if they sit in another room and pointedly ignore the therapist—therapists often are surprised to learn how much information these family members pick up by just being in the background. Eventually their curiosity forces them into the foreground. More often than not, they do join in. In one family in Tacoma, the therapist was 6 months pregnant. Although she met the father during the first session, he never came into the living room after that. After about the first 2 weeks, though, he started darting out of the bedroom to give her gifts as she was leaving. Once a banana ("Bananas are good for pregnant women."), once a bag of marshmallows. One time, the therapist was ill and a male team member substituted for her. The father gave him a Playboy magazine as he left. Clearly the father was involved and appreciative even though he chose not to participate directly.

Family members like in-home services. Not only is it more convenient and functional for them, but many comment that it helps alleviate some of their embarrassment at having to ask for services. They feel less subservient and vulnerable and say that it's more like having a friend or family member come over to help. This conceptualization is more comfortable for most than that of the traditional caseworker, social worker, or doctor/patient roles. Clients are more likely to experiment with new options when they feel comfortable.

Flexibility in Services Delivered

In addition to flexibility in scheduling and length of sessions, we think it is important to tailor service packages to the needs of individual families.

The goal of all services is to enable families to resolve their own problems. They may request help in meeting such basic needs as food, clothing, or shelter. They may work on using public transportation, budgeting, nutrition or relationships with school or other social service personnel. Help is also available regarding child development, parenting, communications, anger management, assertiveness and general problem resolution skills. Staff members are expected to have such a wide array of options available to them in any one situation that they can feel free to respect client values and beliefs about interventions. If family members are uncomfortable with behavioral interventions, they may like Rational Emotive Therapy. If they do not respond to Rational Emotive Therapy, they may feel comfortable with values clarification. The service options are limited only by the creativity of the worker and her teammates.

We have been asked why we use highly trained workers, usually with Master's Degrees, to help clients meet basic needs. There are many reasons we believe it is important to involve highly skilled professionals in hard service delivery rather than delegating those tasks to a paraprofessional. A basic goal of Family Preservation Services is to teach families the skills necessary to provide for themselves. While it appears to take fewer skills to provide many concrete services, and in some communities it is fairly easy to find food, housing, or transportation, it is very complicated to teach clients how to perform these tasks and to advocate for themselves. Particularly in New York City, it is an extremely difficult, stressful, and time consuming task to navigate and manipulate even the simplest of agency procedures for obtaining services.

Dividing a family among helping professionals according to tasks that need to be addressed, such as using a professional for therapy and a paraprofessional to deliver concrete services, is often difficult to coordinate and can prove confusing for the family. In addition, we have found that providing concrete services, such as cleaning an apartment or driving a client to the grocery store, is a terrific way to engage clients. Most client families have already been through many therapists. They often believe that the therapists cannot or will not really help. When a therapist provides a concrete service, the client is often surprised and grateful to see that the therapist actually can help. This client is often more willing to begin sharing information or to accept the workers suggestions once the therapist has demonstrated that she/he does more than "talk therapy."

We also have found that clients often are the most open and willing to share information when they are involved in doing concrete tasks with their therapist such as washing the dishes or going to the food bank. Somehow, when people have part of their minds on other things, it often becomes easier for them to let out their deeper, more vulnerable, more complicated feelings and beliefs. It is important that the person who receives this information is the one who is best able to respond and act on it. That person is the therapist.

Using one worker to provide both hard and soft services also helps reduce the compartmentalization of family difficulties and provide a better overall plan. A worker learns a lot about the clients when they spend time on hard services together. It's a good way to observe client's skills in being assertive, handling frustration, etc. More important, the therapist can take advantage of "teachable moments" when providing concrete services, while a less experienced or skilled individual would be unable to do this. Overall, the worker has a more complete perspective and first hand impression of the problems or difficulties the family is experiencing.

Intensity

We have chosen to provide as intense a service as possible because we believe that the most change can occur when people are really upset. We want to be able to see families when they are in crisis, and to respond rapidly and thoroughly to mini-crises that occur during our involvement. In order to maintain this capacity for rapid, comprehensive response we need to keep our caseloads very low. In order to keep our costs reasonable, we need to keep the length of intervention to the minimum necessary to safely stabilize the family without placement.

Worker Caseload

At Homebuilders, workers carry two cases at a time. This allows them the time to provide specific psychoeducational interventions as well as to help meet the basic hard service needs of the family. Overall, Homebuilders therapists see the same total number of families in a year as do therapists in many traditional counseling programs, but the services are concentrated to take advantage of the time when the family is in crisis and experiencing the most pain, and as a result, most open to change.

Workers lose accessibility when they see more than two families at a time. They cannot be as responsive to the needs of six families as they can be to two. Despite the existence of a good back-up system, this lack of accessibility could compromise client safety and possibly result in a tragic event.

Therapists also lose flexibility when they deal with more families. It is harder to stay on with one family, when they happen to need more time, if another family is scheduled shortly thereafter, and maybe another one after that. In addition, Therapists with larger caseloads are on call to more families. Clients who are in crisis or experiencing multiple problems seem to benefit most from immediate responses from their therapist. The smaller the caseload, the more likely it is that the therapist can respond quickly to client crises and concerns, and the greater the impact the therapist can have.

Time constraints can also limit the hard services aspect of the intervention. Providing hard services and teaching families how to gain access to those services is often the most time-consuming part of the intervention. An entire afternoon or day can be spent at the welfare office or a doctor's office, or enrolling a youngster in an after-school program. It would be difficult to find that kind of time if one had to carry responsibility for many families.

We have heard concerns about costs of the two-family caseload being prohibitive. Some who voice these concerns feel more comfortable with therapists seeing six families for 3 months, or twelve families for 6 months. Ironically, these patterns lead to an identical number of families being seen per worker per year (twenty-four). (Actually, most Homebuilders and other family preservation workers serve around twenty families per year because of time for vacations, illnesses and case extensions.) It is important to consider the total number of cases handled during a year rather than just the total being served at any one point in time.

With more traditional services, for example, child welfare guidelines suggest twenty cases per child protective services worker (Child Welfare League of America Standards for Child Protective Service, Revised Edition, 1973, p. 60). Often these cases are open for a year, leading one worker to serve a comparable number of cases per year to the average Homebuilders therapist. Group homes may serve fewer than ten children per year with six to ten workers. This could mean only one case (or fewer) per worker per year. Psychiatric hospitals can have a similar staff to client ratio. Viewed with a yearly perspective, twenty cases per therapist per year is not an unreasonably low expectation.

We also like to keep the caseload low because of concerns about worker burnout. Most families served by Homebuilders are very needy in a number of areas and the therapists' experiences with each family are often very intense. Without adequate time to spend with client families, it is difficult for the therapist to keep track of everything that is going on. In addition, trying to cover more than two families at a time can make being on 24-hour call such a burden as to be unfeasible.

Brevity

Homebuilders usually see families for only 4 weeks, although extensions (up to a total of 8 weeks) are not uncommon, especially in the Bronx, where the wheels of bureaucracy turn more slowly than in the West. We originally adopted the short time period because crisis intervention theorists (Parad, 1965) believe crises and the opportunities they present usually last no longer than 6 weeks.

To many, 4–8 weeks seems like a very short time. Often others in the community are skeptical that significant change can occur in a month or so. Clients, too, often express a desire for more time. It is possible that more could be accomplished with some families if the intervention were longer. Therapists sometimes say they would like more time to work with their clients. A longer intervention would possibly give therapists more time to link their client up with community resources that have waiting lists.

Why, then, have we set 4 weeks as a goal? For one thing, experience has shown us it is usually long enough to prevent placement. There are many differences between Homebuilders and more traditional approaches that make it feasible for Homebuilders to produce change more rapidly. Clients are in crisis. They are seen, sometimes for long, consecutive periods of time, in the settings where the problems are taking place. They see therapists when they need them, for as long as they need them. Because of the low caseload carried by their workers, it is possible for clients to get, in 4 weeks, the equivalent number of hours that one would receive in 1 year of outpatient therapy. One participant in a training workshop referred to the short-term approach as a "microwave" intervention, where the outcome is comparable to longer term models.

There are a number of advantages to an intensive, short-term intervention. Paramount is the expectation that change can occur rapidly. The Home-builders therapist discusses the 4-week time frame with the client family during the first home visit, and continues to refer to it frequently throughout the intervention period. For many families, it is an astounding notion that things could just change, rapidly. They are flattered by someone's belief that they can achieve goals. This expectation seems to influence the client and the therapist so that both are more willing to "give it their all." The expectation that change can occur rapidly is positive for many clients. They are relieved to hear that their problems may not drag on for months or years. It helps clients gear up for a big effort.

The brief time frame also helps keep both the therapist and the client focused on the specific goals, as well as on what interventions are or are not working. Furthermore, when they know there is a definite time period available, it is much more likely that they will use the time productively. With their therapist, families are continually reassessing priorities and possible avenues of change. We believe this assessment process is an important skill for them to have and we hope they use it long after we are gone.

After 4 weeks, many clients have reached a plateau and are ready to take a break from the hard work of changing their lives. Having the intervention go beyond 4 weeks also makes it more difficult for workers to maintain the intensity of their effort and keep their energy level up. Usually, the crisis is over within a month. Once it is past, we lose many of the motivators of a crisis and make much less progress on goals. Continuing to push for progress may be counterproductive beyond this point. For many it is like going on a successful diet and getting into a size 12 dress. Not everyone is interested in becoming a size 8 or 10.

Moreover, we have found that the success rate of averting out-of-home placement does not appear to be influenced by the length of the intervention. Over the years at Homebuilders, we have tried varying the length of the intervention. We have experimented with 8 week, 6 week, and 4 week interventions, maintaining identical goals and intensity. Our gradual decrease in intervention from an average of 8 weeks to 4 weeks, because of pressure to serve more clients, did not make a difference in our overall success rate. Informal data at Homebuilders indicate that if a family has not been able to profit from the 4- to 8-week intervention, their situation is unlikely to really turn around after that time. When we do extend cases for much longer, our success rate drops significantly.

For the agency, the time limit helps us to keep costs down, serve more cases, and make possible lower caseloads per therapist. Longer interventions cost more (unless we also increase the caseloads). The increased cost and/or length of the intervention can be difficult to justify to funding sources that want to pay only for prevention of placement and can point to documentation that it is possible to prevent placement with 4 to 6 weeks of service. In addition, a shorter intervention helps prevent worker burnout and stress by limiting the amount of time that staff are expected to cope with any one set of problems.

Even though we recommend a 4-week goal for the intervention period, this time limit should be considered a guideline, not an absolute limit. It is important to remember that, although most cases can be terminated in 4 weeks, there will be some families that need more time and some families that need less time. It is also important to remember that this guideline must always remain secondary to the program's basic goal of helping most families avert placement by learning to cope with their problems.

Limited Objectives

Our comfort with the short time limit of our intervention is closely related to our program goals. At the end of 4 weeks, we are very rarely finished to the point where clients feel they have accomplished all that they can, or where therapists feel they have offered all that they are able to provide. Usually, there is some unfinished business. Most families are getting along much better, but most still have some problems coping with their emotions. Their houses are not always clean. The children do not go to school 100% of the time.

Our goal is not to make the perfect family. For one thing, we do not know what perfect families look like. If the goal of our service was to have the maximum effect on the family, to help them change as much as they possibly can, the total hours needed could be unlimited. In our experience, no one is ever finished growing or learning.

If the goal is to prevent out-of-home placement, then one needs only as many hours as it takes to resolve the immediate crises and teach whatever skills the clients need to be able to maintain the family without intensive help. At Homebuilders, program goals are limited: to prevent the need for out-of-home placement and to teach families the basic skills necessary to remain living together. In some cases, families still need services. What we have done is help them to attain a level of functioning that will allow them to benefit from more traditional services. For example, most of our families could not get themselves to weekly appointments at a counseling agency at the time they were referred to us. They were too disorganized, too angry, too discouraged to make it. At the end of Homebuilders intervention, however, they may have different ideas about what "help" can be like. They have had an experience where putting in time with a therapist began to pay off for them. They are usually getting along quite a bit better with each other and have more energy for getting to appointments.

We also believe that some of the situations facing our clients are not problems that can be resolved, no matter how much time is available with a therapist, but rather predicaments to be endured as gracefully as possible and coped with as effectively as possible. For example, a woman bound to a wheelchair is going to have a difficult time raising two young children by herself. Parenting skills will help, as will social support, but the going will be rough. Similarly, the wife of a navy man is probably going to feel lonely, frightened, resentful and abandoned some of the time she is left home with five kids. She can learn to decrease the panic she feels. She can make new friends and develop more positive relationships with her children, but she will still be lonely, and there will still be a big gap in her life. In the Bronx, many families live in dangerous neighborhoods with substandard housing and drug abuse all around. They can learn to be assertive with landlords and to use housing advocates effectively. They can learn to stay off the streets at night and to teach their children to say "no." They can learn to bear some of the pressures with less emotional strain. But life will still be difficult. All family members will still live in far more danger than any of us would like to see. Life offers all of us some challenges and most of us some burdens. Social services like Homebuilders cannot and should not be expected to fix everything.

Staffing

We believe that the most efficient, cost-effective, and least intrusive structure is to use a single therapist per case, with team back-up. Each therapist is responsible for conducting the entire intervention for each of his or her clients but has ready access to the larger team for support and back-up.

Using a team of two therapists—one professional and one paraprofessional—to see families can seem appealing, especially when you consider the intensity of the service, the 24-hour accessibility of the therapist, the severity of the problems faced by the client population, and the emphasis on accountability. A team of two therapists would probably be safer going to and from families, especially in some urban areas. The team approach may also feel more comfortable to some planning groups that are concerned about finding one person who is willing or able to provide a wide range of hard and soft services.

As a general rule, two heads are better than one, and two observers are better than one, so most therapists initially believe they would like working in teams. They feel that using two therapists might reduce the total number of weeks necessary for the intervention because two people would be working with each family. In addition, the two therapists could share being on call. It also is helpful to have two people to model good communications and problem solving for the family.

There are, however, a number of compelling reasons for using a single therapist supported by team back-up. For one thing, a major goal of Family Preservation Services is to develop a no-lose consensus plan for each family. The therapist's duty is to everyone. If one person is responsible for all family members, he or she is motivated to get as much information as possible from all family members for a good synthesis. If family members are assigned to different workers, the therapists sometimes tend to advocate for their particular clients rather than for the family as a whole.

It is easier for the family to learn to trust and relate to one person rather than two. It is difficult enough to talk with one stranger about all your weaknesses and perceived inadequacies, about all the times you were hurt and did not know what to do about it. We think it may be more than twice as hard to really open up to two new people. For many clients it may be impossible. For many families, one of their problems is having so many different workers pushing them in different directions. One worker may think the mother needs to be more firm; the other worker may think she needs to be more understanding. Minimizing this pressure and confusion is helpful.

Using a team takes more planning, debriefing, and record keeping time. Information can easily be lost between the two team members, and neither may really have a view of the big picture. It is also more difficult to do spontaneous interventions; that is, to identify an opportunity and to take advantage of it and teach. Often a therapist is responding to the immediate situation and has no time to plan or coordinate with someone else about the skill that needs to be taught. In addition, it is not uncommon for team workers to disagree about family directions. Control can become a big issue between team members and any hard feelings between the two workers can have an impact on the intervention. Family members also find it difficult to know whom to call when they are in a crisis. It can also be very time consuming for co-therapists to consult about and coordinate their interventions.

There are also disadvantages in dividing the work in the intervention according to task, such as using a professional for therapy and a paraprofessional to provide concrete services. Frequently, the person who provides concrete help has a much closer relationship with the family as a result of the amount of time spent with its members. As a result of the closeness of that relationship it is not only difficult for the hard service person to keep family members from talking about "therapy" issues, but it is also possible for the "therapist" to feel left out of or impeded by that relationship. The paraprofessional may also feel upset that he or she is paid much less than the professional team member despite the fact that he/she probably has accomplished just as much or more with the family.

Using a team to see each family can blur accountability. Therapists often do not feel as much of a sense of accomplishment when things go well because they have to share credit with another team member. In contrast, when things are going poorly, it is hard to determine whether the problems lie with one worker or the other, or the interaction between the two.

In addition, especially at the beginning of the intervention, it is helpful to minimize the number of "helpers" on the scene. We have had clients referred with as many as fifteen different case managers, each one thinking he or she was in charge. Sometimes the number of conflicting messages received by social service personnel can itself be a major problem. We want to help reduce confusion and fragmentation, not add to it.

Workers usually feel safer in teams, and in some situations this may be the case. There is some evidence, however, that when they travel in teams—especially at night—two workers may appear more threatening to clients who are upset. In Seattle, for example, pairs of mental health commitment officers are more likely to be attacked by clients than are individual workers.

All these aspects of the model—the rapid response to referrals, the accessibility of workers at home during evenings and weekends, the time available for families, the location of the services, the staffing pattern, the low caseloads, and the brief duration of services—produce a much more powerful intervention than one that utilizes only one or two of these components. It is impossible to have the intensity and flexibility we would like with a large caseload. It is impossible to maintain focus, responsiveness to crisis, and accessibility if the intervention drifts on for too long a period. We urge others considering replication of Homebuilders to try the whole package first and tailor it to their communities if they encounter difficulties. If they eliminate one aspect, such as the short time frame or the low caseload, they are likely to decrease the power of the overall intervention far more than they can realize without first attempting the whole model.

We believe that most families deserve strong, effective support in attempting to learn productive ways to cope with overwhelming problems before children are placed outside the home. So far, this combination of program strategies is the most powerful we have seen.

Evaluation

The Homebuilders Program has been evaluated in many different ways. At this point, we would like to summarize a number of the methods of evaluation and results of various studies. Each has its own set of limitations, but taken as a whole, we believe they provide encouraging evidence that we do prevent placement and help families learn to resolve some of their presenting problems.

One of the most basic issues has been the program's ability to actually prevent placement. We track clients by phone, letter, and the Washington State Department of Social and Health Services computer systems to see whether or not they get placed. Until 1982, we followed clients for 3 months past intake. Although client populations varied slightly, an average of 94% avoided out-of-home placement for at least 3 months. Since 1982, we have tracked clients for 1 year after intake. For this time period, 88% avoided placement. Placements include state-funded foster, group, psychiatric, or correctional care settings. We do not count as placement situations where a child goes to live with extended family members or another parent or brief respite care of less than two weeks.

Once the issue of placement is addressed, we are then concerned with the cost effectiveness of the model. We want to know how the costs of Homebuilders compare with the costs of out-of-home placement. In Washington State, we obtain information regarding the average costs of different out-of-home placements from the Washington State Department of Social and Health Services. We take the average cost per time period and multiply it by the average length of stay to get the average cost per client. We compare these costs to the actual costs of Homebuilders. Assuming all cases would have been placed, costs of Homebuilders were $31,646,857 less than the average costs of placement. A summary of this information is shown in Table 3.3.

This information is heartening. Using these cost differences, we can also form some hypotheses about the number of placements that would have to be averted in order to justify the initial cost of a program. For example, if an average group care placement costs $22,373 and it costs $200,000 per year to begin a program, only 8.9 placements (200,000 divided by 22,373) must be averted in order to recoup program costs.

These figures are very interesting to legislators and policy makers, but they do have some limitations. We do not know for sure that clients we see would have been placed. The cost comparisons are narrow, involving only the cost of Homebuilders and out-of-home placement, when, in actuality, many other services and resources may have been utilized.

We have conducted two studies designed to examine the issue of whether clients referred to Homebuilders really would have been placed. The first, in 1976–1977, involved overflow clients who were status offenders referred from the Pierce County Juvenile Court. In this group, 73% of the clients who were seen by Homebuilders were not placed. Of the clients who were not served by Homebuilders (because we were full), 72% were placed. The second comparison study involved overflow mental health cases referred by the Pierce County Office of Involuntary Commitment. In this study, 100% of the comparison cases and 20% of the treatment cases were placed.

Of course whether or not a child gets placed is only part of our concern. We want to know not only if a child is placed, but how he and his family are functioning. We have tried to find out if they are really better off after Homebuilders involvement. One of our best ways of tracking client progress is the Goal Attainment Scaling that is the foundation of our recordkeeping system. Two to four goals are set with each family and then rated weekly regarding progress. If progress does not occur, the treatment plan is changed.

We have also used a number of more formal measures of client functioning. In the 1980 Mental Health Study, we found improvements on the Global Assessment Scale and the Child Behavior Checklist.

Table 3.3. Homebuilders Cost Effectiveness with Various Client Populations, 1974–1986[a,b]

Client population category	Numbers served	Success rate 3 mos after termination[a] (%)	Potential placements	Cost of potential placements ($)	Cost of Homebuilders ($)	Cost difference between placement and Homebuilders placement ($)
Families in conflict	1,262	94	66% Foster care 32% Group care 2% Psychiatric care	7,030,520 9,038,692 1,125,000	3,281,200	13,913,012
Child abuse/neglect	1,198	95	88% Foster care 9% Group care 3% Psychiatric care	7,574,044 2,416,284 1,620,000	3,114,800	8,495,528
Delinquency	250	92	37% Foster care 63% Group care	784,920 3,512,561	650,000	3,647,481
Child mental health	123	83	13% Foster care 87% Residential treatment	135,040 3,068,546	319,800	2,883,786
Child mental health study[d]	25	83	100% long-term psychiatric care	2,572,500	128,250	2,444,250
Developmental disability	45	95	100% Foster care	379,800	117,000	262,800
Total	2,928	94		39,257,907	7,611,050	31,646,857

[a]The cost effectiveness of Homebuilders' family preservation model has been evaluated by comparing the average cost of Homebuilders with the average costs of projected out-of-home placements. The average cost of Homebuilders is obtained by dividing program costs by the total number of clients served. Costs of placements are obtained by multiplying the average costs per day or month by the average length of stay. 1986–1987 costs of placement were obtained from the following Washington State Department of Social and Health Services figures:

Table 3.3. (continued)

	Average length of stay (mos)	Average cost per month ($)	Total cost per client ($)
Homebuilders			2,600
Foster care: CPS	19.4	370	7,186
Foster care: FRS, DD, Delinquent, Mental health	19.4	435	8,440
Group care	13	1,721	22,373
Residential treatment	13	2,206	28,678
Acute psychiatric hospitalization	4	11,250	45,000
Long-term psychiatric care	14	7,350	102,900

[b]Portions of 1982 data are unavailable due to change in parent agency.

[c]Since 1983, follow-up data are available for one year after intake. Those data show an overall success rate of 88%.

[d]Specific mental health project conducted in 1979.

One limitation of these methods is that they involve verbal reports about behavior instead of actual observations of the behavior. There is also the possibility of a regression phenomenon. Since all the clients we assist are in crisis, it is reasonable to believe that there would be improvement on some of these measures over time without intervention.

We have also relied heavily on client feedback as a means of assessing the effectiveness of our intervention and the degree to which goals were actually met. We contact clients routinely, 3 and 12 months after intake. A summary of 1 year's client feedback information is shown in Table 3.4

In the previously mentioned mental health study, we also obtained ratings from parents regarding improvements on presenting problem behaviors. A summary of those reports is shown in Table 3.5.

In one study funded by the Administration for Children, Youth and Families, client mothers, children and therapists were interviewed within 24 hours after a session to determine events that were helpful or non-helpful, the degree of helpfulness/non-helpfulness, the responsibility attribution for the event, and the correlations of all these with the ultimate outcome of the case. Trained judges were able to reliably assign 1120 critical incidents into eight thematic categories. The most significant finding in this study

Table 3.4. Homebuilders 1985 Client Feedback Survey: King, Pierce, Snohomish, and Spokane Counties

1. Do you think this outcome is the best for your family at this time?
   a. For families where child is living at home:

Yes	204	(85%)
No	21	(8%)
Not sure	16	(7%)

   b. For families where child is living out of home:

Yes	13	(59%)
No	5	(23%)
Not sure	4	(18%)

2. Was Homebuilders helpful or not helpful to your family?

5 Very helpful	190	(67%)
4	58	(20%)
3	25	(9%)
2	5	(2%)
1 Not helpful	4	(1%)
0	2	(1%)

3. Did you find Homebuilders more or less helpful than other counseling you have had?

More helpful	151	(87%)
Equal	13	(8%)
Less helpful	8	(3%)

Table 3.4.   (continued)

4. How helpful was the previous counseling you had?
       5 Very helpful   27   (27%)
       4   8   (8%)
       3   16   (16%)
       2   19   (19%)
       1 Not helpful   28   (28%)
       0   3   (2%)
5. Would you recommend Homebuilders to a family in a situation similar to your family's?
       Yes   263   (97%)
       No   5   (2%)
       Not sure   3   (1%)
6. Was it helpful that your therapist came to your home for appointments?
       Yes   269   (98%)
       No   5   (1.5%)
       Not sure   1   (.5%)
7. Did you feel that your therapist really cared about your family?
       Yes   202   (99%)
       No   —
       Not sure   2   (1%)
8. Did your therapist schedule appointments at times that were best or most convenient for you?
       Yes   274   (99%)
       No   1   (.5%)
       Not sure   1   (.5%)
9. Did you feel that the therapist really listened and understood your situation?
       Yes   269   (97%)
       No   7   (2%)
       Not sure   2   (1%)
10. Was your therapist available to you when you really needed him/her?
       Yes   272   (99%)
       No   2   (1%)
       Not sure   —
11. Was your therapist on time for appointments?
       Yes   180   (97%)
       No   5   (3%)
       Not sure   —
12. Did your therapist ever seem to take sides?
       Yes   11   (5%)
       No   225   (94%)
       Not sure   3   (1%)

Table 3.5.   Parent and Therapist Ratings of Improvement of
Presenting Problems in Homebuilders Mental Health Study

Problems	No. cases with problem at intake	Parent/therapist ratings of condition at termination (%)		
		Worse	Same	Better
Disorientation	5			100
Delusions	3			100
Hallucinations	2			100
Inappropriate affect	8			100
Assault to others	13			92
Social isolation	9		44	56
Lack of cooperation	11		10	90
Lack of motivation	7			100
Dependency	12			100
Depression	16	6	6	88
High suicide potential	8			100
Drug abuse	6	16.5	16.5	67
Alcohol abuse	6		75	25
Learning disability	4		75	25
Sexual assault to others	1			100
Thought disorder	1			100
Affective disorder	5			100
No school	10		30	70
Anxiety	17	6	18	76
Medical problems	2		100	
Problems with anger	17	6		94
Sleep disturbance	3		33	67
Hyperactivity	7		14	86
Impaired judgment	15		20	80
Impaired communication	13		15	85
Obsessional rituals	2			100
Speech impairment	2		100	
Delinquent acts	8	12	25	63
Poor impulse control	12		25	75
Psychosomatic illness	3		33	67
Phobias	7			100
Peer problems	11		36	64
Physical handicap	1		100	
Assault to property	9		22	78
Averages		1.5	17	81.5

was the importance of the provision of concrete services in helping to avert placement.

Limitations of client feedback measures are that clients may be telling us what they think we want to hear. Also, their comments may not be linked to actual changes in problem behaviors.

Homebuilders have also been evaluated formally and informally by many outside auditors and evaluators, including the American Criminal Justice Institute, the Washington State Legislature, the Washington State Department of Social and Health Services, the Washington State Office of Research and Evaluation, and the National Institute of Mental Health. Outside auditors and evaluators have limits, too. They usually begin by focusing on goal attainment ratings and costs, but as they get closer to the client stories in the records, and if they talk with clients themselves, they rapidly shift to concern about what is really happening in families' lives. Objectivity suffers as compassion rears its subjective head.

More recently, we completed a study funded by the Department of Health and Human Services to evaluate and compare the Homebuilders Program in Washington State with Family Preservation Projects in Utah. Results from this study demonstrated significant improvement in parent and child functioning and social support over the course of the treatment.

As we have mentioned before, however, some of the most important measures of the program's validity are personal accounts of what has really happened with one or two cases. To that end, we present two case summaries.

The Clark Family: Child Abuse

The Clark family was referred to Homebuilders by a public health nurse.[1] The nurse requested that the Homebuilders intervention coincide with the release of the Clark's infant daughter from the hospital. The baby had been born prematurely and had spent the first 3 months of her life in the hospital.

The nurse requested intensive services because she was concerned about the family situation. The Clark's three-year-old son recently had been diagnosed as hyperactive and as having some brain damage. Children's Protective Services and the nurse were also questioning three concussions that the boy had had over the last year. The nurse and CPS were certain that unless Homebuilders was available to see the family, both children would have to be placed in foster care.

The nurse discussed her concerns with the parents, and they consented to allowing a Homebuilders therapist to come to their home. The family had no phone, so the therapist dropped by unannounced for a visit. Mrs. Clark was home at the time, so the therapist asked if she could stay awhile and talk.

After sitting down, the first thing the therapist noticed was the smell of gas leaking from the furnace. Mrs. Clark said she thought she had smelled gas, but hadn't felt

[1]Currently all referrals are routed through the Department of Social and Health Services.

up to walking to the public phone to call her landlord. The family's pediatrician had ordered her to get a telephone installed because of the uncertain condition of the baby, but since her husband was not working regularly, they couldn't afford to pay the installation fee.

The therapist suggested that Mrs. Clark dress herself and the children warmly, open the window and turn the furnace down. While she did that, the therapist went to a public phone and called the landlord to send out a repairman.

When the therapist returned, Mrs. Clark talked about her situation. She said she had been very depressed since the baby's birth, and that she often felt that the child did not belong to her. She was also extremely upset about her son's "wild" behavior. She wondered if the boy had a "bad seed" in him like his uncle who was in prison. She had begun to think that she might kill him rather than watch him grow up to be a murderer like his uncle.

Mrs. Clark was very thin, pale and weak. She had a chronic cold, and had lost her front teeth due to poor health. Now 22, she had had three children and four miscarriages in five years of marriage. She also said she was very lonely. Her husband usually was away from the house from mid-morning to late at night. He worked as an insurance salesman, but he had not sold a policy in five months. The woman told the therapist that every other counselor they had seen had told her that her husband was "rotten" and that she should leave him. She said she loved him and that he didn't beat her. The family had moved to Washington from Idaho several months previously so that they could remain married, yet still be eligible for state aid. Currently they were receiving funds from the WIN program.

The next day the therapist approached a local charitable organization and got the $25 needed to have a telephone installed. She also got two old bedsheets that could be nailed up as curtains, since Mrs. Clark had expressed fears about sitting alone at night with no curtains for privacy. She had told the therapist that one night recently a strange man had been peering in her window. She had been raped once before and was scared it might happen again.

During the next home visit, they focused a lot on the three-year-old son. Mrs. Clark said that she did not love him, and described a variety of what she labeled as self-destructive and wild behaviors that he engaged in. She reported incidents such as him throwing himself backwards off furniture, touching the hot stove and laughing, turning on the kitchen burners, banging his head against the wall until he passed out, biting, scratching, and hitting other people. Although he was three, he still had not started talking. She was concerned that Children's Protective Services would think she was abusing him because he hurt himself so much, and because they locked him in his room at night. The Clarks did this because the boy only slept 2 or 3 hours at a stretch, and if he was not locked in his room, he would go into the kitchen and eat until he vomited. She said CPS thought she should put him in an institution because she couldn't handle him. He would not kiss or show any affection to people. She said he had been removed from the home by Children's Protective Services in Idaho the previous year when she had "a nervous breakdown" and was hospitalized. Since moving to Tacoma, the parents had already voluntarily placed the boy once for 72 hours because the mother felt she "couldn't cope" with him any longer. She was also afraid she might harm him because he made her so angry sometimes.

Before leaving that day, Mrs. Clark and the therapist made a list of what she could do if she felt her son's behavior was so bad that she would want to place him again. The Homebuilder let her know she thought it was a good idea to lock him in his room sometimes and explained the concept of Time Out. The list also included calling the Homebuilder (the family's phone was to be installed the next day). Then they made an appointment to take the son to Mary Bridge Children's Hospital Learning Center to see about enrolling him in a special school program. Finally, the therapist talked with the mother about making some free time for herself, and volunteered to babysit for several hours later that week. Mrs. Clark accepted the offer.

Later that week, the Homebuilder was alone with the children for 5 hours while she was babysitting. She learned a lot about the young boy. She observed him engage in some of the behaviors Mrs. Clark had reported. By the end of the day, however, she determined that he responded to positive reinforcement and Time Out. During the afternoon she taught him to play a kissing game. The information gathered that day was invaluable. It was proof for both the therapist and the mother that the little boy could change, and that he did care about people. His mother cried the first time they played the kissing game.

During the second week of the intervention, Mrs. Clark began to talk more freely about her discontent with her marriage. She said that she knew her husband wasn't really working all the times he was gone. She expressed resentment over the fact that he dressed nicely while she had only one outfit, that he was free to play all day and night while she sat confined in their apartment, that he would not let her get a driver's license but also would not drive her places. Feeling she had reached a teachable moment, the Homebuilder began to talk about territoriality and assertiveness training. The Homebuilder also called the woman's DSHS caseworker and got authorization to get her front teeth replaced.

Mr. Clark was beginning to get curious about what was happening. One day he stayed home to meet the therapist. While his wife was at the dentist, he and the Homebuilder spent several hours talking. He shared his own frustrations about having to be on welfare. The Homebuilder told him that she wanted him to be a part of the counseling process and he agreed to attend the next session. After their discussion he seemed more willing to participate.

During the last weeks of the intervention, the therapist focused primarily on teaching the parents some behavioral child-management skills. The son had begun attending Mary Bridge school program, and Mrs. Clark rode the bus with him every day. The Homebuilder was pleased to see this, as it gave the mother a chance to watch the teachers, and to make friends with the staff there. Mrs. Clark reported having some positive feelings about her son, and no longer felt she should send him away. She also began to feel much better about herself. She had temporary caps on her teeth, and began to smile more. She was also beginning to gain a little weight.

As the end of the intervention approached, the therapist and Mrs. Clark explored ways she could continue counseling. She decided that she wanted to go back to a counselor at the mental health center. She had seen the counselor a couple of times right after the baby was born last summer, and thought she could trust her. She made an appointment.

During her last week with the family, the therapist helped the Clarks move to a better apartment in the neighborhood where they felt safer. It wasn't until after the move that the family found out the Mary Bridge bus would no longer be able to transport the boy to school. Mrs. Clark became very upset, but quickly deescalated herself and began to problem solve. She talked with the counselors at Mary Bridge and followed their suggestion to see if the boy could be transferred to Child Study and Treatment Center's day care program. There were no openings at the Center but he was put on the waiting list.

A follow-up call from this family several months later revealed that although there had been a number of upsetting events that had happened after the Homebuilder left, they were still together as a family. Mrs. Clark had been seeing her counselor and had continued to work on being more assertive. She and her husband were also going for marital counseling. Mr. Clark had quit selling insurance and was enrolled in a job training program. The son was attending the new school, and the mother was participating in a parent education program required by the school. The Clarks reported that their son was starting to talk and did not seem as "wild." The infant daughter was doing fine as well.

Homebuilder costs for the Clark family intervention totalled $2,937. If the mother had been placed in a psychiatric hospital, the cost of hospitalization would have been $5,926. If the two children had been removed by Children's Protective Services, the cost of their placement would have been $15,000 or $7,500 each. Total costs would have been $20,926.

Gary: Mental Health

This case was referred to Homebuilders by the Office of Involuntary Commitment. There were several major problem areas. Gary, a 15-year-old boy, had severe behavior problems and was suspected of being pre-psychotic or of having a severe character disorder.

Gary had violent temper outbursts daily; he would scream obscenities and end up on the floor sobbing he should be killed or that he would kill someone else. Gary had punched dozens of holes in the walls and doors of his parents' house. Once he put all his bedroom furniture in a pile and chopped it into little pieces. His 12-year-old sister was in a body case from a spinal operation. He would spit in her face and hit her. One time a babysitter locked herself in the parents' bedroom during a fight with Gary. He took a pellet gun and shot at the door.

When the therapist went to the home, it became evident that the family was violent, not just the boy. During one disagreement the stepfather put a gun to Gary's head and marched him out to the car, tied one of the boy's legs to the bumper, and threatened to drag him if he didn't shape up. The stepfather has said, "I'm going to kill him or me if this doesn't get better." At other times, the stepfather had hit Gary with pieces of wood and scratched his face with his fingernails. The mother spat at Gary.

Many fights centered around Gary not doing chores, even though he was around home all day. He had been expelled from school. Teachers said, "Everybody hates him. You can't trust him for a minute. The only emotion he feels is anger." The parents' relationship was very strained due to family problems; the stepfather had walked out twice in the last 6 months. Both parents told the therapist that a divorce seemed imminent.

The therapist spent several days just listening in order to let everyone make sure their version of the problem had been fully understood. All expressed relief and all expressed interest in learning different ways to cope. The mother was the first to make a major change; she learned active listening so that when Gary started to yell at her, instead of yelling back, she was able to help him calm himself down. This resulted in a rapid reduction of his outbursts. The boy was also trying to notice what triggered his anger. He began to learn Rational Emotive Therapy to tell himself calming statements. The stepfather also began working on other ways of expressing his frustration. All family members learned to recognize when their frustration and anger was beginning to build and to construct "I" messages before the situation got out of control.

The stepfather began leaving lists of chores for the boy to do each day. Gary's allowance was contingent upon task completion. The school was unwilling to give Gary another chance, so the therapist arranged for a tutor to come to the home.

At the end of 5 weeks, there had been only two major outbursts. Gary was doing 80% of his chores and getting almost straight A's in his work with the tutor. His mother said, "I don't feel afraid anymore." On one occasion the therapist provided child care so that the parents could take a brief vacation, during which they renewed their commitment to their marriage. The relationship between Gary and his stepfather remained strained. Since the family lived in a remote area of the county and it would be difficult for them to locate appropriate ongoing services, the family decided they would rather have weekly follow-up sessions with the Homebuilder therapist instead of one extra week of intensive service.

Two years later, the therapist ran into the boy at the county fair. He was still living at home. Out-of-home placement was no longer an option. Homebuilders cost was $4,200. Hospitalization would have cost the State of Washington over $36,000.

References

Child Welfare League of America (1973). *Standards for child protective service (revised edition)*. Washington, DC: Author.

MacGregor, R., Ritchie, A. M., Serrano, A. C., and Schuster, F. P., Jr. (1964). *Multiple impact therapy with families*. New York: McGraw-Hill.

Parad, H. J. (1965). *Crisis intervention*. New York: Family Services Association of America.

Chapter 4

Family-Based Services and Public Policy: Context and Implications

Brenda G. McGowan

Introduction

Homebuilders, one of the more sophisticated models in the current range of family preservation services, illustrates both literally and figuratively the ambiguities and paradoxes inherent in our policy framework for families and children at risk. The very name of this program embodies some of the core values undergirding the American social welfare system, as does its philosophy and its mode of operation.

A splendid program by all accounts, this is an intensive, short-term, crisis intervention service that aims to prevent unnecessary out-of-home placement of children by teaching families "to handle their own problems rather than continually relying on the state to rescue them when things get rough" (Kinney *et al,* this volume, Chapter 3). Carefully directed to families that cannot remain intact without outside help, Homebuilders is cost effective, makes expert use of modern interventive technology, and emphasizes concepts of nuclear family autonomy, independence, optimism, pragmatism, and hard work.

These characteristics, all very consonant with current trends in child welfare policy, clearly contribute to the apparent success of the program. Yet, some of the factors that lead to programmatic success—narrowly defined target population, crisis orientation, residual definition of need, limited service objectives, and high value on family autonomy and independence—reflect policies that are dysfunctional when viewed from the perspective of the total population of families and children at risk. The very invention of family preservation services such as Homebuilders—excellent as these programs may be—testifies to the failure of past and current social policies to insure provision of the institutional supports required to enable parents to meet their children's developmental needs.

Using the Homebuilders program as an exemplar, this chapter will examine the interplay between policy and practice in the field of family and children's services. Historical shifts and tensions leading to the present system of service delivery will be described in the first section. This will be followed by a discussion of the current policy framework for provision of family and children's services. Ongoing policy dilemmas will be analyzed in the third section; the final section will examine the educational and policy implications of the family preservation experiment.

Historical Shifts in Public Policy

In the early days of this country there was no explicit public policy related to child welfare. Children were regarded as the property of their parents and had no special rights. Those who survived beyond infancy were defined as an economic resource and expected to help with household and farm labor at very young ages. The thought of state intervention in family life for the benefit of the child was never even entertained. A few private institutions for orphans were established during the Colonial period, but most orphaned children were cared for informally by relatives or neighbors and expected to serve the same economic functions as children born to a family.

The only group of children thought to require any special attention from public authorities were children of paupers. There was a meager system of public assistance in place for such families termed "outdoor relief." Because of the fear that these children would acquire the "bad habits" of their parents, they were frequently farmed-out to families who agreed to maintain them for a contracted fee, or indentured, or placed in a public almshouse. No effort was made to provide services to poor children or parents in their own homes. Moreover, little thought was given to the right of the community to intervene in such situations. It was simply assumed that paupers, who were socially condemned, had forfeited their right to plan for their children.

This rather laissez faire pattern of care for children in need began to change radically during the nineteenth century due to the many shifts occurring in the social order at that time. Widespread economic growth led to the emergence of a bourgeois class in which the labor of women and children was not required at home, and influential citizens had the time and resources necessary to focus attention on the developmental needs of children. As a consequence of the massive waves of immigration during the 1800's, increased urbanization, and the economic and social havoc wreaked by the Civil War and the Industrial Revolution, low-income families began to face new hazards. Large numbers of poor children were left alone on the streets, frequently engaging in criminal behavior in order to survive.

Many new programs were initiated in order to respond to these challenges. The first major shift in social provision was the development of large numbers of voluntary and public institutions designed to care for dependent children as well as for those who were orphaned. Repeated investigations and exposes of the horrendous conditions in these institutions led to the creation of a new approach to care called free foster homes. This concept was promulgated by Charles Loring Brace, who established the Children's Aid Society in New York in 1853. As a way to save children from the evils of the city and give them proper moral training and work habits, he recruited what were defined as "good Christian homes" located in rural areas of the Midwest and upstate New York to care for homeless and destitute children that were picked up on the streets and shipped out in trainloads from the city.

In a very parallel but somewhat later development, Martin Van Buren Van Arsdale established a statewide voluntary agency in Illinois in 1883, the Children's Home Society, to provide free foster homes for dependent children. Both of these efforts were widely replicated, thus institutionalizing the foster care tradition that persists today. By the end of the century there were Children's Aid Societies in most of the major Eastern cities, and Children's Home Societies had been established in 36 midwestern and southern states by 1916. Children's institutions, particularly those organized under sectarian auspices and those designed for black children, continued to flourish during this time, thus creating a sharp increase in the total number of children placed outside their own homes.

Several other developments of the late nineteenth century related to the provision of family and children's services have direct relevance to current policy issues surrounding the provision of family preservation services. One was the increasing recognition that children who commit criminal acts should be treated differently from adults and the subsequent establishment, first of "reform" schools for delinquent youth, and later, of community-based probation programs and the juvenile court. A second major initiative of this period was the founding of the Charity Organization Society in 1877, a movement that aimed to rationalize charity and promote individual reform by sending volunteer friendly visitors into the homes of poor people to provide advice and serve as role models for parents. This first systematic effort to promote family well-being by the provision of individual case services provided a context and a model for the development of the social work profession and for what later became family service agencies. Although the settlement house movement that evolved at the same time also helped to shape the profession, it seemed to have little impact on the structure and objectives of the early family service and child welfare agencies.

Perhaps the most important development of this period in relation to the provision of children's services was the establishment of the early Societies for the Prevention of Cruelty to Children. The first was founded in New York in 1874, and by 1900 there were 250 such agencies in various parts of the country. Although published accounts of the activities of these societies suggest that the early leaders saw their primary function as prosecution of parents, not protection of children, they gradually assumed broader responsibilities. Moreover, their establishment signaled an emerging recognition of society's right and obligation to intervene in family life when necessary to protect the welfare of children. This view and the associated concept of minimally acceptable standards for child rearing have been central in all subsequent debates about appropriate service provision for families and children at risk. Commenting on the gradual elevation of children's rights in relation to parental prerogatives, Bremner (1971, p. 117) noted:

> As the state intervened more frequently and effectively in the relations between parent and child in order to protect children against parental mismanagement, the state also forced children to conform to public norms of behavior and obligation. Thus the child did not escape control; rather he experienced a partial exchange of masters in which the ignorance, neglect, and exploitation of some parents were replaced by presumably fair and uniform treatment at the hands of public authorities. The transfer of responsibilities required an elaboration of administration and judicial techniques of investigation, decision, and supervision.

Thus it can be seen that although the actual services available to families and children at the turn of the century were quite primitive and meager, the major patterns of service provision had been established. Moreover, the stage had been set for the elaboration of policies and programs that has occurred in more recent years. The first half of the twentieth century witnessed increasing professionalization, bureaucratization, and specialization of family and child welfare services. Public and voluntary agencies expanded in size and scope, volunteers were replaced by specially trained paid staff, professionals became preoccupied with meeting clients' mental health needs, and states began to assume increased responsibility for delivering, financing and regulating services. Despite all this activity, until the past two decades, there were few real changes in the objectives of service or the types of help provided.

However, there were several initiatives at the federal level that have had significant impact on the delivery of services in more recent years. The first White House Conference on Children was called in 1909 to consider provisions for care of dependent children. The delegates at this conference went on record as supporting the principle of maintaining children in their own families whenever possible and not depriving them of home life "except for urgent and compelling reasons" (Bremner, 1971, p. 365). Although the delegates expressed preference for private charity rather than public relief, major efforts were subsequently directed toward passage of mothers' pension laws authorizing states to provide public assistance to parents without other sources of income to enable them to sustain their children at home.

Despite the initial opposition of Mary Richmond, Edward Devine, and some of the other early leaders of the social work profession (Abbott, 1938), all but two states had passed such laws by 1935. Also, a consensus gradually emerged among professionals in child welfare about the importance of maintaining children in their own homes. The annual report of the Children's Aid Society in New York in 1923 reflects this view (Thurston, 1930, p. 138):

> There is a well-established conviction on the part of social workers that no child should be taken from his natural parents until everything possible has been done to build up the home into what an American home should be. Even after a child has been removed, every effort should be continued to rehabilitate the home and when success crowns one's efforts, the child should be returned. In other words, every social agency should be a *"homebuilder"* (emphasis added) and not a "home breaker."

This statement could obviously serve as a motto for the family preservation movement today. But the very fact that it took over 50 years to establish a "Homebuilders" program says much about the strength of the forces opposed to this approach.

Another significant federal initiative, the establishment of the United States Children's Bureau in 1912, demonstrated Congressional recognition of the federal government's responsibility for dependent children; and the mandate given to the Bureau to "investigate and report . . . upon all matters pertaining to the welfare of children and child life among all classes of our people . . ." suggested a public responsibility to monitor the well-being of all children, not just those posing special problems for the community. The Sheppard-Towner Act of 1921 later gave the Bureau responsibility for administering grants-in-aid to states for maternal and child health care, thus creating a model for federal funding of direct services to children and parents. Again, these initiatives were not without conflict. The Sheppard-Towner Act was the subject of vitriolic attacks from the time it was first introduced until it was allowed to lapse in 1929. Opposition to the program was justified by allegations of socialist leanings among the leaders of the Children's Bureau (Bremner, 1971, pp. 1010–1025).

The one other development of the early twentieth century that has important ramifications for service delivery today was the passage of Titles IV and V of the Social Security Act of 1935. Title IV, Grants to States for Aid to Dependent Children, now known as AFDC, provided federal matching funds for state grants to families with dependent children; and Title V,

Part 2, Child Welfare Services, later subsumed under Title IV-B, provided federal funding to develop child welfare services, particularly in rural areas, and to strengthen the states' role in administering these services. Although there was little, if any, coordinated planning prior to passage of this law, by 1938 all but one state had submitted plans for coordinated delivery of child welfare services (Bremner, 1971).

Both of these programs were funded modestly and suffered from numerous implementation problems, but they created the framework for federal child welfare policies today. As the author has commented previously, AFDC has "undoubtedly contributed more than any other social program to the goal of enabling children at risk of placement to remain in their own homes" (McGowan, 1983, p. 69). This lesson cannot be ignored in current deliberations about the potentials and limitations of family preservation services. Title IV-B quickly demonstrated that limited federal funds can be used to shape the ways in which such larger pools of state and local monies are expended, thus providing a model for those eager to effect changes in patterns of service delivery. The law authorizing Title IV-B funds, in an expanded and modified form, continues to be a key determinant of public child welfare expenditures today.

Despite these federal initiatives, continued state expansion and regulation of services, and increased professionalization of staff, no systematic efforts were made until the past 2 decades to implement the concept of family preservation introduced at the first White House Conference on Children. The child welfare field of the early 1960's was a small, relatively closed, residual service system oriented to the care of children outside their own homes. Child welfare services were seldom integrated with voluntary family services, and there were no public family services as such. Quality and coverage were uneven, with some voluntary agencies offering intensive, high quality, specialized services to selected groups of children, while the public agencies and some other voluntary agencies provided minimum care and protection to large numbers of poor, often minority, children. Adoption was defined as an option for healthy white infants, but other children whose parents were unable to provide were allowed to grow up in foster care.

The first major critique of this relatively isolated, self-perpetuating service system was presented in 1959 with the publication of *Children in Need of Parents*, Maas and Engler's study of children adrift in foster care. Additional challenges were posed by the social change efforts, professional reform initiatives, and clients' rights movements of the 1960's, all of which created a climate for the significant policy shifts introduced in the 1970's. Three of the amendments to the Social Security Act introduced during this decade each contributed in some way to the late development of family preservation services. The 1962 and 1967 Amendments, supported by a wide coalition of the leading experts in the social welfare field, reflected clear efforts to establish a comprehensive, publicly funded service system for low-income families, to modify the dysfunctional separation between child welfare and family services, and to insure children living at home the same benefits and services as those available to children in foster care. However, it was a little-noticed, little-debated amendment passed by Congress in 1971, AFDC Foster Care, that has had the more far-reaching, if unintended, consequences for child welfare services. This legislation provided open-ended federal matching funds to states for the care of children living in families eligible for AFDC who are placed in foster care as a result of a judicial determination of need. Although the program provided significant financial relief to states for the costs of children in placement, it offered no incentive to states to develop alternatives to foster care. Consequently, it had the effect of encouraging too frequent and too extended foster placements for children at risk.

A number of other developments of the late 1960's and early 1970's also helped to set the stage for passage of the key pieces of federal legislation guiding the provision of family preservation services today. These included:

- Widespread dissemination of research findings highlighting the potential negative consequences of separating children from their parents;
- Organization of adoptive and foster parent groups dedicated to promoting adoption opportunities for children traditionally considered "unadoptable";
- Initiation of class-action law suits designed to protect the rights of children and secure social benefits for various client groups;
- Rediscovery of the problem of child abuse with widespread publicity about what was termed the "battered child syndrome";
- Promulgation of the concepts of "deinstitutionalization" and "placement in the least detrimental alternative" in deliberations about the adequacy of provision for status offenders, delinquent youth, and other vulnerable groups requiring specialized care;
- Expansion of the boundaries of traditional family and child welfare agencies that took advantage of new sources of federal funding to increase services and reach out to new populations at risk;
- Introduction of the concept of child advocacy and establishment of numerous public, voluntary, and professional groups dedicated to protecting the interests of various groups of children.

Reformulating the Policy Framework

As costs and expectations increased simultaneously, issues related to the delivery of children's services began to assume greater importance on the public policy agenda. Federal and state legislators who formerly had been content to leave such matter to the discretion of local and state administrators and voluntary associations were pressured from all sides to begin to take action. Four federal laws passed during the period from 1974–1980, together with the corresponding state statutes and plans, create the framework for much of the current activity related to the provision of family preservation services.

Child Abuse Prevention and Treatment Act of 1974

A response to increased media coverage of problems of child abuse and to agitation in the medical community about the newly identified battered child syndrome, this act, PL 93-247, created the National Center on Child Abuse and Neglect. It provides limited funding—$26 million in FY 1987—for demonstration projects to states complying with a series of regulations related to establishment of statewide systems for reporting and investigation of complaints of suspected child abuse and neglect.

The law fails to specify the conditions that should be defined as child abuse or neglect or the evidential standards for reporting. Moreover, although the intent of the legislation is conveyed clearly in its title, the implementing regulations focused attention on mandatory reporting and investigation, not prevention and treatment. Consequently, this law has had the effect of greatly enlarging the pool of children coming to the attention of public authorities as potentially in need of care and protection, without providing the resources or guidelines necessary to enable states to deal more effectively with this population.

Juvenile Justice and Delinquency Prevention Act of 1974

This law, passed in response to widespread concern about inappropriate confinement of juvenile delinquents and status offenders, reflected another effort to use federal funding as a stimulus to state reform. It authorizes modest funds ($70 million for FY 1987) to support state efforts to improve juvenile justice systems and to create alternatives to the traditional, very costly detention and correctional facilities. To be eligible for funding, states are required to develop state plans insuring the removal of status offenders from juvenile detention and correctional facilities, separation of juveniles from adults in jails and prisons, and eventual removal of all youth from these adult facilities. This program has stimulated substantial state progress in diverting status offenders from the juvenile justice system and separating youth from adult offenders, but the funding has never been sufficient to encourage widespread development of community-based alternatives for delinquent youth.

Title XX, Grants to States for Social Services

This amendment to the Social Security Act, initially perceived as a landmark bill authorizing the first major social services program, was designed to promote self-sufficiency and prevent current and future dependency by supporting the development of comprehensive, effective, goal-directed services to children and adults at risk. It provided 75% federal matching funds to states for a broad range of services, stipulating only that one service be directed toward each of five goals related to promoting self-support and self-sufficiency, preventing abuse and neglect, and preventing inappropriate institutionalization. This law, part of the Nixon Administration's "new federalism," aimed to give increased authority and responsibility to the states, while limiting costs.

Although this legislation mandated development of comprehensive state social services plans and required citizen participation in the planning process, it retained the $2.5 billion ceiling on social service expenditures enacted by Congress in 1972. Thus, the law ultimately had the effect of increasing the competition among various interest groups within each state for what—with inflation—became more limited social service funds. (The total appropriation for FY 1987 was only $2.7 billion.) Despite these limitations and the amendments imposed by the Social Services Block Grant of 1981, Title XX has become a major source of child welfare funding, providing approximately 30% of the budget for state child welfare services in 1982 (Burt and Pittman, 1985).

Adoption Assistance and Child Welfare Act of 1980

This comprehensive law, PL 96-272, was enacted after several years of Congressional reform efforts, receiving widespread support from a broad coalition of public officials, child welfare professionals, advocacy groups, and client organizations. It was proposed in response to repeated studies and exposés documenting the fiscal and human costs of child welfare agencies' failure to offer services to children and parents in their own homes, to provide appropriate care and treatment for children in placement, or to discharge children quickly to their biological families or into adoptive homes (e.g., Fanshel and Shinn, 1972; Bernstein, Snider, and Meezan, 1975; Gruber, 1978; Knitzer *et al.*, 1978; Persico, 1979). Consonant with a number of court decisions and recent changes in state statutes requiring increased protections for parents' rights and more careful monitoring of children in placement, the law was also motivated by reports of various cost-effective programs that helped to prevent placement and/or effect early discharge from care (e.g., Jones *et al.,* 1976; Pike, 1976; Burt and Balyeat, 1977; Emlen, *et al.,* 1978; Stein, *et al.,* 1978; Maybanks and Bryce, 1979).

PL 96-272 adopts what Knitzer and Allen (1983, p. 120) have described as "a carrot-and-stick approach to redirect funds away from inappropriate, often costly, out-of-home care and toward alternatives to placement." Replacing the AFDC Foster Care Program with a new Title IV-E, Foster Care and Adoption Assistance Program, this legislation created a conditional ceiling on federal funding for foster care maintenance payments, authorized funding for adoption subsidies for children with special needs, and provided fiscal incentives and penalties related to the development of preventive and reunification services.

Setting forth a comprehensive set of standards for child welfare services, PL 96-272 requires states to establish care review mechanisms—with judicial determination of need and opportunity for parental participation at specified intervals—to ensure that reasonable efforts are made to prevent placement, to arrange placement in the most appropriate setting, and to discharge children to permanent homes in a timely manner. The law also specifies that case plans be developed to insure placement "in the least restrictive, most familylike setting available located in close proximity to the parents' home, consistent with the best interests and needs of the child." To facilitate aggregate data collection and monitoring, PL 96-272 mandated that states establish statewide information systems and conduct a onetime inventory of all children in care longer than 6 months.

Passage of this law made prevention of placement and permanency planning explicit objectives of federal child welfare policy and created incentives for more widespread development of the various types of preventive or family preservation services that had started to evolve in different localities. Since the foster care population had started to decline prior to 1980, probably in response to state legislative and administrative initiatives, it is difficult to determine which changes in child welfare services should be attributed to passage of this law.

By 1982 the requirements for receiving additional funding under the law were defined as major influences on states' long-term planning for child welfare services. Moreover, expenditures for foster care maintenance payments had dropped from almost 75% of all child welfare funds in FY 1979 to less than half in FY 1982, while the proportion of funds allocated for preventive and protective services increased from 8% to just over 23% during the same period (Burt and Pittman, 1985). Yet despite these apparent successes, Congress appropriated $697 million to fund Title IV-E (foster care and adoption services) in FY 1987 and only $222.5 million for Title IV-B (preventive and reunification services research, demonstration, and training grants). These figures suggest again the enormous difficulties inherent in any effort to develop alternative service provisions for children at risk. Moreover, the recent increase in the total foster care population, including many children previously discharged from care, raises questions about the viability of permanency planning as a universal policy objective.

What is very clear from even a casual perusal of the professional literature or from informal conversations with workers and administrators in various states is that the terms of the child welfare debate, definitions of success, expectations of professional staff, and allocation of decision-making responsibilities have all shifted markedly since this law was passed. Although these changes are often cited in discussions of the relative merits of mandated permanency planning, they indicate little about how well the substantive intent of the law is being implemented. As Stein and Gambrill (1985, pp. 91–92) have commented:

> Whether workers are developing case plans in accordance with the guidelines described in the law, whether case reviews are substantive or whether reviewers are merely rubber-stamping plans made, whether administrators are utilizing the data from information management systems to facilitate planning for children are only some of the issues that should be addressed if the intent of the law is to be realized. Unless implementation is monitored, the framework created by the Act may be little more than a house of cards.

Dilemmas of Policy Implementation

Although obstacles to policy implementation must always be anticipated, what could not be predicted prior to passage of PL 96-272 or any of the earlier laws were the Reagan Administration's efforts to dismantle most of the major federal social programs established to strengthen family life and enhance child development. This mean-spirited campaign to strip families of needed social resources by repealing laws, reducing funding, deregulating programs, and restricting eligibility has been well-documented and will not be described in any detail here. However, we must emphasize that those attempting to implement the newer concepts of family support and preservation have had to struggle to do this in what can only be described as an environment hostile to the well-being of poor families. The potentials and limitations of family preservation services must be evaluated in this context.

There seems a cruel irony in the fact that those who have long argued the need to provide services designed to maintain children in their own homes are being given the opportunity to demonstrate the viability of this approach at the very time when obstacles to family preservation are mounting. When one-quarter of all young children and almost half of those in young families are living in poverty (Children's Defense Fund, 1988), when increasing numbers of families are plagued by problems of homelessness, poor nutrition, unemployment and underemployment, substance abuse, and ill health, one must maintain very limited expectations of what can be accomplished by even the most skilled and well-designed clinical service interventions. And those concerned about "child welfare" may need to question whether prevention of placement is always a desirable or realistic goal.

State and local governmental units, as well as agencies in the voluntary sector, have attempted to replace lost federal funds by reaching out to new sources of funding and instituting new efficiencies in service arrangements, but they have not been able to substitute for the heavy cutbacks in major entitlement programs. To survive, they have started to emphasize provision of crisis-oriented, "last ditch" services to those most in need, deferring provision of more routine, preventive care. As a consequence, child welfare agencies, always an end-of-the-line resource for families unable to meet the needs of their children through more normative means, are now being confronted with increasing numbers of families experiencing profound social, economic, and emotional problems. And although they have fewer resources with which to address these problems, public expectations and scrutiny of their efforts have increased.

The recent, widespread interest in family preservation services is very understandable in this context because these programs promise—and frequently deliver—quick, low-cost, positive results for a number of troubled families that no one else has been able to help. The danger is that their very success may divert attention from the noxious social forces leading to crises in family functioning, obscure the need for other less intrusive community supports, and heighten the tendency to blame families unable to respond to this approach.

The policy dilemmas posed by the development of family preservation services must be examined from this perspective. To ignore the regressive social climate in which these programs are being implemented would do them a grave injustice.

Balancing Child Protection and Family Preservation

A long-standing policy dilemma not addressed explicitly by the Child Abuse Prevention and Treatment Act of 1974 or the Adoption Assistance and Child Welfare Act of 1980 is the question of what constitutes minimally acceptable levels of parenting. How should the child's right to protection from harm be balanced against the family's right to privacy and autonomy? When do the risks of maintaining children in their own homes outweigh the risks of removing them from their parents? The 1974 law sanctions widespread state intervention in family life in order to protect children, whereas the 1980 law mandates clear protections against unwarranted public intervention in family life.

Despite extensive overlap in the target populations addressed by these two laws, federal policy-makers have not attempted to reconcile their sometimes conflicting objectives. Instead, public officials and judges in various localities have been left with the task of fashioning an incremental body of state laws, regulations, and court decisions to govern situations of apparent tension between the goals of protecting children at risk of parental harm and preventing or limiting out-of-home placement. Although some of the legal tensions could be resolved by more precise statutory definitions of the parent–child situations covered by each law, current levels of knowledge do not permit accurate prediction of the relative benefits and harms to children that may be posed by alternative interventive approaches. In fact, available research findings raise questions about the interventive assumptions inherent in both laws.

To illustrate, a relatively small proportion of reports of child abuse and neglect (57% of those made by professionals and 35% of those made by lay people) are confirmed after investigation. Moreover, the best available estimates indicate recidivism rates of approximately 50% in families that do receive some intervention or treatment (Stein, 1984). In contrast, despite the reported egregious neglect of some individual children in foster care, repeated research suggests that 70 to 80% of those who grow up in foster care do quite well (Kadushin, 1978). Consequently, although more careful specification of the characteristics of children in need of protective and/or permanency planning services might lead to more equitable treatment, it cannot be assumed that this would necessarily lead to better outcomes for children at risk, the presumed intent of both laws.

Family preservation services, most of which are based on the assumption that carefully timed home-based intensive intervention with families at risk may help to prevent child maltreatment and avert out-of-home placement, reflect the effort to find programmatic solutions to this policy of balancing risks. However, these programs pose a number of other issues.

Making Reasonable Efforts

PL 96-272 requires judicial determination that "reasonable efforts" have been made to enable children to stay safely at home before placement in foster care, but reasonable efforts are not operationally defined. As a result, there is wide variation among the states regarding the extent and range of services available for families at risk, and wide variation among judges within each state about what constitutes an acceptable level of effort to prevent placement of children coming before the court. A publication of the National Council of Juvenile and Family Court Judges, Child Welfare League of America, Youth Law Center, and National Center for Youth Law argues that to make reasonable efforts to maintain children in their own families, each state must maintain a comprehensive range of income supports, concrete and counseling services including housing, child care, respite care, substance abuse treatment, mental health counseling, family services, parent training, and transportation (National Center for Youth Law, 1987). Family preservation services are appropriately identified as only one component of the required range that should be made available to families at risk.

Although the key actors in the development of intensive, home-based family services are clear that these should be viewed as only one component of a continuum of care, recent developments in a number of states suggest that service planners may be overemphasizing provision of family preservation services to the exclusion of other needed family supports. The reasons for this trend are obvious: limited fiscal resources; early, if sketchy, reports of cost effectiveness; the national penchant for seeking quick-fix solutions; and a deep-seated aversion to long-term dependency. What is often ignored in the rush to institutionalize these services is the fact that they are based on a crisis intervention model, which assumes the capacity for independent functioning once balance is restored. Unfortunately, not all parents have the emotional, cognitive, social or economic resources necessary to enable them to function independently on a consistent basis. They can maintain loving homes and meet their children's basic development needs only if they are provided a range of supports on a sustained basis, perhaps until their children are grown. The question that must therefore be addressed is how much help should be extended to families at risk. Does the mandate to make reasonable efforts extend beyond a time-limited intensive intervention? Are we as a society willing to make the long-term commitment to children's well-being that we demand of parents? At what cost?

Objectives and Targeting

Although Homebuilders programs and other types of family preservation services are being established in a number of states, there is currently a great deal of ambiguity about the objectives of these services and their target population(s). Some programs aim to enhance family functioning, while others are geared only to preventing out-of-home placement of children. Some target families in which children are at risk of abuse or neglect; others include families in which children are at risk for placement because of delinquent behavior or mental illness. In Maryland, family preservation services are tied to the child protection system, but help is offered *prior* to investigation of alleged abuse or neglect. In Florida, family preservation services are not provided until *after* the investigation of the need for child protection, but they are also offered to families whose children may be placed because of their own behavioral difficulties. In Minnesota, where children's services have recently been reorganized around the provision of family preservation services, there are notable differences by county in the identification of target population(s). Hennepin County, for example, has chosen to concentrate on adolescents at risk of placement, whereas Ramsey County is targeting its services on young children at risk (A. J. Kahn and S. B. Kamerman, 1988, pers. commun.).

These differences in the nature of the target population, timing of interventions, and desired outcome have obvious cost implications. Moreover, unless explicitly recognized, they are likely to result in contrasting assessments of the effectiveness of such services. Current knowledge does not permit a precise specification of the relative merits of these alternative approaches. What can be assumed is that earlier intervention with a wider pool of families in which children may be at risk is likely to have a broader effect; but given the costs of such a venture, this could be at the price of targeting limited resources on those most at risk of imminent placement. Further research is needed to help clarify risk criteria and to identify which types of risk situations are most likely to benefit from which types of services. However, additional knowledge will not resolve the value questions inherent in the decision to target services at a narrowly defined population likely to be most at risk of child placement, or to reach out to a larger population of families who could benefit from services, even if placement might be averted without such intervention.

Allocating Responsibilities for Service Delivery

PL 96-272's requirement that states make reasonable efforts to prevent and limit foster care placement assumes public (federal, state, and/or local) responsibility for financing preventive services. Decisions regarding specific service arrangements are left entirely to the states. Thus multiple questions arise regarding appropriate auspices and structure for the delivery of services, linkages between preventive and protective services, case and program accountability mechanisms, criteria for service monitoring and evaluation, responsibility for service integration, and legal and service boundaries. Some of these are clearly technical questions requiring careful analysis of the cost-benefits associated with alternative approaches. Others involve value judgments that have a direct impact on allocation of public funds and equity of treatment for families at risk.

Space limitations do not permit through discussion of all of these dilemmas. What can be noted are some of the core issues related to auspices and service arrangements. As indicated above, current federal policy suggests that the states are responsible for planning, financing, and monitoring preventive and protective services for children at risk. Moreover, involuntary intervention in family life has long been viewed as an intrusion on parental rights that requires statutory authority and should be undertaken only by designated public officials.

The provision of intensive home-based services to families in which there have been allegations of child abuse and neglect poses a unique challenge in this context. Because the interventive model requires a level of worker autonomy, flexibility, and skill that is extremely difficult to achieve in a public bureaucracy, many states are choosing to contract these services out to voluntary agencies. Yet the contracting process does not relieve the state of its core child protective and oversight responsibilities. Thus states must develop suitable procedures for monitoring the quality of service provision and insuring rapid state intervention when the safety of a child is threatened.

Unfortunately, such regulatory and accountability mechanisms can have the effect of structuring and routinizing services in a way that undermines the creativity, resourcefulness, and speed of response that contracting is expected to promote. Although some states have long traditions of purchasing selected services from the voluntary sector, the increased reliance on contracting for provision of protective and preventive services highlights the need for more careful study of the anticipated and unintended consequences of various types of contracting procedures, the impact on various subgroups within the population at risk, and the implications for the distribution of power and resources among different interest groups.

Other organizational dilemmas are posed by the multiple funding streams and regulatory structures governing delivery of services to children and families. Although bureaucratic arrangements vary from state to state, all must address problems of case integration and program coordination. Families with children at risk of placement almost by definition require multiple sources of support. Yet access to the various educational, health, housing, income maintenance, legal, and social service systems is frequently controlled by a complex web of eligibility criteria and application requirements that function to exclude rather than include families in need. Regardless of whether intensive, home-based service programs are based in the public or voluntary sector, or whether they come under the jurisdiction of the social service, child protection, mental health, or juvenile justice system, in order to be effective they must be able to help their clients obtain speedy assistance from other service agencies.

Despite the recent spread of family preservation services, there has been little systematic analysis of such issues as where best to locate these programs organizationally, how to pool funding and staff from diverse sources in order to expand internal program resources, or which types of case management and interagency coordinating mechanisms are most likely to facilitate integrated service delivery.

There is, of course, a political risk inherent in any effort to make more explicit links between family preservation services and other human service resource systems because such endeavors focus attention on more of the true costs associated with placement prevention, i.e., the costs of resources that are provided in addition and/or extend beyond intensive, home-based family services. Since one of the reasons for initiation of these services is their assumed cost effectiveness, any pooling of additional outside resources could diminish interest in this model of service delivery by seemingly suggesting that it is not viable financially. On the other hand, it can be argued that the "reasonable efforts" mandate requires provision of whatever resources are needed to sustain family functioning and that speedy, coordinated service delivery ultimately reduces both the human and fiscal costs that accrue from societal neglect of children at risk.

Policy Implications

The long historical struggle to address the legal, moral, fiscal, and practice dilemmas posed when parents seem unable or unwilling to care adequately for their children suggests the enormity and complexity of this task. Family preservation services are an important new development in this context, offering an innovative, intensive practice technology for work with high-risk families that may reduce foster care placement without increasing risk of child abuse or neglect or diminishing parental privacy and autonomy. The early reports of service effectiveness and cost efficiency are promising, leaving little doubt that this development should be encouraged and that further expansion, replication, and experimentation are warranted.

However, the history of child welfare services also attests to the imprudence of seeking a single solution to the problem of children at risk. Foster care, a social invention developed to meet the needs of children at risk in their own homes and communities, was redefined in the 1970's as a social problem to be prevented. Permanency planning mandates introduced under PL 96-272 to limit foster care placements are now being challenged by recent research findings suggesting that some children may do better in foster care than in their own homes (Barth and Berry, 1987; D. Fanshel, 1988, pers. comm.). Current knowledge does not permit us to predict the long-term impact of intensive, home-based services.

Family preservation services must not be viewed as a panacea. These are categorical programs able to help only one segment of the total range of families and children in need of support and are organized to provide limited types of case services. They cannot address the socioeconomic forces that contribute to tensions and inadequacies in family functioning nor can they provide the long-term assistance and/or specialized treatment required by some parents and children. Thus it is essential to maintain realistic expectations of what these programs can and cannot do.

For family preservation programs to function effectively, they must be offered as one component of a continuum of family and children's services that includes community-based, developmental and early intervention programs; family life education; individual, marital, and family counseling; group services for youth; information, referral, and advocacy services; respite care; homemaking, day care, and day treatment resources; mediation services; and foster homes, group homes, and residential treatment facilities. It is also essential that these programs.be given the capacity to command needed resources from other human service agencies including health, housing, income maintenance, education, mental health, substance abuse, job training, and employment.

Although child protective and family preservation services are theoretically distinct, in practice there is a great deal of overlap and blurring of boundaries because these programs work with many of the same families and the service demands are increasing. In 1986, reports of alleged abuse or neglect were filed on an estimated 2.2 million children, an increase of over 90% since 1981 (Children's Defense Fund, 1988). The current effort to extend and institutionalize family preservation services poses a risk in this context because these programs, like child protective services, could be easily overwhelmed by numbers and/or overregulated and constrained by procedures designed to monitor and routinize service delivery. To maintain the objectives, integrity, and potential effectiveness of family preservation services, efforts should be made to implement several of the key recommendations offered repeatedly to strengthen child protective services (Stein, 1984; Forsythe, 1987; McGowan, et al., 1986). These include (1) reducing the range of cases requiring mandatory reporting and investigation so resources can be targeted on those most at risk; (2) providing alternative, voluntary entry points to service to permit families to obtain help before crises emerge; and (3) separating investigation of child abuse reports from direct service provision.

Another risk posed by the current interest in expanding family preservation services in the public sector is that this may increase pressure to institutionalize a specific model of service. As the history of social work practice illustrates, premature closure on a single approach can blind practitioners to alternative, newer sources of knowledge (Germain, 1970). Although the Homebuilders program offers significant promise, it is obviously too soon to determine which of the family preservation models are most cost-effective with which types of clients in which community contexts or even whether the various programs should rely on a single model of practice. Similarly, little is known about the staffing patterns, training resources, and organizational arrangements that can best facilitate delivery of effective services to families at risk. Therefore, it is essential that funding patterns and accountability demands be flexible and be designed to reward innovation, not routinization, of service delivery.

Although the record of family preservation services to date favors continued expansion and replication, it would be irresponsible to make a major public investment in these programs without investing simultaneously in a series of modest studies designed to examine the short- and long-term cost benefits of alternative service structures and practice technologies. At a minimum this research agenda should include:

- Longitudinal studies with clear control groups aimed at assessing the impact of these services over time;
- Evaluation of the efficacy of alternative program models (time frame, practice technology, entry point to service) with similar client populations;
- Identification of the ways that alternative structural arrangements (auspices, staffing patterns, degree of integration with other service systems) may facilitate and/or hinder implementation of specific program models;
- Evaluation of the cost benefits of alternative methods for monitoring contract compliance and insuring case accountability;
- Analysis of the impact of different child protective service structures on the delivery of family preservation services;
- Examination of the ripple effects that initiation of family preservation services may have on other components of the service delivery network in different community contexts.

Finally, it should be noted that the simultaneous introduction of a range of family preservation services in a number of different states offers an unusual opportunity for the federal government and/or or more foundations to sponsor a serious developmental research project aimed at identifying the most effective practice approaches for helping high-risk families. Such a broad-scale natural experiment in social programming is rare and should be examined empirically. The knowledge accrued from such an effort could help to reduce the historic ambiguities inherent in current child welfare policy and promote more effective service delivery to high risk families.

Implications for Social Work Education

Although the Council on Social Work Education mandates inclusion of at least one course on social policy in the required curricula of all schools of social work, students often complain that the content in these courses has little relevance to their actual practice. What many fail to understand, except at a very abstract level, is how much prevailing public policies shape their practice roles and objectives. Similarly, students often view social policies as given, assuming that practitioners can have little influence on policy formulation and implementation.

The story of the development of family preservation services could yield real educational benefits in this context because it offers a very current and graphic example of the interrelationship of policy and practice. The primary objective of these services—prevention of placement—makes sense only if viewed against the backdrop of forces that led to passage of PL 96-272. And new practice approaches such as the one developed by Homebuilders are required to implement the goals of this legislation.

As a case study, the record of Homebuilders' establishment, expansion, and replication could be used to illustrate important teaching points related to professional participation in social action. These include:

- Ways direct service practitioners can influence policy formulation and implementation at different governmental levels;
- The leadership, creativity, resources, and commitment such efforts demand;
- The multiple change tactics employed to effect even modest service reform;
- The political and structural obstacles to more rational or radical service planning.

Such an exercise could be discouraging to students impatient to create immediate change. Yet the reality is that social reform in this country occurs on a very halting, incremental basis. Moreover, social workers can usually influence the process of change only by working in close concert with other interest groups and political forces. It is important for students to absorb these lessons early in their careers so they are prepared to tolerate temporary setbacks and to acquire the advocacy skills required to be effective over the long haul.

At a different level of analysis, the family preservation service experiment highlights several core educational dilemmas that deserve further debate within the profession. First, given the obvious linkages between policy, administration, research, and practice, why do we persist in organizing most of our courses by method rather than by field of practice? How can we better prepare students to grasp the multiple determinants of practice in the "real world" without sacrificing their development of specialized knowledge and skills? What are the trade-offs inherent in using particular service initiatives such as Homebuilders to teach a selected range of professional skills?

Second, as recent efforts to implement the objectives of PL 96-272 indicate, public funding decisions are shaped primarily by value choices, political interests, and economic constraints, not by empirical research and rational decision-making processes. Yet, program evaluations are usually designed to assess the effectiveness of specific practice technologies, not to answer questions about the viability of a particular policy or the adequacy of the resources allocated to its implementation. Given these realities, social work educators must consider how best to prepare students for professional practice in a policy context of what is at best limited rationality. Is the current heavy emphasis on data-based practice necessary and appropriate? What other types of knowledge and skill are essential? How do we teach students to function effectively in this context without jading their appreciation for the scientific knowledge which should undergird every profession?

Finally, recent increases in categorical funding and in external monitoring of service programs have the effect of constraining professional autonomy regarding the nature, scope, and extent of client services. Yet the Code of Ethics of the National Association of Social Workers (1979, p. 3) states clearly that social workers' primary responsibility is to their clients and that they "should retain ultimate responsibility for the quality and extent" of the services they perform. This shift in public policy could pose serious ethical dilemmas for individual practitioners working with clients whose needs do not fit regulatory guidelines or assumptions. Although there are unlikely to be any clear answers to these dilemmas, social work educators must begin to address these questions more directly and to help students develop more explicit guidelines for professional decision-making.

References

Abbott, G. (1938). *The child and the state,* vol. II. Chicago: University of Chicago.

Barth, R., and Barry, M. (1987). Outcomes of child welfare services under permanency planning. *Social Service Review, 61,* 71–89.

Bernstein, B., Snider, D., and Meezan, W. (1975). *Foster care needs and alternatives to placement.* Albany: New York State Board of Social Welfare.

Bremner, R. H. (Ed.). (1971). *Children and youth in America: A documentary history,* vol. II. Cambridge: Harvard University.

Burt, M. R., and Balyeat, R. R. (1977). *A comprehensive emergency services system for neglected and abused children.* New York: Vantage.

Burt, M., and Pittman, K. (1985). *Testing the social safety net.* Washington, DC: Urban Institute.

Children's Defense Fund. (1988). *A call for action to make our nation safe for children: A briefing book on the status of American children in 1988.* Washington, DC: Author.

Emlen, A., *et al.* (1978). *Overcoming barriers to planning for children in foster care.* Portland, OR: Regional Research Institute, Portland State University.

Fanshel, D., and Shinn, E. (1972). *Dollars and sense in foster care of children: A new look at cost factors.* New York: Child Welfare League of America.

Forsythe, P. (1987). Redefining child protective services. *Protecting Children, 4,* 12–16.

Germain, C. (1970). Casework and science: A historical encounter. *In* R. W. Roberts and R. H. Nee (Eds.), *Theories of social casework,* pp. 3–32. Chicago: University of Chicago Press.

Gruber, A. (1978). *Children in foster care: Destitute, neglected, betrayed.* New York: Human Sciences Press.

Jones, M. A., Neuman, R., and Shyne, A. W. (1976). *A second chance for families.* New York: Child Welfare League of America.

Kadushin, A. (1978). Children in foster families and institutions. *In* H. S. Maas (Ed.), *Social service research: Reviews of studies,* pp. 90–148. Washington, DC: NASW.

Knitzer, J., and Allen, M. L. (1983). Child welfare: Examining the policy framework. *In* B. G. McGowan and W. Meezan (Eds.), *Child welfare: Current dilemmas, future directions,* pp. 93–141. Itasca, IL: Peacock.

Knitzer, J., Allen, M. L., and McGowan, B. G. (1978). *Children without homes.* Washington, DC: Children's Defense Fund.

Maas, H., and Engler, R. (1959). *Children in need of parents.* New York: Columbia University.

Maybanks, S., and Bryce, M. (1979). *Home based services for children and families: Policy, practice, and research.* Springfield, IL: Charles C. Thomas.

McGowan, B. G. (1983). Historical evolution of child welfare services. *In* B. G. McGowan and W. Meezan (Eds.), *Child welfare: Current dilemmas, future directions,* pp. 45–90. Itasca, IL: Peacock.

McGowan, B. G., Bertrand, J. A., and Kahn, A. (1986). *The continuing crisis: A report on New York City's response to families requiring protective and preventive services.* New York: Neighborhood Family Services Coalition.

National Association of Social Workers. (1979). *Code of ethics of the National Association of Social Workers.* Washington, DC: Author.

National Center for Youth Law. (1987). *Making reasonable efforts: Steps for keeping families together.* Report of the National Council of Juvenile and Family Court Judges, Child Welfare League of America, Youth Law Center, and National Center for Youth Law. San Francisco: Author.

Persico, J. (1979). *Who knows? Who cares? Forgotten children in foster care.* New York: National Commission on Children in Need of Parents.

Pike, V. (1976). Permanent planning for foster children: The Oregon Project. *Children Today, 5,* 22–25, 41.

Stein, T. J. (1984). The child abuse prevention and treatment act. *Social Service Review, 58,* 302–314.

Stein, T. J., and Gambrill, E. D. (1985). Permanency planning for children: The past and present. *Children and Youth Services Review, 7*(2/3), 83-94.

Stein, T. J., Gambrill, E. D., and Wiltse, K. T. (1978). *Children in foster homes: Achieving continuity of care.* New York: Praeger.

Thurston, H. W. (1930). *The dependent child.* New York: Columbia University.

Chapter 5

Theories Guiding Home-Based
Intensive Family Preservation Services

Richard P. Barth

Kurt Lewin's observation that there is "nothing so practical as a good the-ory" is widely accepted. Conversely, nothing is likely to be as impractical as an intervention based on a weak theory. Whereas effective interventions do not always have close ties to theory, programs guided by better theories should more readily prevent the unnecessary placement of children. Inten-sive family preservation services (IFPS) draw on four major theories for articulating ideal service delivery systems and treatments: crisis intervention theory, family systems theory, social learning theory, and ecological theory. An implicit acceptance of crisis intervention theory is something of a given by most agencies offering IFPS, whereas consensus on the merits of fam-ily systems theory and social learning theory has not been reached. Family systems theory is a difficult to define but widely accepted model for social work practice. Social learning theory is the best articulated of the theories and has strong roots in psychology and a few social work bailiwicks. Ecolog-ical theory is primarily a natural sciences metaphor for social science-based practice, but varied interpretations of this metaphor in practice may have great impact on services.

This chapter addresses each of these theories and their derivative practices and describes their contribution to the delivery of IFP services. The general evidence indicating the usefulness of the theories and services based on them is reviewed. The junctures between theories and approaches are considered as are aspects of these services needing better articulation.

Crisis Intervention Theory

Crisis intervention theorists differ in how they organize and conceptualize crises. Generally, however, the "crisis" is the hazardous event that cannot be resolved with customary resources or problem-solving approaches (Caplan, 1964). The "crisis reaction" is the state of upset or disequilibrium that exists during the attempt to resolve the situation.

Crisis theory and intervention focus on everyday people confronted with untenable circumstances rather than on individuals whose deviant behavior is long-standing and a product of "mental disease;" on precipitating events rather than predisposing environmental and personal factors; and on high-risk situations rather than high-risk populations (Auerbach, 1983). Crisis intervention theories were not designed to address family circumstances characterized by "mental disease" or comparable long-lasting impairments (e.g., substance abuse) *and* untenable circumstances *and* predisposing stress *and* precipitating emergencies among high-risk populations in high-risk situations. Crisis theory initially described individual and not family reactions to developmental and natural crises. Family stress theory (McCubbin and Patterson, 1983) and family treatment that includes crisis intervention have only begun to integrate these domains (Everstine and Everstine, 1983).

Crisis theory poses that crisis reactions are self-limiting; that is, symptoms disappear or are "worked through" (with varying degrees of successful adaptation) in a brief time—approximately 4 to 6 weeks from onset (Bloom, 1980; Darbonne, 1967). Recent evidence fails to flatter the theory. The amount of time required before a crisis is resolved and an individual adapts and regains his or her equilibrium cannot easily be measured. Reasonable efforts to measure coping with cancer surgery suggests a range of responses from 4 weeks to 5 years (Krouse and Krouse, 1982; Ray, 1978) and for rape victims the recovery ranges from 4 to 6 months postrape to 3 years for those experiencing the most severe and sudden attacks (Ellis *et al.,* 1981). Comparable time studies for family crisis reactions have not been reported. The idea that individuals or families reach new "homeostatic" arrangements after 4 or 6 weeks, or any other uniform time period after a crisis is simply a notion. Child welfare research has not satisfactorily estimated the typical amount of time that elapses between a parent's complaint that a child is beyond control and the family's decision to exclude the child from the home. Nor is it clear how long it takes before a family loses their motivation to resume the care of a child who was removed from the home.

Crisis research and theory do not begin to inform us about the length of time a family can be provided with services and attain a successful outcome. We have some evidence that families that have not been reunified by 18 months after the child's removal will never be reunified (Jones *et al.,* 1976). Reviews of family therapy outcome research (e.g., Wells, 1981) suggest that "short-term interventions have equal, if not better, improvement rates than lengthier treatment" (p. 292). But this may be attributable more to the failure of interveners to maintain their level of services to families or because more difficult families take longer and change less. Families may not be following the assumed path of failing to maintain the motivation to use the services because they plateau at a new level of "homeostasis." Since motivation is an interaction between the individual and the service provider and not an independent condition of an individual or family (Barth, 1986), a family's effort to resolve a family crisis is probably in great part dependent upon the service provider's interest in having the situation resolved.

Lewis' (1982) operational description is that a crisis is an event that has resulted in a sudden *discontinuous* change in functioning. Yet, the evidence is not compelling that families behave differently after a report of child abuse (assuming that is the most common crisis experienced by families who receive IFPS) than they did before. The present position of most developmentalists is away from that of "developmental crises" (Erikson, 1959) toward a view of change that is more continuous than discontinuous, more incremental than abrupt, and more even than uneven (Brim and Kagan, 1980). Assumptions that families are markedly different or are on the way to becoming markedly different as a result of a crisis are best treated gingerly.

As crisis theory is applied to families, the family's crisis reaction is considered atypical of their other, more competent, reactions. Crisis theory assumes that services offered during that disequilibrium are better able to help families find adaptive resolutions. On the other hand, the helping messages of crisis services may be obstructed by family members' reduced ability to function as individuals and as a family at a time of confusion and discontinuity. Crises represent opportunities, but they are also stressors that draw on resources necessary for change. Families may, of course, vary in this respect with some in essence saying "I'm glad you're here to help now" and others saying "I have no time for that now." Early crisis theory cited evidence that stress and learning are related along an inverted U-shaped curve so that too much or too little crisis-related arousal worked against learning more adaptive strategies (e.g., Janis, 1969). This evidence is consistent with recent evidence that the higher prestress arousal the less the poststress adjustment, and the less the prestress arousal the better the poststress adjustment (Auerbach, 1983). Both early and late versions of crisis theory suggest that intervention will work best with families not in full crisis state.

The type and timing of responses made by families at the point of crisis (often the result of a report of child abuse) is unclear. In an early report, Homebuilders described key elements of the model as follows:

> It reaches families while they are in crisis. Intakes are seen within 24 hours of referral. Family members are more willing to experiment with new ideas and new behaviors when their pain seems most unbearable. The Homebuilder's presence at a stressful time, and the sharing of large amounts of information, form a bond which makes successful therapy more likely (Behavioral Sciences Institute, 1981, p. 2).

Evidence that intervening at the point of crisis is most beneficial because the crisis response facilitates openness and change is missing. The importance of this element to the effectiveness of the service is also unclear. The assumptions that waiting lists or delays in commencing services will thwart effective services are not based on convincing evidence.

Family Systems Theory

Perhaps no belief about treatment is held more widely by social workers than the belief that family systems theory is a valuable ally. Virginia Satir (1967) has been, arguably, the social worker with the most influence among social workers in the last half century. Although Satir is not often associated with home-based interventions, her interest in family therapy began while working as a school teacher and after visiting more than two hundred families and often intervening in the role of "visiting teacher." After leaving that position, Satir began her career as a social worker and family therapist. A proponent of Gregory Bateson's early efforts (Bateson *et al.,* 1956) with systems theory and a devotee of humanistic psychology (Rogers, 1957, 1961), Satir succinctly describes the classic social work view in a chapter marking 30 years of practice:

> All systems are balanced. The question is, what price does each part of the system pay to keep it so? The rules which govern a family system are derived from the ways parents maintain self-esteem and, in turn, form the context within which the children grow, and develop their self-esteem. Communication and Self Worth are the basic components (Satir, 1982, p. 12).

Even though Satir's recent profile among family therapists has been lower than Minuchin and Haley and the MRI group, her view of family systems theory continues to be assumed by many family systems practitioners. Like Satir, most family therapists cannot describe family systems theory without reference to family therapy. It is not a theory which is often studied or discussed on its own merits. It is inextricably linked to family therapy.

Family systems theory has spawned or fostered numerous forms of family therapy. The best known family therapies, and their most renowned developers, include structural family therapy (Minuchin *et al.,* 1967), Bowenian intergenerational family therapy (Bowen, 1978), strategic family therapy (Haley, 1963; Rabkin, 1977), and the Mental Research Institute's interactional view (Bodin, 1981; Watzlawick *et al.,* 1974). Even the experts in the field do not reliably distinguish approaches; as an example, Gurman *et al.,* (1986) place Stanton and Todd's (1979) excellent work with heroin addicts under the structural heading whereas Stanton at times describes his work as strategic

(Stanton, 1981). The merging of family therapy approaches continues and the field's early emphasis on differences between theories is receding.

For the purposes of this chapter, the family treatment model that will be discussed is structural family therapy. This is among the most widely known and practiced of the family therapies in part because Minuchin and his colleagues have disseminated the approach through writing and training with unparalleled success. Although elements of the model are based on the sociological theories about organizational power and structure, in practice family system (and even psychodynamic) influences enter in. In a recent poll of the readership of the Family Therapy Networker, 34% of respondents described themselves as eclectic, 18% as structural, 12% as systemic; and only 2% described themselves as behavioral (Rait, 1988). Structural family therapy also incorporates aspects of Haley's original strategic therapy and interactional family therapy. In the home-based family services world, the structural approach to family treatment is the most widely used and, next to social learning, the best tested approach (e.g., AuClaire and Schwartz, 1986; Showell, 1988). Still, the eclectic influences on the delivery of family therapy are certainly great.

Family Systems Practice Models

Many family therapists would agree that the general structures that a family develops to carry out its functions can be functional or dysfunctional depending on the specific family tasks and the family context. The family system or structure (these are not truly synonymous but are often used as such) is assessed along three dimensions: boundary, alignment, and power. Boundaries are the rules defining who participates and how in each type of family task. Common boundary problems addressed in structural family therapy include the parental right to control privileges and the basic responsibilities of adolescents. Alignment refers to ways that family members have of working together or in mutual opposition to each other or to other family subsystems. Alignment problems might arise when one parent, while agreeing that the parents have the right to set rules, consistently contradicts or subverts the rules set by the other parent in sympathy for the child. Power is the relative force of each family member on the achievement of family functions. Power determines who will prevail in developing boundaries and shaping alignments. The general assessment and intervention strategy is to determine the issues around which to explore and intervene; to assess the family structure along the dimensions of boundaries, alignment, and power; and to set goals related to changes in family structure.

The process of family therapy varies somewhat according to the family's challenges, but a few characteristics can be generalized. Cotherapy does not have a clearly defined niche within structural family therapy (Stanton, 1981). This is partly due to the technical problems of maintaining control over the changes in structure targeted during each treatment session. Structural family therapists typically prefer to see all family members together, but do have a way of thinking about various strategies for including different family subsystems: *joint* processes involve seeing all family members together; *concurrent* processes are interviews with different groupings of the family; and *sequential* processes involve resolving issues with different parts of the family during phases of the treatment. The extent to which this flexibility is used by structural family therapists may, in part, depend on how strongly their training emphasized the systemic roots of this approach. The majority of contact time appears to be spent seeing the family jointly. Structural family therapists typically see families for an hour at a time (Stanton, 1981) and, for more serious families, from 4 to 7 months (Minuchin *et al.*, 1978; Rait, 1988).

A few key techniques in structural/systemic family therapy are familiar to most family therapists. They include: *joining* (accommodating the therapist's style to the family style); *enactment* (identifying and addressing miscommunications and unsuccessful family interactions in the therapy session); *restructuring* (promoting patterns of parent–child interaction that are neither overinvolved nor underinvolved and that have a parent-in-charge); *reframing* (redefining the meaning of events and reality to promote morale and effective problem solving); and *creating intensity* (motivating change by pushing a family or dyad past its threshold of comfort with the present pattern of relating).

The Hennepin County IFPS project (AuClaire and Schwartz, 1986) describes their services as using a structural family therapy approach. (Of the practice techniques they reported using less than half the time, the majority were cognitive or behavioral.) According to AuClaire and Schwartz (1986), their staff were not expert at family therapy but endeavored to apply structural family therapy techniques to: build a mutually trusting relationship with the family; identify and build on existing family strengths; establish parents as authority figures; value the client as a person; express empathy; change the structure within the family; delineate family boundaries; take a nonjudgmental stance; elicit information to clarify the situation; and express interest and feedback to family members to confirm or promote their understanding.

Structural family therapists are also encouraged to limit their participation to the minimum that is necessary to set in motion the family's natural healing resources (Colapinto, 1982). Whereas the model aspires to create structural changes in families that improve the family's ability to manage future events, the model does not offer specific theory-based strategies designed to ensure the maintenance of the family changes after therapy stops. Yet, structural family therapists may address issues critical to the maintenance of change. A case in point is Montalvo's intervention with a firesetting child, as described by Minuchin (1974). Although the child's firesetting disappears after the first session, Montalvo stays in contact with the family for 18 months. He works with the child's teachers, holds sessions in the family home and encourages the older child's development. Minuchin writes, "Although changes within a family can be effective, to be lasting such changes cannot be achieved in isolation from a family's circumstances. Working with the family in its context is essential to modifying and then perpetuating the modifications" (p. 239).

Social Learning Theory

The last decade and a half has witnessed growing appreciation for social and cognitive contributors to family behavior change (Mahoney, 1974; Kendall and Braswell, 1985; Barth, 1986). Albert Bandura, the wizard of social learning, clarified the importance of cognitions in the regulation of behavior (Bandura, 1977). Whereas rewards and penalties following a behavior are known to influence the likelihood that children or parents will use that behavior again, this likelihood is mediated by expectations. A family member's low expectations that they can change or that their efforts to change will result in changes in the family will reduce motivation to learn and use new skills. Such expectations may aptly describe the likelihood or may be mistaken. Expectations often change as behavior changes. Behavior, beliefs, and affect are believed to influence each other reciprocally. Social learning theory diverges from a psychodynamic approach—but is consistent with a strategic family therapy approach—in rejecting the belief that changes in thinking and feeling necessarily antecede changes in behavior.

The other great contribution of Bandura and the social learning theorists arises from their grasp of the way that family members learn from each other. Their research clearly shows that the power of rewards, penalties, and expectations are, at times, developed through direct experience but are also facilitated by observation. From these findings, technologies have developed for teaching parents and children skills for self-management (e.g., Barth *et al*, 1983; Gaudin and Kurtz, 1985; Wolfe and Sandler, 1981). These technologies emphasize the importance of demonstrating skills that can be used, encouraging practice of those skills by children and parents (either in on-the-spot role plays or during homework assignments), and providing cognitive rehearsal and preparation for future efforts.

Social learning theorists and practitioners have a sometimes uneasy alliance with therapists employing strategies developed in Rational Emotive Therapy (RET) (Ellis, 1962; Ellis and Bernard, 1983). RET was initially regarded with reservation by social learning-based therapists because of its heavy reliance on confrontation and the unconventional ways of its founder. Recently, RET has moved farther into the mainstream of psychotherapy and behavior therapy. Still, some fundamental differences exist between social learning approaches and RET. Ellis (1980) distinguished them by indicating that RET views problem behavior (and emotions) as symptomatic of an underlying belief system that constitutes the core of maladjustment; whereas cognitive–behavioral approaches do not attempt to modify the overall philosophy and assumptive world of clients through the use of disputational methods but are more problem-focused and define goals in terms of specific behavior change. The impact of RET on clients is not nearly as clear as that of other techniques coexisting under the broad rubric of social learning-based treatment techniques. Still, RET's reliance on the systematic teaching of skills for increasing clients' competencies and on theoretical assumptions about the role of cognitions in shaping behavior place RET within the social learning realm. Homebuilders employs a range of techniques based on cognitive views of behavior espoused in RET.

Social Learning Practice Models

Research on IFPS provides imprecise partraits of the theoretical and practice orientation of service providers. Clearly, the most influential provider of such services is Homebuilders, which relies on a multiple-component model but is fundamentally a social learning-based program. Social learning approaches to family therapy began at approximately the same time as structural family therapy and family systems therapy, but, in contrast, have a smaller following. Early reporting of such work described it as "reprogramming the social environment" (which often meant changing the family) or as "parent training," or "behavior modification" (Patterson *et al.,* 1967). During its early years, family therapy gained its widest use with adolescents who were beyond parental control. In contrast, social learning theorists' population of concern for nearly two decades was younger children. Social learning-based approaches have highlighted the "family" for only the last decade (e.g., Fleischman *et al.,* 1983; Mash *et al.,* 1976; Patterson, 1975). It was not until 1985 that the journal *Child Behavior Therapy* was renamed *Child and Family Behavior Therapy.* Structural and systems theorists and practitioners have often misunderstood social learning-based approaches, arguing falsely that "psychodynamic and behavioral approaches localize problems in individuals, (whereas) the problem unit from an eco-systemic perspective invariably involves several people" (Tavantzis *et al.,* 1985, p. 73). This status seems to be shifting of late, as Gerald Patterson, a social learning therapist and researcher, has recently received major awards from the American Family Therapy Association and the American Association for Marriage and Family Therapy.

Although social learning strategies were successfully employed with small children and with adolescents in group care, strategies for working with families' conflict in home settings have been somewhat recent additions to the social learning field (e.g., Hall, 1984; Kinney *et al.*, 1977; Patterson and Forgatch, 1987). The use of social learning techniques with parent–adolescent conflict shows promise (e.g., Szykula *et al.*, 1982) but is complicated by some difficulties in effecting lasting change (Kirigan *et al.*, 1982; Wolf *et al.*, 1987). The evaluations of Homebuilders, which has served many families with adolescents and relies heavily on social learning concepts and strategies, attest to the efficacy of a social learning approach. Unfortunately, social learning approaches retain ugly duckling status in the swan-filled waters of family therapy. Aside from being seldom understood and often misrepresented, they are also more difficult to learn because of a limited pool of skilled trainers and supervisors.

Social learning-based family therapists endeavor to identify patterns of family interactions that punish competent family membership. Therapists seek to change low expectations for good experiences in the family, and promote family members' ability to reward each other by reciprocally changing their behavior. When family members have low expectations that efforts to change will be rewarded, despite evidence to the contrary, interventions may focus on exercises that enhance rethinking of the situation. Techniques drawn from Rational Emotive Therapy with adults may be employed with parents and, with modification, with adolescents to increase the accuracy of appraisals about the possibilities for positive outcomes (DiGiuseppe, 1983).

In practice, social learning-based approaches with families vary in their structure during cases and between cases (Barth, 1986). They may include parent training—in which the therapist works with the parent and the small child or children to promote effective parenting, parent consultation—in which the therapist works with the parent(s) but not the child, and parent–adolescent communication training and problem solving—in which all family members are involved. Perhaps because social learning approaches began addressing parent–child dyads, this approach is less concerned than conventional family therapy models that all family members participate simultaneously. (Family therapy approaches are moving to a problem-focused rather than family-focused approach and are increasingly flexible on this account.)

Social learning-based treatment programs have recently begun to give more attention to effects of the broader social environment or ecology on family functioning. Evidence about the influence of social support or social coercion on a parent's ability to follow through with effective and positive parenting practices learned during behavioral family therapy has prompted such concern (Wahler and Dumas, 1984). These concerns are in keeping with the longstanding commitment to providing assistance to families that generalizes beyond the clinic—that is, at least into the home—and lasts beyond the period of treatment. Attempts to promote generalization and maintenance of treatment gains have long called for work with teachers, employers, probation officers, and peers. Such work could extend the influence of social learning-based models well beyond the family. To date, however, there is little technology for doing so.

Outcome Research

Outcome research on crisis intervention, conventional family systems treatments, and social learning-based family therapy complements the nascent research on the efficacy of home-based services (i.e., AuClaire and Schwartz, 1986). Crisis intervention evaluations are weakest and stand apart. Family systems interventions have not yet been directly compared to social learning interventions. Still, some points of comparison can be identified. Less can be said about crisis intervention efforts since, as previously discussed, crisis intervention has not been adequately conceptualized or operationalized for outcome research.

Crisis Intervention Services

The value of theories can be determined by whether the interventions they spawn produce results that are superior to other theories or no theory at all. A profile of research on outcomes of crisis interventions is difficult to draw, however, because almost any treatment can be defined as crisis intervention given that almost any untoward event that precedes the onset of treatment may be vilified as the crisis. "Crisis intervention, neither in practice nor from an evaluative stand point, has evolved in any coherent fashion from crisis theory or its attendant assumptions . . . . Virtually every system of psychotherapy or behavior change includes crisis intervention in its domain" (Auerbach, 1983; p. 19). All crisis intervention efforts do, at least, share a commitment to intervening at the earliest point after the crisis. The most thorough crisis intervention research efforts have been evaluations of Samaritan suicide centers. These are mixed: one early study indicated that these centers reduce the suicide rate (Bagley, 1968), but a subsequent and more sophisticated investigation (Jennings *et al.,* 1978) found no difference. When research on crisis intervention efforts was summarized by Auerbach (1983), the conclusion reiterated Williams and Polak's (1979) summation—no systematic research has tested the efficiency of crisis intervention as a technique. At present, there is no forceful theoretical or evaluative argument for drawing on crisis theory or crisis intervention constructs to boost the helpfulness of

IFPS. Comparative program evaluations should consider whether the ability to respond immediately, the use of "beepers," and the absence of waiting lists contribute a significant amount to program outcomes; alone, crisis theory is not a trustworthy guide for program design.

Systemic or Structural Family Therapy

In assessing the effectiveness of family therapy approaches, this chapter draws heavily on the work of Gurman, *et al.*, (1986) who have made careers of encyclopedic and skillful reviews of this literature. They argue that " . . . the practice of family and marital therapy leads to positive outcomes. Family therapy no longer needs to justify its existence on empirical grounds. . . . Indeed, we believe that the progress achieved in the last few years offers the basis for even more confidence about the salience of systemic thinking and practice than did the research we reviewed in 1978" (p. 570). According to those well-known reviewers of the family therapy field, systemic, nonbehavioral family and marital therapies are considered to have some beneficial effect in about two-thirds of cases and to be better than no treatment or conventional treatments. In a study of work with youth called "delinquents" (but more like our current status offenders) in Utah, Parsons and Alexander (1973) demonstrated that a family therapy approach that included structural and behavioral components outperformed client-centered family therapy, psychodynamic–eclectic family therapy, and no treatment.

Social Learning Treatment

The efficacy of social learning-based treatments is also well documented. No other intervention for families with antisocial children has been investigated so carefully and shown such favorable results (Kazdin, 1984; Gurman, *et al.*, 1986). In an integrative table providing overall estimates of the effectiveness of various marital and family therapies for specific disorders and problems, Gurman *et al.* (1986) identify social learning-based approaches as having more established effectiveness than structural therapy. Social learning approaches have probable or established effectiveness in work with six categories of disorder—conduct disorders of children, substance abuse, juvenile delinquency, marital discord, anxiety disorders of adults, and adult schizophrenia. Structural family therapy, which has been far less tested than the social learning approach, has demonstrated probable or established effectiveness in two categories—substance abuse and psychosomatic disorders of children and adolescents. In sum, the social learning basis for therapeutic interventions shows power (not just promise) in helping individuals and families with a wide range of family difficulties. Noteworthy in this review

(Gurman *et al.*, 1986) is the lack of direct evidence about the effectiveness of either approach in addressing families that are neglecting, abusing, or sexually mistreating their children. Reviews of behavioral approaches to child abuse treatment (e.g., Reid, 1985) and recently documented successes (e.g., Szykula and Fleischman, 1985) suggest the promise of social learning-based approaches. One social learning-based project for helping abusive families found success only after moving the therapists into the home because changes in parenting witnessed in the clinic did not transfer to the home (Goldstein *et al.*, 1985). Significant studies of family systems interventions with child maltreating families are more scarce. Frankel's (1988) review addresses just that question and reveals a paucity of evidence that maltreated children receive better quality care following home-based family centered services of any kind.

The Blending of Family Systems and Social Learning Models

Differences between social learning theory and family systems theory may differ more than their practices. Table 5.1 lists ten theoretical assumptions gleaned from the literature that may distinguish family systems from social learning theory and provides this author's ratings of how much each treatment approach relies on each assumption. There appears to be as much agreement as disagreement. Social learning theory is better articulated than family systems theory, but rarely makes assumptions that family systems theory rejects. However, social learning theorists reject some assumptions closely held by family systems theorists—especially the theory that established ways of functioning may have to become dysfunctional before change will occur.

Family systems and social learning theorists and practitioners share many techniques—often unaware. For example, Tavantzis *et al.* (1985) describe a home-based structural family therapy approach for delinquents at risk of placement. They argue that while most social learning and home-base prevention projects appropriately treat the family as the unit of service, these programs receive little cross-fertilization from the structural, strategic, and systemic models of family therapy. Yet, their own ecosystemic view of problems that lead to placement could have been copied from a social learning program manual:

> . . . the premise is not that delinquency is caused by prior unfortunate experiences in the family . . . . Rather, it is assumed that how problems are maintained is more important than how they originated—that present causes are more relevant than past causes. The emphasis, therefore, is on how problems persist as an aspect of current, ongoing disturbances in family life (p. 75).

Table 5.1. Theoretical Assumptions of Family Systems, and Social Learning Theory

	Family systems[a]	Social learning theory
1. The behavior of every family member is related to and dependent on all the others	Hi	Hi
2. Each event is multiply determined and no one can be blamed	Hi	Hi
3. Diagnoses of individual pathology supply useful treatment information	Lo	Lo
4. Established ways of operating may have to become highly dysfunctional before families relinquish them and replace them with new ways	Med	Lo
5. Changing negative family behavior is best facilitated by rewarding positive alternatives	Lo	Hi
6. Symptoms reflect difficulties in family functioning	Hi	Med
7. Client's expectation of the outcomes of behavior is a strong determinant of behavior	Lo	Hi
8. Families are hindered from changing their behavior because they lack skills	Lo	Hi
9. Symptoms help to maintain family systems	Hi	Lo
10. Change is facilitated by crisis	Med	Lo

[a] Hi, Theory's reliance on this assumption is high; Med, theory's reliance on this assumption is moderate; Lo, theory's reliance on this assumption is low.

The procedure of complementarity used by structural family therapists (Minuchin and Fischman, 1981) has aspects very similar to social learning's "behavioral analysis." Under either label, therapists help family members understand how each individual's behavior is contingent on responses from other family members.

Family systems theorists argue about the importance of avoiding systemic confusion caused by having multiple outside helpers with conflicting roles and plans (Coopersmith, 1983). They also caution against therapists trying to change the child directly or offering the child limits, consistency, affection, or understanding that parents do not provide because of the danger of undermining the parents' position in the family (Tavantzis *et al.,* 1985). Social learning-oriented service providers would agree with both of these concerns.

There are many references to homework in the structural family therapy literature (Minuchin and Fischman, 1981; Colapinto, 1982). Only 1% of family therapists in Rait's (1988) study indicated they never assign homework or tasks. Yet, the therapists in the Hennepin County Project (Au-Claire and Schwartz, 1986) were less likely to indicate that they assign homework. Homework has different characteristics and purposes in each approach. Structural family therapists use homework to change family relationships, whereas social learning therapists are more likely to use it to build skills. For example, in order to improve the parents' ability to make joint decisions, a structural family therapist might ask both parents to review their child's school work each day to decide if he warranted subsequent privileges. The social learning therapist might encourage the same action to ensure that the youth receive ample reward for satisfactory school work, thereby increasing the subsequent likelihood of school success.

Table 5.2 lists therapist techniques employed by the 8 home-based structural family therapy workers in AuClair and Schwartz (1986), rated by frequency of use. The ratings in column 2 of the table represent the social learning approach. When workers from the same project rated items used to evaluate Homebuilders training, they agreed on 66% of the items that described ideal Homebuilder's practice, with the strongest disagreement on "it is the worker's job to motivate family members," "never insist that all family members participate," "rarely confront family members," and "provide hard services including moving, cleaning, and grocery shopping."

Differences between Family Systems and Social Learning Practices

Although the similarities in the practice of structural family therapists and social learning family therapists seem to exceed the differences, the differences are not insignificant. Social learning- and family systems-based treatment models have clear contrasts. Proponents of both perspectives find some aspects of the other approaches—or at least their often selective impressions of them—to be naive, peculiar, and even harmful. Perhaps the most significant objection of social learning therapists is that structural family therapists do not treat clients as colleagues and instead, purposefully demonstrate their control over the family by such means as reseating clients. Family systems practitioners might counter that they empower families by drawing on the families' strengths and that social learning approaches tend to demean clients by assuming that they lack skills for solving problems. Further, they would argue that all interventions include elements of power and control. And unless this use of control by any therapist is preceded by considerable effort to join with the family and to develop a positive alliance through the demonstration of warmth, empathy, and genuineness, families are less likely to have positive outcomes (Wells, 1981). Indeed, the therapists in AuClaire and Schwartz (1986) indicate that expressing empathy and joining were their most frequent activities.

Table 5.2. Techniques Employed in Family Systems[a] and Social Learning-Based Programs

		Family systems[b]	Social learning theory
1.	Build a mutually trusting relationship with the family	Hi	Hi
2.	Identify and built on existing family strengths	Hi	Hi
3.	Establish parents as authority figures	Hi	Hi
4.	Value the client as a person	Hi	Hi
5.	Express empathy	Hi	Hi
6.	Change the structure within the family	Hi	Lo
7.	Delineate family boundaries	Hi	Lo
8.	Take a nonjudgmental stance	Hi	Hi
9.	Elicit information to clarify the situation	Hi	Hi
10.	Express interest and feedback to family members to show that they are understood	Hi	Hi
11.	Prepare a written contract outlining methods to achieve measurable goals	Lo	Hi
12.	Provide didactic training to parents in child management techniques	Lo	Hi
13.	Address and work with family of origin issues	Hi	Lo
14.	Create a system of rewards to encourage specific behavior changes	Med	Hi
15.	Rehearse communication or problem-solving skills	Lo	Hi
16.	Engage in therapeutic work specifically with the family dyad	Lo	Med
17.	Explicitly provide direction for family member's behavior during a session	Lo	Lo
18.	Instruct family members in concrete methods to change behavior by demonstrating the desired behavior	Lo	Hi
19.	Connect the family with other helping resources in the community	Lo	Med
20.	Structure the therapeutic session to get family members to interact to illustrate dysfunctional patterns	Lo	Lo
21.	Reinforce (positively or negatively) a client's thoughts or feelings	Med	Hi
22.	Be aware of your own feelings during a session and express them to clients	Med	Lo
23.	Reinterpret events for family members to give them an alternative	Med	Med
24.	Encourage and suggest possible actions to family members	Med	Med
25.	Teach family members methods that will help them solve problems more effectively	Med	Med

[a]Family systems rankings are adapted from AuClaire and Schwartz (1986).
[b]Hi, high reliance on technique; Med, medium reliance on technique; Lo, low reliance on technique.

At times, the differences between approaches may be more striking. A Homebuilder therapist would likely hold family sessions in the family's living room with the TV on, keep the initial talk breezy, and listen a lot to all who pass by. A structural family therapist would more likely tell family members to turn off the TV, move to the kitchen table, and sit where the therapist wants them to sit. Homebuilder's therapists extol such naturalistic assessment methods as identifying teachable moments and building relationships based on a collegial approach. Structural family therapists seek more control over the family session.

Many family systems theorists would reject such social learning techniques as teaching a parent to use "time out" and developing point and reward systems to increase a child's positive actions. These might be considered patchwork approaches that would not have lasting impact without more complete changes in dimensions of the family system. Such strategies might be considered naive by family therapists because they inadvertently interfere with the family system without leading family members to recognize the need to redo family rules, redraw family boundaries, or redistribute family power. If family therapists used time out, they would be less likely to go through the procedure in great detail and would, instead, more often assume that if the family could not implement the procedure, it indicated a dysfunctional family structure rather than a skill deficit.

Ecological or Not Ecological: Is That the Question?

The actual practices of therapists working under the guidance of family systems or social learning-based approaches may differ most strikingly according to their theoretical allegiance to an ecological systems model. An ecological orientation argues that individuals cannot be understood separately from their transactions with the environment (see Germain and Gitterman, 1980; Maluccio, this volume, Chapter 6). It encourages assessment of the client's skills for coping with the environment and proposes interventions to reduce the misfit between the environment's offerings and the client's capacities and needs. Although nearly every practitioner aspires to this lofty and diffuse goal, there are widely varying views on whether therapists should principally work to directly change the environment or to build the family's capacities.

Neither social learning theory nor family systems theory clarifies the impact on family functioning of the family's access to basic resources for safe and healthy living. Although Aponte (1976) among family therapists and Wahler and Graves (1983) among social learning researchers have clarified the significance of extrafamilial forces on intrafamilial coping, none clearly specifies the priority that addressing problems in housing, financial assistance, and education should be given in the therapeutic scheme. Nor do they detail techniques for countering environmental stressors. Although a family systems approach can be broadened into an ecological approach (Hartman and Laird, 1983) and social learning theory can be applied to advocacy and achieving community change (Weisner and Silver, 1981), these applications are not promoted in the treatment approaches these theories have spawned. As a result, some therapists in programs that employ a structural family therapy model will not accompany clients to the employment service division or attend a child's special education Individual Educational Plan meeting. They would argue that the client's ability to succeed in these encounters should be assessed and promoted within the family therapy sessions. Other therapists with the same theoretical stripes participate vigorously in directly influencing those environmental resources and view those actions as compatible with a broader family systems view (Aponte, 1976). Implementing the ecological model calls for assuming such practice roles as teacher, mediator, advocate, and organizer (Germain and Gitterman, 1980). Social learning-based approaches have well elaborated technologies for teaching and mediation, but offer little guidance related to the skills of advocate and organizer.

Of the theories considered here, ecologically-based interventions have the highest level of concern with addressing environmental impingements on a family or child's functioning. The need for interventive efforts to span home, school, and community is explicit in the theory (Garbarino, 1982). The emphasis of the ecological model is to determine ways to achieve family goals rather than to modify family structure or provide new skills for family interaction. Whereas teaching skills may be compatible with an ecological perspective (Barth, 1986; Whittaker *et al.*, 1986), changes in family structure or skill are not assumed to be necessary to attain family goals in all programs. Indeed, some longstanding and successful intensive home-based service programs like the Emergency Family Care Program in California invest the majority of their interventive activities on linking families with needed resources and few of their efforts on changing client behavior via family therapy or social learning-based approaches. They do not assume that families lack skills or have dysfunctional family structures.

Conclusions

In the absence of compelling head-to-head research comparisons between models of intensive family preservation services, how do program planners, practitioners, and educators decide which theories to use to guide their interventive efforts? One approach is to assume the equivalency of family treatment and conclude that it is a matter of taste. Worthington (1987) plays a variation on that theme by proposing that the likelihood of success of different family treatment approaches depends on the match between a family's response to the transitions and the model of intervention. Yet, outcome reviews indicate that the improvement of families, children, and adults above no-treatment comparison groups appear to be consistently more impressive for social learning-based interventions than they are for other approaches (Casey and Berman, 1985; Gurman *et al.,* 1986; Pecora *et al.,* 1987). We can all be sure, however, that such comparisons will not substantially alter the face of family preservation services. Developmentally, the field is a long way from determining the best unilateral approach or what mix of family systems, social learning, and ecological interventions are most effective. None of the theories are wrong—they are all just incomplete. So are the most common variants of family therapy.

For example, family systems theorists are farther along in incorporating a developmental approach in their work than are social learning theorists, who do not often address issues of individual development or family life cycle in their work (cf. Harris and Ferrari, 1983). This family developmental process holds that family systems pass through predictable life stages, involving new methods of coping with the demands of the environment (Carter and McGoldrick, 1980). Families pass through various transition points (e.g., the first child attending school or the challenges of adolescence) with varying ability and the family system may fail to operate at some point. At these times, family systems will benefit from a range of outside interventions to help them get back on track. "This theoretical framework allows the family therapist to view the problems which are present in the family as 'breakdowns' in the family's evolutionary quest" (Koman and Stechler, 1985, p. 7). At present, family developmental models have little supporting data and serve largely as a heuristic for considering problems arising as family members cope with developmental dilemmas. Still, they provide a useful reminder of developmental processes at work and are an aid to intervention. This concept of the evolving family is considerably more useful than the historical homeostatic model of families that it is dislodging. Family systems/structural and social learning-based models should pay more heed to developmental theories, and endeavor to identify which families with children of what ages can best benefit from what levels and types of interventions.

Social learning approaches may provide families with more assistance because they use more behavior change strategies. As previously observed, many of the core elements of family therapy are also employed by social learning therapists. But, social learning therapists do more than conventional family therapists. Social learning therapists are also likely to use parent training, teach time out, develop contracts, help clients practice cognitive restructuring, and train clients in self-management skills. The proven ability of these approaches to change family behavior cannot be denied—yet they are often ignored by family therapists. Programs which also draw on ecological theories and encourage linkages to formal and informal resources have additional and powerful assets.

The history of family therapy is closely bound with family systems theory. Family therapy with high risk families is now in danger of becoming handcuffed by an overallegiance to variants of family systems theory which exclude social learning and ecological procedures. This exclusion is based on skimpy theoretical grounds and overlooks the possibility that those procedures may give a family new tools for self-regulation and sovereignty. Available theories of family behavior are simply not sufficiently proven to rule out the use of techniques with demonstrated efficacy.

A challenge for structural family therapists is to incorporate useful behavior-changing techniques from the social learning literature. A classic example is treatment of firesetting—a problem that raises instant concerns about the need for out-of-home placement. Although the aforecited report of Montalvo's efforts shows that structural family therapy can help a child over come firesetting tendencies, there are clear and tested social learning-based protocols and procedures for assessing and treating firesetters (see Barth, 1986). Educators of family therapists must strive to become familiar with such technologies and teach family therapists how to integrate such techniques into their family work.

While arguing for the integration of social and cognitive techniques into all practice, the author is concerned that a social learning-based approach will be viewed as a technological rather than theory-based approach. Both social learning and family systems approaches may become technological insofar as the therapist seeks to match a certain technique with a certain family constellation, rather than apply a unique intervention on the basis of a thorough assessment and flexible intervention procedures inspired by the family's interests, capabilities, and needs. Social work educators and trainers will do well to ground themselves and their students in the psychology of individual behavior change to complement their family systems orientation. At the same time, social learning-based therapists have much to do to integrate developmental and ecological theories into their work.

Providing intensive family preservation services is one of the more challenging activities that a therapist can undertake. Core helping skills that are common to family systems and social learning approaches may make a difference to families—especially if they are buttressed by the timely provision of work in the family's broader ecology. Family systems theory, social learning theory, and ecological theory—and many of the techniques derived from them—are often complementary and agreeable. When their proponents begin to draw on each other's resources, the field will move into a more promising era.

Implications for Teaching and Research

Social work education is moving toward offering practice models and techniques that will assist families to stay together and thrive. Ecological models, structural family therapy, task-centered practice, and even social learning-based interventions are gaining greater currency. Many issues require analysis and capable instruction, however, before graduates will be prepared to lead the development of family preservation services. These include:

- Developing models for assessing which families are at short-term risk of needing to place one or more children and which may be at risk of inadequate parenting across the childhoods and adolescences of all their children;
- Clarifying the best strategies for helping clients to become their own case managers and behavior changers;
- Integrating social learning and human development models so that knowledge of life's influences can be better used to help clients alter their circumstances;
- Articulating the potential and limits of skill training—which families will learn which parenting or self-management skills, taught in which way?
- Teaching individual assessment of psychopathology in a way that is consistent with ecological and social learning theories;
- Keeping ecological and family systems theories from becoming mental mush with little more meaning than "everything affects everything."

Research challenges are no greater and no less. Experimental studies that vary the duration of services are also needed given that the theory and evidence in support of lasting effects of brief interventions is not yet persuasive. In our present state of knowledge, even descriptive studies on family preservation services are well worthwhile. Efforts to address the following could result in significant contributions to family and child welfare research.

- What are the outcomes for chronically neglectful families with young single mothers and several small children?
- Do the outcomes for families on waiting lists differ from those served more promptly?
- What are the outcomes for families who receive several doses of IFPS?
- How much advantage would families gain from participating in a less intensive version of IFPS following the conclusion of conventional IFPS?

References

Aponte, H. J. (1976). The family school interview: An ecological approach. *Family Process, 15,* 303–311.

AuClaire, P., and Schwartz, I. M. (1986). *An evaluation of the effectiveness of intensive home-based services as an alternative to placement for adolescents and their families.* Minneapolis: University of Minnesota, Hubert H. Humphrey Institute of Public Affairs, Center for the Study of Youth Policy (mimeo.).

Auerbach, S. M. (1983). Crisis intervention research: Methodological consideration and some recent findings. *In* L. H. Cohen, W. L. Claiborn, and G. A. Specter (Eds.), *Crisis intervention,* 2nd ed. New York: Human Sciences Press.

Bagley, C. (1968). The evaluation of a suicide prevention schema by an ecological method. *Social Science and Medicine, 2,* 1–14.

Bandura, A. (1977). *Social learning theory.* Englewood Cliffs, NJ: Prentice-Hall.

Barth, R. P. (1986). *Social and cognitive treatment of children and adolescents.* San Francisco: Jossey-Bass.

Barth, R. P., Blythe, B. J., Schinke, S. P., and Schilling, R. F. (1983). Self-control training for child abusers. *Child Welfare, 62,* 313–324.

Bateson, G., Jackson, D. D., Haley, J., and Weakland, J. (1956). Toward a theory of schizophrenia. *Behavioral Science, 1,* 251–264.

Behavioral Sciences Institute. (1981). *First year Homebuilder mental health project report.* Tacoma, WA: Author.

Bloom, B. L. (1980). Social and community interventions. *Annual Review of Psychology, 31,* 111–142.

Bodin, A. M. (1981). The interactional view: Family therapy approaches of the Mental Research Institute. *In* A. S. Gurman and D. P. Kniskern (Eds.), *Handbook of family therapy,* pp. 267–309. New York: Brunner/Mazel.

Bowen, M. (1978). *Family therapy in clinical practice.* New York: Jason Aronson.

Brim, O., and Kagan, J. (Eds.). (1980). *Constancy and change in human development.* Cambridge: Harvard University Press.

Caplan, G. (1964). *Principles of preventive psychiatry.* New York: Basic Books.

Carter, E., and McGoldrick, M. (1980). *The family life cycle.* New York: Gardner.

Casey, R. J., and Berman, J. S. (1985). The outcome of psychotherapy with children. *Psychological Bulletin, 98,* 388–400.

Colapinto, J. (1982). Structural family therapy. *In* A. M. Horne and M. M. Ohlsen (Eds.), *Family counseling and therapy.* Itasca, IL: F. E. Peacock.

Coopersmith, E. I. (1983). The family and public service systems: An assessment method. *In* B. P. Keeney (Ed.), *Assessing in family therapy.* Rockville, MD: Aspen.

Darbonne, A. (1967). Crisis: A review of theory, practice and research. *Psychotherapy: Theory, Research and Practice, 4,* 49–56.

DiGiuseppe, R. A. (1983). Rational–emotive therapy and conduct disorders. *In* A. Ellis and M. E. Bernard (Eds.), *Rational-emotive approaches to the problems of childhood.* New York: Plenum.

Ellis, A. (1962). *Reason and emotion in psychotherapy.* Secaucus, NJ: Lyle Stuart & Citadel.

Ellis, A. (1980). Rational-emotive therapy and cognitive behavior therapy: Similarities and differences. *Cognitive Therapy and Research, 4,* 325–340.

Ellis, A., and Bernard, M. E. (Eds.). (1983). *Rational-emotive approaches to the problems of childhood.* New York: Plenum.

Ellis, E. M., Atkeson, B. M., and Calhoun, K. S. (1981). An assessment of long-term reaction to rape. *Journal of Abnormal Psychology, 90,* 263-266.

Erikson, E. H. (1959). *Identity and the life cycle* (Psychological Issues Monograph 1). New York: International Universities.

Everstine, D. S., and Everstine, L. (1983). *People in crisis: Strategic therapeutic interventions.* New York: Brunner/Mazel.

Fleischman, M. J., Horne, A. M., and Arthur, J. L. (1983). *Troubled families: A treatment approach.* Champaign, IL: Research Press.

Frankel, H. (1988). Family-centered, home-based services in child protection: A review of the research. *Social Services Review, 562,* 137-157.

Garbarino, J. (1982). *Children and families in the social environment.* New York: Aldine.

Gaudin, J. M., and Kurtz, D. P. (1985). Parenting skills training for child abusers. *Journal of Group Psychotherapy, Psychodrama and Sociometry, 38,* 35-54.

Germain, C. B., and Gitterman, A. (1980). *The life model of social work practice.* New York: Columbia University.

Goldstein, A. P., Keller, H., and Erne, D. (1985). *Changing the abusive parent.* Champaign, IL: Research Press.

Gurman, A. S., Kniskern, D. P., and Pinsof, W. M. (1986). Research on the process and outcome of marital and family therapy. *In* S. L. Garfield and A. E. Bergin (Eds.), *Handbook of psychotherapy and behavior change* (3rd ed.). New York: Wiley.

Haley, J. (1963). *Strategies of psychotherapy.* New York: Grune & Stratton.

Hall, J. A. (1984). Empirically based treatment for parent-adolescent conflict. *Social Casework, 65,* 487-495.

Harris, S., and Ferrari, M. (1983). The developmental factor in child behavior therapy. *Behavior Therapy, 14,* 37-53.

Hartman, A., and Laird, J. (1983). *Family-centered social work practice.* New York: Free Press.

Janis, I. L. (1969). Some implications of recent research on the dynamics of fear and stress tolerance. *Social Psychiatry, 47,* 86-100.

Jennings, C., Barraclough, B. M., and Moss, J. R. (1978). Have the Samaritans lowered the suicide rate? A controlled study. *Psychological Medicine, 8,* 413-422.

Jones, M. A., Neuman, R., and Shyne, A. W. (1976). *A second chance for families: Evaluation of a program to reduce foster care.* New York: Research Center, Child Welfare League of America, Inc.

Kazdin, A. E. (1984). Treatment of conduct disorders. *In* J. Williams and R. Spitzer (Eds.), *Psychotherapy research: Where are we and where should we go?* New York: Guilford.

Kendall, P. C., and Braswell, L. (1985). *Cognitive-behavioral therapy for impulsive children.* New York: Guilford.

Kinney, J. M., Madsen, B., Fleming, T., and Haapala, D. A. (1977). Homebuilders: Keeping families together. *Journal of Consulting and Clinical Psychology, 45,* 667-673.

Kirigin, K. A., Braukman, C. J., Atwater, J. D., and Wolf, M. M. (1982). An evaluation of teaching-family (Achievement Place) group homes for juvenile offenders. *Journal of Applied Behavior Analysis, 15,* 1–16.

Koman, S. L., and Stechler, G. (1985). Making the jump to systems. *In* M. P. Mirkin and S. L. Koman (Eds.), *Handbook of adolescents and family therapy.* New York: Gardner.

Krouse, H. J., and Krouse, J. H. (1982). Cancer as crisis: The critical elements of adjustment. *Nursing Research, 31,* 96–101.

Lewis, M. S. (1982). Topological relationships among crisis variables. *Psychotherapy: Theory, Research and Practice, 19,* 289–296.

McCubbin, H. I., and Patterson, J. M. (1983). Family transitions: Adaptations to stress. *In* H. I. McCubbin and C. R. Figley (Eds.), *Stress and the family: Volume I: Coping with normative transitions.* New York: Brunner/Mazel.

Mahoney, M. J. (1974). *Cognition and behavior modification.* Cambridge: Ballinger.

Mash, E. J., Handy, L. C., and Hamerlynck, L. A. (Eds.). (1976). *Behavior modification and families: Theory and research,* Vol. 1. New York: Brunner/Mazel.

Minuchin, S. (1974). *Families and family therapy.* Cambridge: Harvard University.

Minuchin, S., and Fischman, H. C. (1981). *Family therapy techniques.* Cambridge, MA: Harvard University.

Minuchin, S., Montalvo, B., Guerney, B., Rosman, B., and Schumer, F. (1967). *Families of the slums.* New York: Basic Books.

Minuchin, S., Rosman, B. L., and Baker, L. (1978). *Psychosomatic families: Anorexia nervosa in context.* Cambridge: Harvard University.

Parsons, B. V., and Alexander, J. F. (1973). Short term family intervention: A therapy outcome study. *Journal of Consulting and Clinical Psychology, 41,* 195–201.

Patterson, G. R. (1975). *Families.* Champaign, IL: Research Press.

Patterson, G. R., and Forgatch, M. (1987). *Parents and adolescents: Living together. Part I: The Basics.* Eugene, OR: Castalia.

Patterson, G., McNeal, S., Hawkins, N., and Phelps, R. (1967). Reprogramming the social environment. *Journal of Child Psychology and Psychiatry, 8,* 181–195.

Pecora, P. J., Fraser, M. W., and Haapala, D. (1987). *Defining family preservation services: Three intensive home-based treatment programs* (Research Report #1, Grant #90-CW-0731/01, Office of Human Development Services). Salt Lake City: Social Research Institute.

Rabkin, R. (1977). *Strategic psychotherapy.* New York: Basic Books.

Rait, D. (1988). Survey results. *The Family Therapy Networker, 12,* 52–56.

Ray, C. (1978). Adjustment to mastectomy: The psychological impact of disfigurement. *In* P. C. Brand and P. A. Van Keeps (Eds.), *Breast cancer: Psychosocial aspects of early detection and treatment.* Baltimore: University Park Press.

Reid, J. B. (1985). Behavioral approaches to intervention and assessment with child abusive families. *In* P. H. Bornstein and A. E. Kazdin (Eds.), *Handbook of clinical behavior therapy with children.* Homewood, IL: Dorsey.

Rogers, C. (1957). The necessary and sufficient conditions of therapeutic personality change. *Journal of Consulting Psychology, 22,* 95–103.

Rogers, C. (1961). *On becoming a person.* Boston: Houghton Mifflin.

Satir, V. (1967). *Conjoint family therapy,* rev. ed. Palo Alto, CA: Science & Behavior Books.

Satir, V. (1982). The therapist and family therapy: Process model. *In* A. M. Horne and M. M. Ohlsen (Eds.), *Family counseling and therapy.* Itasca, IL: F. E. Peacock.

Showell, W. H. (1988). Adoptive families use FT well, according to Oregon findings. *Family Therapy News,* January–February, p. 4.

Stanton, M. D. (1981). Strategic approaches to family therapy. *In* A. S. Gurman and D. P. Kniskern (Eds.), *Handbook of family therapy,* pp. 361–402. New York: Brunner/Mazel.

Stanton, M. D., and Todd, T. C. (1979). Structural family therapy with drug addicts. *In* E. Kaufman and P. Kaufman (Eds.), *The family therapy of drug and alcohol abuse.* New York: Gardner.

Szykula, S. A., and Fleischman, M. J. (1985). Reducing out-of-home placements of abused children: Two controlled field studies. *Child Abuse and Neglect, 9,* 277–284.

Szykula, S. A., Fleischman, M. J., and Shilton, P. E. (1982). Implementing a family therapy program in a community: Relevant issues on one promising program for families in conflict. *Behavioral Counseling Quarterly, 2,* 67–79.

Tavantzis, T. N., Tavantzis, M., Brown, L. G., and Rohrbaugh, M. (1985). Home-based structural family therapy for delinquents at risk of placement. *In* M. P. Mirkin and S. L. Koman (Eds.), *Handbook of adolescents and family therapy,* pp. 69–88. New York: Gardner.

Wahler, R. G., and Dumas, J. E. (1984). Changing the observational coding styles of insular and noninsular mothers: A step toward maintenance of parent training effects. *In* R. F. Dangel and R. A. Polster (Eds.), *Parent training,* pp. 379–416. New York: Guilford.

Wahler, R. G., and Graves, M. G. (1983). Setting events in social networks: Ally or enemy in child behavior therapy? *Behavior Therapy, 14,* 19–36.

Watzlawick, P., Weakland, J., and Fisch, R. (1974). *Change: Principles of problem formation and problem resolution.* New York: W. W. Norton.

Weisner, S., and Silver, M. (1981). Community work and social learning theory. *Social Work, 26,* 146–150.

Wells, R. A. (1981). The empirical base of family therapy: Practice implications. *In* E. R. Tolson and W. J. Reid (Eds.), *Models of family treatment,* pp. 248–305. New York: Columbia University.

Whittaker, J. K., Schinke, S. P., and Gilchrist, L. D. (1986). The ecological paradigm in child, youth, and family services: Implications for policy and practice. *Social Service Review, 60,* 483–503.

Williams, W. V., and Polak, P. R. (1979). Follow-up research in primary prevention: A model of adjustment in acute grief. *Journal of Clinical Psychology, 35,* 35–45.

Wolf, M. M., Braukman, C. J., and Ramp, K. A. (1987). Serious delinquent behavior as part of a significantly handicapping condition: Cures and supportive environments. *Journal of Applied Behavior Analysis, 20,* 347–359.

Wolfe, D. A., and Sandler, J. (1981). Training abusive parents in effective child management. *Behavior Modification, 5,* 320–335.

Worthington, E. L. (1987). Treatment of families during life transitions: Matching treatment to family response. *Family Process, 26,* 295–308.

Chapter 6

Family Preservation Services and the Social Work Practice Sequence

Anthony N. Maluccio

Throughout its history, the social work profession has periodically high-lighted and reaffirmed its traditional commitment to practice with and in families, especially in such settings as child welfare, family services, and mental health. As noted in Chapter 1, currently such commitment is reflected in the growing emphasis on family preservation services or home-based, family-centered programs for multiproblem or high-risk families (e.g., Bribitzer and Verdieck, 1988).

In line with this emphasis, social work practice in the area of family preservation services should be explicitly integrated into the curricula of graduate social work programs, to prepare social workers who can contribute to the strengthening of families and the prevention of unnecessary out-of-home placement of children and youth. Building on this premise, this chapter considers ways of achieving such integration, particularly in the direct practice sequence, following a review of the values, knowledge areas, and skills most pertinent for professional practice in family preservation services.

Values, Knowledge Areas, and Skills

Several chapters in this book consider in depth the range of values, knowledge areas, and skills that are required for competent performance in family preservation services, in general, and the Homebuilders model, in particular. These chapters cover much of the content that should be incorporated in the education of social workers and others engaged in family preservation services.

Here we review the central themes or content areas, to highlight what social workers need to learn in order to engage in intensive family preservation practice with multi-problem or high-risk families. The emphasis is on values, beliefs, and attitudes; knowledge areas and theoretical perspectives; and skills or competencies.

Values, Beliefs, and Attitudes

Kinney *et al.* (this volume, Chapter 3) discuss a variety of values, beliefs, and attitudes that influence the strategies used in the Homebuilders model. For the most part, these may be regarded as guidelines for family preservation practice in general. They include:

- Focusing on the family as the unit of help or attention;
- Respecting each family's and family member's strengths, potential, natural strivings toward growth, and capacity for change;
- Emphasizing staff members' roles in teaching or helping family members to develop coping and mastery skills, rather than "treating them;"
- Shifting from an illness or deficit orientation to a health/growth orientation in understanding and working with the family;
- Instilling hope and enhancing motivation in family members;
- Regarding clients as colleagues or partners in the helping process;
- Empowering families to "do" for themselves;
- Valuing cultural diversity;
- Supporting staff members in their efforts to help families.

Knowledge Areas and Theoretical Perspectives

The values, beliefs, and attitudes outlined above are buttressed and complemented by a range of knowledge areas and theoretical perspectives from psychology, sociology, biology, anthropology, and other fields. Barth (this volume, Chapter 5) reviews a number of theories that guide family-based services: in particular crisis intervention, which underscores the potential for change when human beings in crisis are offered quick, timely, and focused help; family systems theory, which has led to a variety of family therapy models; and social learning theory, which offers a range of strategies for teaching skills in areas such as parenting.

In addition to the above theories, Homebuilders and other family preservation models reflect various conceptual perspectives, although they may not have been explicitly delineated by the developers or proponents of the models. These include the following:

- *An ecological perspective,* which offers a broad conceptual lens for analyzing human behavior and social functioning within an environmental context. This perspective draws from such fields as ecology, systems theory, anthropology, and organizational theory (Bronfenbrenner, 1979; Germain and Gitterman, 1980; Whittaker *et al.,* 1986).

- *A developmental perspective,* which provides a frame of reference for understanding a family and its members in relation to goals and needs that are common to all persons and families, as well as in relation to their own particular aspirations, needs, and qualities. This perspective draws from knowledge of the stages and tasks of the family life cycle and the biopsychosocial principles of individual growth and development.

- *A competence-centered perspective,* which stresses that human beings have an innate drive to achieve competence in their dealing with environmental challenges. This perspective supports practice methods and strategies that promote the effective functioning of children, parents, and families. It draws from ego psychology; psychodynamic psychology; and learning, developmental, and family systems theories (Maluccio, 1981).

- *A permanency-planning perspective,* which embodies a mandate to maintain children in their own homes or, if necessary, place them permanently with other families. Permanency planning draws from a philosophy underscoring the value of rearing children in a family setting; a theoretical perspective stressing that stability and continuity of relationships promote a child's growth and functioning; and programs and methods focused on contracting, decision-making, and goal planning (Maluccio *et al.,* 1986).

As illustrated in Fig. 6.1, the ecological, developmental, competence, and permanency planning perspectives lead to an integrative conceptual framework for family-centered child welfare practice. Such a framework seems well suited to family preservation practice, for which it provides theoretical support and guidance in such ways as the following:

1. Regarding the family as the central unit of service or focus of attention, whenever possible and as much as possible. Human beings can best be understood and helped within their significant environment, and the family is the most intimate environment of all. It is here that children develop and form their identities and many of their com-

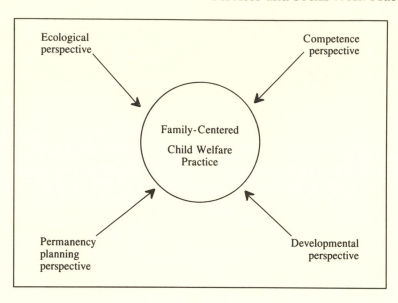

Figure 6.1. An integrative framework for family-centered child welfare practice.

petencies. There is extensive evidence regarding the crucial role of bonding, family connectedness, and continuity of relationships with parental figures in the growth and development of children. Moreover, the family has the potential to provide resources throughout the life cycle, especially as its members are sustained and supported by various services (Hartman and Laird, 1983).

2. Viewing parents and children within a person-in-environment framework; that is, as engaged in ongoing, dynamic transactions with each other and with their environment and in a continuous process of growth and adaptation. In other words, family members are seen as "open systems" that are spontaneously active and essentially motivated to achieve competence in their coping with life demands and environmental challenges (Germain and Gitterman, 1980).

3. Understanding family systems, the relationships between families and their environments, and the significant sources of support as well as stress and conflict encountered by families (Garbarino, 1982; Whittaker and Garbarino, 1983). Workers can then assess more objectively the complex personal and environmental factors affecting parents and children, and arrive at more appropriate treatment plans and recommendations.

4. Appreciating the unique qualities, styles, and needs of different ethnic, racial, and cultural groups, and thus facilitating the provision of services that are culturally relevant, particularly for minority children and families, who constitute a disproportionate number among those coming to the attention of child welfare agencies.

5. Directing professional help to the interaction between the family and its environment. There should be efforts to effect change not only in the parents or other family members, but also, and more importantly, in their environment, so that it may become more nutritive and supportive (Germain and Gitterman, 1980). This involves, above all, the provision of environmental opportunities and social supports that are necessary to sustain and promote each person's efforts to grow, achieve self-fulfillment, and contribute to others. Such supports are essential if the family is to fulfill its potential as a nurturing force and as a setting for maximum development of each member's competence, identity, and autonomy.

Skills or Competencies

The values and attitudes, knowledge areas, and theoretical perspectives outlined thus far support an extensive range of skills or competencies required for practice focused on family preservation. These are delineated by Kinney *et al.* (this volume, Chapter 3) in relation to the Homebuilders model and by Jackson (1987), Lloyd (1984) and others for other models.

In-depth consideration of the requisite skills is beyond the scope of this chapter, and the reader is referred to the works cited above. By way of illustration, however, it may be useful to note some of the areas in which particular skills or competencies need to be highlighted and nurtured in the training and education of social workers and others in the human services:

- Assessing and utilizing family strengths;
- Assessing, modifying, and utilizing the environment;
- Assessing severe pathology, chronic substance abuse, and the potential for violent behavior;
- Goal planning, including setting clear, specific, and limited goals on the basis of careful assessment;
- Using time frames and setting time limits;
- Decision-making;
- Contracting with families;
- Combining concrete and clinical services;

- Using informal as well as formal helping resources;
- Teaching life skills, especially skills in parenting, problemsolving, negotiation, communication, behavior management, and mood management;
- Collaborating with a variety of service providers;
- Understanding and working with the policies, rules, and procedures of a variety of child welfare programs;
- Tailoring services to the needs of each family, with flexibility in use of self on the part of the worker, in accessibility of worker, in location of service, and in selection of strategies;
- Offering crisis intervention services;
- Providing intensive services;
- Responding quickly to a family's direct or indirect request for help;
- Engaging families in their home settings;
- Using termination as an aid in empowering families, and facilitating networking and referrals to ongoing services when needed.

Implications for Direct Practice Curriculum

The values, knowledge areas, and skills outlined above are in one form or another incorporated in the direct practice curricula of graduate schools of social work. This is not surprising: much of this content has long been considered essential in the preparation of social workers, regardless of the particular specialization or agency setting in which they may be interested.

The typical curriculum thus includes at least the essence of what students need to know in order to be able to implement a family preservation model in their practice. This of course does not mean that students are actually prepared to do so upon graduation. Much more needs to be done to prepare them for providing family preservation services at a high level of competence. In particular, students need help to integrate content on values, knowledge, and skills into their practice in a coherent, responsible, and effective manner.

Achieving such integration requires systematic training in family preservation practice and one or more of its models. It calls for what Whittaker and Tracy (this volume, Chapter 1) delineate as "the value of studying a whole cloth, practice approach, *as it is presently practiced:* treatment techniques, organization/administration, knowledge base and evaluation," rather than studying fragments of different models or approaches. Such systematic training contrasts with the pattern of infusing content about different practice models throughout the curriculum, a pattern which is at present more typical in graduate social work education.

While the latter pattern has the advantage of exposing all students to a variety of practice models and their theoretical underpinnings, it also embodies major limitations: dilution of essential content; unevenness in emphasis, fragmentation of practice strategies and concepts, learning more about the "trees" and less about the "forest;" and inadequate commitment to—or insufficient proficiency in—the application of a specific model. In general, diffusion leads to knowledge and value changes in the learner, whereas specialization leads to skill development *plus* gains in knowledge and values.

The issue of specialization versus diffusion continues to be alive and well in many other social work curriculum areas, such as content on minorities, women, and ethics. Given the current political reality and the structure of existing curricula, it seems most useful at this point to offer a variety of options for teaching and learning family preservation practice in graduate schools of social work. Accordingly, the rest of this chapter will consider issues and strategies for: (1) teaching family preservation throughout the curriculum, and (2) teaching family preservation practice as a specialization.

Teaching Family Preservation Throughout the Curriculum

Although the "diffusion" approach has certain limitations, it can be employed to achieve a variety of purposes that can ultimately help strengthen the delivery of family preservation services in agencies throughout the community. These include sensitizing students to the values and concepts underlying family preservation; enriching students' practice with diverse client populations through teaching selected skills and techniques on family preservation; helping students to integrate content from other courses into their own knowledge base; and promoting students' interest in further specialized study in the area of family preservation.

Teaching Opportunities.   Whatever the nature of its organization in a particular school, the direct practice curriculum offers numerous opportunities to help achieve the above purposes by introducing and/or emphasizing content pertaining to family preservation. Some examples follow.

Courses in Human Behavior and the Social Environment provide an excellent base for conveying the significance of the family in human development, since content on family structure, function, and development is generally included. Presentation of such content can underscore the value of preserving families and instill in students a commitment to avoid unnecessary removal of children from their families. Additionally, there can be emphasis on factors such as poverty and racism that place stress on families, and on the social supports required to enable families, and parents in particular, to carry out their functions (Bronfenbrenner, 1979; Garbarino, 1982).

Research courses can bring in examples of studies in such areas as prevention of out-of-home placement, prevention and treatment of child maltreatment, impact of loss and separation on children and parents, and evaluation of family-based intervention programs, including the effectiveness of the Homebuilders model. Through examination of these studies and participation in research projects, students can be empowered to examine their own practice as well as their agencies' programs in relation to the philosophy of family preservation. They can thus move toward a more knowledge-based, empirically derived practice not only with high-risk families but also with clients in general.

Courses in the area of Social Welfare Policies and Services can further promote students' examination of agency practice and service delivery, as well as the values inherent in various family preservation models. Such examination can range from analysis of federal policies and programs pertaining to families, to analysis of service systems in the community, to critique of a specific agency's programs.

In addition, as considered by Pecora (this volume, Chapter 7), a program such as Homebuilders can be used as a case study to demonstrate the issues and opportunities that emerge in efforts to implement family preservation services. Students can thus learn what and how agencies need to change to be more supportive of family preservation goals and values. For students in the direct service curriculum such learning is essential, as it deepens their appreciation of the impact of structural and organizational factors on their practice with particular families.

Direct practice courses—whether they are organized along the lines of integrated practice, specific methods, or substantive specializations or concentrations—offer opportunities to reinforce content on family preservation. These opportunities can complement or build on those provided through courses in the Research, Human Behavior and the Social Environment, and Social Welfare Policy and Services sequences.

A specific component focusing on family preservation should be required of all students in direct practice. Instructors can select and emphasize case illustrations involving families with children at risk of out-of-home placement. These illustrations are readily available in child protective services and other child welfare settings; but they are also found in most practice contexts, including health and mental health, juvenile justice, mental retardation, income maintenance, and schools.

These cases can offer rich opportunities for teaching values and competencies required for direct work with families in general. They can also be used to highlight and reinforce numerous principles and strategies—such as contracting, goal setting, empowering families, and teaching skills—that are at the heart of Homebuilders and other models. Case discussion can focus on ethical issues involved in family-based services, and students can be helped to appreciate and deal with ethical dilemmas arising in any intervention with a family.

Teaching and learning in practice courses must be complemented by appropriate field work experience. In most field placements, students work with families who often include children or youth at risk of removal from the home. In these cases, students must confront the reality of issues covered theoretically in classroom courses—issues such as assessing the family's adequacy to meet the child's needs, considering the appropriateness of out-of-home placement, dealing with the dilemma of protecting the child versus preserving the family, or making a permanent plan for the child. Field instructors can help students to approach these and other issues from the perspective of family preservation, thus sharpening the students' skills in helping to enhance family functioning and maintain children in their own homes.

Integrative field seminars, which are required by some schools of social work, could be another teaching vehicle. These seminars typically include students from diverse agencies, concentrations, or specializations. Students could be encouraged to examine selected cases from a family preservation perspective. In particular, case discussion could focus on what could be done—or could have been done—by the social workers and other service providers to help preserve the family.

It would also be interesting to create as a model laboratory a field practicum in specialized agencies or specialized units within public child welfare agencies. This would be similar to the model of student units popular some years ago, but it would focus on new practice approaches. The unit would involve faculty leadership and students from different methods and concentrations. Students would practice and learn about implementing family-centered child welfare services from a variety of perspectives.

Teaching Family Preservation Practice as a Specialization

Infusion of content on family preservation services into the curriculum, while valuable in itself, does not adequately prepare social workers for specialized practice in this area. As reflected in the overview of values, knowledge, and skills presented earlier in this chapter, there is much that social workers must learn to become competent practitioners with high-risk families. In essence, they need to specialize. Toward this end, additional opportunities can be developed and offered to interested students, as discussed later.

Courses in Family and Children's Services.   Many schools have some form of specialization or concentration in the areas of child welfare or family and children's services. Typical courses cover child welfare, family treatment, practice with children and adolescents, and related topics (Maluccio, 1985).

One of these courses could be enriched either by including a substantial component on family preservation or by reshaping the course on the basis of the philosophy and practice of family preservation. The course could be adapted to the needs and interests of students. It could emphasize, for example, either organizational and administrative aspects or practice principles and strategies of family preservation services. Such an enriched or reshaped course would serve as a systematic introduction to the topic and as a stimulus for further specialization by the students through additional courses and/or field practice experiences.

Course on Family Preservation Services.   Another option would be to create a new course focused exclusively on family preservation. This option could be considered in addition to—or instead of—modification of an existing course.

The purpose of the new course would be to provide students with an in-depth, comprehensive understanding of family preservation services and practice. The course could be organized as a systematic, comparative examination of various models and approaches and include the following content areas, among others:

- Theoretical framework underlying family preservation programs and practice;
- Definition of family preservation services and relationship to child welfare in general, permanency planning in particular, and other service systems such as mental health, mental retardation, and juvenile justice;
- History, philosophy, and rationale;
- Organizational and political context and policy framework;
- Comparison of different models—common or generic features, unique characteristics, theoretical underpinnings, program structure and outcomes;
- Evaluation of effectiveness of different models;
- Development, implementation, and management issues.

Course on Homebuilders.   A generic course such as the one outlined above could be followed by an even more specialized course concentrating on a single practice model. The Homebuilders model is highly recommended for a number of reasons. First, it has a strong empirical base, having been developed through direct practice and ongoing experimentation. Second, it is characterized by a coherent and carefully articulated framework of values, knowledge, skills, and strategies; and, third, its effectiveness with high-risk families has been empirically demonstrated.

Whatever model is selected as the focus, the purpose of this course would be to enable social workers to attain a high level of understanding of the approach and to practice it competently. In line with this purpose, and as Whittaker and Tracy suggest in Chapter 1, it would be crucial to teach the model as a "whole cloth" and to present its organization, treatment, approaches, evaluation, and other aspects in an integrated manner. The course would also be an excellent vehicle for helping students to integrate various curriculum components that are now taught separately, such as core knowledge, values, practice skills, and organizational issues.

It would also be essential that students enrolled in the course have a concurrent field placement in a family preservation program supporting course objectives. Selection of agency and field instructor and collaboration between field agency and school would obviously be crucial, although beyond the scope of this chapter.

Additional Opportunities. The suggestions offered thus far have been geared to students enrolled in schools of social work and are intended to provide them with opportunities to specialize in the area of family preservation services. It is equally as important to consider ways of achieving the same purpose for social workers and other human service professionals who have already obtained an advanced degree in their discipline.

One alternative would be to permit some of these graduates to enroll in specialized courses such as those outlined above. A potentially more useful option would be to create a postgraduate certificate program focused on teaching family preservation practice. Such a program could be developed by tailoring some of the course offerings outlined in this chapter to the needs and qualities of advanced students, in conjunction with related field practice experiences in family preservation.

Although details would have to be worked out, a certificate program could be modeled after existing school programs in such areas as aging, substance abuse, and family and children's services. Such an approach would help meet the demand for skilled practitioners that has been forecast, as agencies throughout the country introduce or expand family preservation services for high-risk families.

Teaching Methods and Aids

Teaching family preservation content in the direct practice curriculum can build on typical methods and aids, such as case presentations and curriculum modules dealing with specific aspects of family preservation practice. Teaching aids and outlines may be developed or adapted from a range of materials in the literature, such as the following:

- Introduction to family preservation services, including history, rationale, structure, and legal framework (e.g., Edna McConnell Clark Foundation, 1985).

- Definition and classification of family preservation services by dimension—such as treatment model, program structure, and program outcome (e.g., Pecora, *et al.,* 1987).

- Descriptions of exemplary programs (e.g., Homebuilders model in Kinney *et al.,* this volume, Chapter 3; Iowa model in Lloyd, 1984; National Resource Center on Family-Based Services, 1983; and the Maryland model in Jackson, 1987).

- Program reviews, critiques, and evaluation reports (e.g., Halpern, 1986; Kaplan, 1986; Landsman, 1985).

- Texts on family-based services (e.g., Bryce and Lloyd, 1981; Maybanks and Bryce, 1979).

- Annotated bibliographies on family-focused interventions (e.g., Friedman and Street, 1985).

Additional tools need to be developed, particularly audiovisual aids that can bring alive the practice of family preservation and stimulate both faculty and students. Although currently there are numerous case records and videotapes on family therapy, in general they do not make explicit the theme of family preservation.

Another strategy, as often employed in practice courses, is to bring staff members of family preservation programs into the classroom as consultants, resource persons, or co-teachers. Their participation through these roles would be invaluable, especially as a school begins to focus on this area of teaching. Family preservation programs would be a good area for faculty-agency staff exchanges, since both agencies and schools are new at some aspects of these approaches.

Faculty Development

Incorporating family preservation content into the curriculum, whether by infusion or specialization, is likely to require some faculty development in most schools of social work. This can include traditional approaches such as obtaining consultation or participating in workshops led by staff members of exemplary family preservation programs. Faculty can also participate in practice-based research, especially research on experimentation with—and evaluation of—different approches to family preservation.

In addition, selected faculty members and field instructors could be involved in internships or other training activities at a program such as Homebuilders. Such involvement is ultimately the best way to become immersed in the model, be excited by it, and learn enough to teach it. As faculty members and field instructors thus become renewed and committed to a real-life model, they will be better able to teach it and to infuse pertinent content throughout the curriculum. Such collaboration could be promoted through offering joint faculty–agency appointments to selected faculty members and agency staff.

Conclusion

Direct practice curricula in graduate schools of social work hold numerous opportunities for reinforcing, expanding, or introducing content on family preservation services and practice. Schools need to determine whether to exploit these opportunities through a broad-based curriculum approach, some form of specialization, or a combination of methods.

Although the best format or approach for a particular school may be argued, the need to do something is evident: specialized content is increasingly required to enable social workers and others in the human services to achieve the goals of empowering and preserving vulnerable families and avoiding the unnecessary placement of children and youth out of their homes.

To contribute to these goals, schools of social work must enrich or expand the social work practice sequence through more explicit attention to family preservation. In particular, as suggested in this chapter, schools can consider adopting an integrative framework for family-centered child welfare practice; exposing all students to content on values, knowledge, and skills in family preservation; providing opportunities for specialization in this area of practice to interested students; and promoting faculty–staff exchanges and collaboration with exemplary programs or agencies offering family preservation services.

References

Bribitzer, M. P., and Verdieck, M. J. (1988). Home-based, family-centered intervention: Evaluation of a foster care prevention program. *Child Welfare, 67,* 255–266.

Bronfenbrenner, U. (1979). *The ecology of human development.* Cambridge: Harvard University.

Bryce, M., and Lloyd, J. (Eds.). (1981). *Treating families in the home: An alternative to placement.* Springfield, IL: Charles C. Thomas.

Edna McConnell Clark Foundation. (1985). *Keeping families together: The case for family preservation.* New York: Author.

Friedman, R. M., and Street, S. (1985). *Family-focused interventions: An annotated bibliography.* Tampa, FL: University of South Florida, Florida Mental Health Institute, Research and Training Center for Improved Services for Seriously Emotionally Disturbed Children.

Garbarino, J. (1982). *Children and families in the social environment.* New York: Aldine.

Germain, C. B., and Gitterman, A. (1980). *The life model of social work practice.* New York: Columbia University Press.

Halpern, R. (1986). Home-based early intervention: Dimensions of current practice. *Child Welfare, 65,* 387-399.

Hartman, A., and Laird, J. (1983). *Family-centered social work practice.* New York: Free Press.

Jackson, S. (1987). *Intensive family services: A family preservation service model.* Maryland Department of Human Resources.

Kaplan, L. (1986). *Working with multi-problem families.* Lexington, MA: Lexington Books.

Landsman, M. J. (1985). *Evaluation of fourteen child placement prevention projects in Wisconsin—1983-1985.* Iowa City: University of Iowa, National Resource Center on Family Based Services.

Lloyd, J. C. (1984). *Basic family-centered curriculum for family service workers and parent aides.* Iowa City: University of Iowa, National Resource Center on Family Based Services.

Maluccio, A. N. (Ed.). (1981). *Promoting competence: A new/old approach to social work practice.* New York: Free Press.

Maluccio, A. N. (1985). Education and training for child welfare practice. *In* J. Laird and A. Hartman (Eds.), *A handbook of child welfare: Context, knowledge, and practice,* pp. 741-759. New York: Free Press.

Maluccio, A. N., Fein, E., and Olmstead, K. A. (1986). *Permanency planning for children: Concepts and methods.* New York: Tavistock.

Maybanks, S., and Bryce, M. (Eds.). (1979). *Home-based services for children and families: Policy, practice, and research.* Springfield, IL: Charles C. Thomas.

National Resource Center on Family-Based Services. (1983). *Family-centered social services: A model for child welfare agencies.* Iowa City: University of Iowa, Author.

Pecora, P. J., Fraser, M. W., and Haapala, D. (1987). *Defining family preservation services: Three intensive home-based treatment programs.* Salt Lake City: University of Utah, Graduate School of Social Work, Social Research Institute.

Whittaker, J. K., and Garbarino, J. (1983). *Social support networks: Informal helping in the human services.* New York: Aldine.

Whittaker, J. K. Schinke, S. P., and Gilchrist, L. D. (1986). The ecological paradigm in child, youth, and family services: Implications for policy and practice. *Social Service Review, 60,* 483-503.

Chapter 7

Designing and Managing Family Preservation Services: Implications for Human Services Administration Curricula

Peter J. Pecora

Family preservation services represent one of many exciting treatment models for improving family functioning and preventing child placement that are being implemented throughout the country in child welfare, mental health, developmental disability, and juvenile justice agencies. Previous chapters in this monograph have discussed the evolution, treatment approaches, policy issues and research findings associated with family preservation services (FPS), with particular focus on the Homebuilders model. Yet there are a variety of administrative issues associated with designing, implementing, evaluating, and managing FPS programs.

This chapter will discuss some of these issues and illustrate their utility for teaching administrative content in graduate schools of social work or other human service educational programs. In particular, three areas related to administration of FPS will be addressed: (1) program and organizational design; (2) personnel management; and (3) financial management, fundraising, and cost–benefit analysis.

The Political and Organizational Context
of Family Preservation Services

As with virtually all human service programs, FPS agencies or programs function within a political and organizational context, which heavily influences how the services are organized and delivered. For example, FPS have expanded during the past 10 years, in part because it was recognized that permanency planning was a necessary but insufficient response to minimizing the number of children being placed in substitute care. The widespread impression that FPS is a cost-effective alternative to traditional child welfare services has also increased its popularity as fiscal austerity and program accountability became some of the important themes during the 1980s.

Family preservation services were also promoted because of their "ideological fit" with some of the concerns and priorities that were raised during the last 2 decades. Many of these concerns were translated into law by a diverse group of advocates as part of PL 96-272 (the Adoption Assistance and Child Welfare Act of 1980). Some of the principles that were promoted by this law and the child welfare reform movement that accompanied it were that services be provided in the least restrictive environment and with "reasonable and persistent efforts" to prevent child placement. (See other chapters in this volume, also Pine, 1986.)

While these were some of the driving forces promoting FPS, many child welfare and mental health agencies have been facing a series of budget cutbacks, increasing caseloads, high worker turnover, rising concern about agency liability for leaving children in situations where child maltreatment was a possibility, and union resistance to such job requirements as working evenings and weekends. These fiscal, political, and administrative realities can be used to illustrate the complexity of developing, implementing and managing FPS in a turbulent organizational environment. And they must be kept in mind as we discuss some of the issues associated with designing FPS programs.

FPS Program and Organizational Design Issues

There are a variety of program design issues that must be addressed and structural components that must be established when developing a FPS program. Most of these components and decisions are representative of those associated with developing and managing any human service program in such a way that organizational excellence is maximized (Patti, 1983, 1987). But the purpose and organizational context of many FPS programs pose some unusual challenges. These design issues provide an opportunity for social work educators to illustrate course content in administration, community organization, program planning, and supervision classes with challenges currently faced by FPS administrators.

For example, it is important to examine how FPS administrators are developing strategies for maximizing organizational performance in such areas as:

- Output efficiency and delivery of services to intended recipients;
- Acquisition of resources from the agency's environment to expand or maintain services;
- Supervision and involvement of organizational members in a way that maximizes worker satisfaction and productivity while minimizing absenteeism, burnout, and turnover;
- Service effectiveness as measured by client change, client satisfaction, and service quality (Patti, 1985, pp. 2–3).

Social work students need to be able to identify the service elements associated with organizational excellence and the fulfillment of the performance objectives listed above. Some of these elements include: (1) establishing a clear, value-driven agency mission; (2) selection of effective service technology; (3) designing service delivery components that promote service effectiveness and are responsive to client needs; (4) selection of capable personnel; (5) specifying performance criteria and worker appraisal methods; (6) providing high quality supervision; and (7) collection and use of program evaluation and cost–benefit data. These service elements, as they apply to FPS, will be discussed in the sections below drawing upon the work of Patti (1987), Patti *et al.,* (1987), Peters and Waterman (1983), and others.

Establishment of a Clear Agency Mission, Goals, and Objectives

One of the most common characteristics of effective human service organizations is their use of and commitment to a clear, well-defined, value-driven organizational mission (Peters and Waterman, 1983; Selznick, 1984). FPS programs such as Homebuilders have been able to define and articulate their mission in ways that promote staff, client, and public understanding of what it is that they do. Worker job tasks as well as treatment objectives have been well-defined; and even the trademarked name of the program—"Homebuilders"—contributes to its positive image within the communities it serves (see Kinney *et al,* this volume, Chapter 3).

This image and clear sense of mission is bolstered by a supportive ideology: a particular set of values and beliefs about the organizational mission, service technology, and the clients served. Patti (1987), in summarizing some of the literature on organizational excellence, emphasizes that an organization needs "not only clear objectives, structured roles, competent personnel, and adequate resources to perform well, but more importantly, the organization needs values, symbols, and beliefs that attach a social significance to the organization's outcomes and processes, and that help to reconcile ever present ambiguity and uncertainty" (p. 378). The strong commitment to client empowerment and family strengthening held by Homebuilders and many other FPS organizations enhances such an approach to organizational design.

Selection of Effective Service Technology

Many human service organizations recognize that maximizing productivity through people requires a concentration of effort and the use of a well-formulated treatment technology. Despite limitations of our knowledge of human behavior there is a growing body of empirical research and practice wisdom that some agencies are aggressively tapping to provide their staff with the most powerful change technologies available (see for example, Reid and Hanrahan, 1982; Rubin, 1985; Barth, 1986).

FPS administrators and workers, in designing their service approach, should be making careful decisions about the change technology to be used. The empirical evidence and practice wisdom supporting various approaches should be examined. Indeed, many studies of policy and program implementation have emphasized how the need to choose the most effective service technology has been fatally overlooked (Bardach, 1977; Williams, 1980; Williams and Elmore, 1976).

With respect to FPS, determining which theoretical models should guide treatment interventions is complicated by the lack of evaluative research in this area. Furthermore, there are a variety of models and techniques that can be applied, such as family systems and ecologically-based models, and cognitive behavioral approaches that draw upon social learning and other theories (see Barth, this volume, Chapter 5). In addition, although the Homebuilders program has demonstrated the need to use a variety of clinical techniques in combination with concrete services, the choice of which specific clinical techniques and concrete services to emphasize is not clear cut (Fraser *et al.,* 1988; Haapala, 1983). Thus administration students need to be aware of the importance of consciously selecting, refining, and maintaining the agency's service technology. The effort that programs such as Homebuilders put into the orientation and continued training of their therapists is an example of the agency investment that is necessary to operationalize the service technology that is chosen.

Designing Service Delivery Components that Promote
Service Effectiveness and are Responsive to Client Needs

In addition to the selection of a treatment model, program auspice is emerging as an important variable to consider; especially if you are a state administrator who must decide if FPS are to be provided through purchase of service contracts with private agencies, by state program units, or via a mixture of both mechanisms. Private FPS programs have demonstrated some of the highest rates of program effectiveness, but a lack of well-designed research prevents any definitive answer to the question of preferred auspice at this time (Frankel, 1988; Jones, 1985). Yet there are a variety of advantages to delivering FPS through purchase of service contracts with voluntary agencies, such as greater flexibility in staffing, fewer bureaucratic barriers to flexible scheduling, and greater protection of caseload standards (Pecora *et al.,* 1989).

A number of other program design decisions must be made, including choosing which types of clients will be eligible for service (intake criteria), mechanisms for screening prospective clients, length of treatment, work schedules, worker on-call procedures, and caseload sizes (Pecora *et al.,* 1987). In considering these service components, treatment design issues become interrelated with administrative issues as FPS staff consider the various options. For example, how should intake criteria be established for relatively new program models such as FPS? What types of demographic and program evaluation data are necessary to make such a decision? To ensure that clients are actually at "imminent risk of placement," should special placement screening committees be used to examine all FPS referrals?

In addition, clients being served by intensive placement prevention programs often need ready access to their caseworker for assistance in handling family crises that arise during treatment. Deciding how to handle on-call and worker back-up procedures thus becomes extremely important in this type of program if families are to be seen promptly. Finally, selecting worker caseload sizes and duration of treatment becomes intertwined with determining how intensive the service should be. Workers who carry caseloads of 4-6 families for 60-120 days can not provide the same intensity of service as therapists with a caseload of two families for 30 days. What constitutes a reasonable caseload for a given FPS program? What information about service provision, client problems, and worker activity should be used to set caseload standards? Part of social work administration involves setting caseload standards and distributing incoming work in an equitable manner. These issues can be explored with students to illustrate some of the program design challenges associated with social work administration. Furthermore, many of these decisions have implications for personnel management, the focus of the next set of program elements of FPS.

Personnel Management

Social work administration curricula address various aspects of personnel management in introductory administration or supervision classes. Personnel management encompasses the following functions:

- Design and allocation of job tasks and personnel;
- Worker recruitment, screening, and selection;
- Designing and conducting performance appraisals;
- Orienting, training, and developing staff;
- Supervising ongoing task performance, including clinical case supervision;
- Handling employee performance problems;
- Enforcing employee sanctions and dismissing workers (Pecora and Austin, 1987, p. 13).

FPS programs provide a rich resource for assisting students in thinking about the tasks and skills required for selecting quality staff members, specifying performance criteria, choosing a worker performance appraisal method, and supervising workers. These personnel management functions are some of the elements that must be addressed to maximize organizational effectiveness. Their importance for managing FPS programs will be discussed below.

Recruitment, Selection, and Training of FPS Therapists

If clients are the "raw material" for human service organizations, then the FPS therapists constitute the major production equipment. As such, front-line workers represent one of the organization's most precious resources. It is useless for a FPS program to select the most effective service technology if it is unable to hire workers capable of applying the treatment technology in their work with families.

One of the first tasks involved in hiring capable staff members is specification of the knowledge, skills, abilities, and attitudes necessary for effective job performance. Unfortunately, while much progress is being made in specifying the treatment techniques and worker characteristics of successful FPS programs, additional research needs to more fully specify necessary competency levels for FPS workers, both at the time they are initially hired, and later as full-fledged or "journeyman" staff members.[1] In fact, while the majority of FPS programs employ graduate-level social workers, these services are also being provided by personnel with a wide variety of educational backgrounds, including psychology, marriage and family counseling, sociology, recreational therapy, vocational rehabilitation, and education.

A consensus, therefore, regarding what should be the minimum qualifications for FPS therapists does not exist. This complicates agency efforts to prepare position descriptions, recruitment announcements, selection criteria, and interview questions. In response to this lack of information, Homebuilders' administrators have developed their own set of minimum qualifications, and further, employ role play situations during the interview process to help ensure that the persons being hired possess certain counseling skills and the capability to learn others. These selection tasks (and how they are hindered by a lack of consensus regarding minimum qualifications) can be useful examples for teaching about personnel recruitment, screening, and hiring. This situation also has implications for the necessity of social work educational degrees for these positions and for the development of professional standards. That is why it may be valuable for students to discuss the issues raised by Jill Kinney, cofounder of the Homebuilders program, in the case study devoted to therapist screening and supervision that is included at the end of this chapter.

Specifying Performance Criteria and Worker Appraisal Methods

Worker performance appraisal is essentially concerned with systematically assessing how well agency staff members are performing their jobs over a specified period of time. In FPS (and in other areas of the human services), developing measurable performance criteria that are realistic and job-related is a major challenge. For example, consider what performance criteria would be applicable to a FPS therapist, and how these criteria would be measured or their attainment documented. Some of the more gross measures of performance would be the number of children at risk of placement who were maintained in their own homes; number of families where another report of child maltreatment was reported; and number of client complaints.

Contrast the performance criteria listed above with the difficulties involved in specifying what constitutes adequate provision of crisis intervention services, effective teaching of assertion skills, or handling the client termination process in a "professional and sensitive manner." Developing measurable performance criteria for some FPS job responsibilities is very difficult; which is why open-ended, graphic trait, or management by objective type appraisal methods are being used in various forms and combinations in most child welfare agencies (Wiehe, 1980). To better specify performance standards and the behaviors associated with superior versus unacceptable performance, some social work agencies are developing behaviorally anchored rating scales (Pecora and Hunter, 1988).

Presented in Table 7.1 is a description of the major performance appraisal methods currently being used in human services and business. The type of method and the degree of structure required will vary by the size, formality, auspice, and other characteristics of the organization. But many human service organizations are finding that a form of management by objectives provides a satisfactory blend of precision and individuation.

Table 7.1. Major Approaches to Performance Appraisal[a]

1.	Essay/Narrative	Supervisors develop narrative evaluations of the employee's work behavior or job-related personality traits
2.	Graphic (trait) rating scales	Workers are on a 5 to 7 point scale in relation to a series of personality traits, abilities, and other performance factors
3.	Ranking techniques	Workers are rank-ordered in relation to certain traits and each other using straight, alternative, or paired comparison methods of ranking
4.	Forced-choice rating	Key traits or behaviors are identified through a form of job analysis and are inserted into multiple choice questions that require supervisors to choose the trait or behavior that best fits the worker
5.	Management by objectives and results (MBO/MOR)	Workers and their supervisors establish individual performance objectives to be accomplished in a specific time period along with action plans for attainment and methods for monitoring progress
6.	Work standards	Uniform, measurable performance standards are developed to evaluate worker behaviors
7.	Behaviorally anchored rating scales (BARS)	Behaviors necessary to achieve program objectives are identified and then used as scale anchors to rate employee performance
8.	Weighted checklist	Work behaviors are assigned weights according to their importance and supervisors indicate which behaviors are demonstrated by the worker, using a checklist where the weights are omitted
9.	Critical incident	Positive and negative work behaviors or incidents are recorded in relation to mutually agreed upon performance objectives or job tasks
10.	Assessment center	Employees engage in actual or simulated job tasks where their work behaviors can be measured in order to assess current job performance, or more typically, predict their potential for managerial positions
11.	Forced distribution	Raters are forced to place staff on a bell curve where only a certain percentage of staff can receive superior, average, and poor ratings
12.	Field review	Worker appraisal ratings or rankings are reviewed by a small group of supervisors to reasses the appraisal and to develop uniform standards for performance appraisal.

[a]Pecora and Austin (1987).

In addition to selecting performance criteria and methods, the meaningfulness of the various performance criteria must be considered. "If the client values one kind of outcome, the worker values another, and the funding agency yet another outcome, whose definition of success will be used to determine whether the service has been effective?" (Patti, 1987, p. 378)

In selecting both performance criteria and appraisal methods, students should consider that the provision of timely, easy to understand, and caseload-specific feedback to workers is associated with both worker motivation and service effectiveness (Hackman and Lawler, 1971; Patti, 1987; Schoech and Schkade, 1980). Students may find that specifying measurable performance criteria requires not only a knowledge of clinical research and program evaluation, but precise and creative application of the principles associated with performance appraisal.

Providing Quality Supervision

Most FPS cases involve families who are in crisis and have many needs. A high degree of worker autonomy is required as therapists spend the vast majority of their time out of the office. Because of the seriousness and intensity of the cases, workers are required to make critical decisions regarding future risk of child maltreatment and to develop strategies to maintain child safety throughout the case process, including case closure (Holder and Corey, 1987). Consequently, supervision of FPS therapists is one of the most demanding jobs in child and family services—so much so that a project at the University of Washington School of Social Work is developing a competency-based training curriculum on supervising for family-centered practice.

Given the degree of case difficulty and amount of clinical consultation required, how many therapists should a supervisor be allowed to supervise at one time? Because of budget cuts, many human service agencies have increased individual supervisors' span of control to a point where they are unable to fulfill the administrative, clinical, and educational functions of their position (Kadushin, 1985). Because FPS supervisors must balance such diverse roles, what is an equitable number of supervisees? The answer to this question clearly depends upon the nature of the services provided, including the type of clients, clinical interventions employed, worker caseloads, and intensity of the service.

A related issue is the use of group supervision to staff cases and generate strategies for working with particular families.[2] To what extent should group supervision supplement individual worker supervision? What clinical or worker-specific issues are appropriate for individual supervision, but should not be addressed during the group supervision sessions?

Finally, to what extent are FPS supervisors able to balance the provision of staff "consideration" with "setting task structure?" According to studies of supervisory effectiveness, both of these functions must be carried out. Providing consideration involves building relationships, sympathizing, supporting and individualizing workers. Setting task structure concerns setting objectives, clarifying tasks, monitoring and evaluating performance, and providing task-specific feedback (Patti, 1987). A recent 2-year study of the Homebuilders program found a high degree of service effectiveness, low worker turnover, and high worker morale (Fraser *et al.,* 1988). It is likely that quality supervision is one of the major factors accounting for these favorable outcomes, but studies using both qualitative methods and experimental designs are needed to more clearly determine the role of supervision in promoting service effectiveness and worker morale.

These are just a few of the supervision-related issues facing the field of family preservation services. A related concern of many program planners and administrators is the prevention of worker burnout. Because of the intensive nature of many FPS programs, workers may work long hours, including evenings and weekends. Families in crisis place many demands upon the therapists; demands that are accentuated by the short duration of service. To counteract these pressures, programs such as Homebuilders provide large amounts of training, supervisory consultation, and supervisor backup of workers who are on-call. The program also assists workers in recognizing the gains that clients have made through goal attainment scaling and through interviews conducted with clients at case termination. In addition, the agency recognizes individual therapists through awards and by typing positive client comments on multi-colored "hearts and stars" so that they can be posted on a special agency bulletin board. The experience of the program since 1974 is that worker turnover has been surprisingly low, in large part because of these measures.

Social work students will benefit by grappling with personnel management issues such as staff selection, performance appraisal, and effective supervision methods. And given that large salaries, plush offices, and a nine to five workday will not be possible for most FPS workers, what other creative strategies can be devised that will maintain or enhance worker motivation?

Financial Management, Fundraising, and Cost–Benefit Analysis

Many administration sequences in schools of social work include content related to budgeting, general types of accounting systems, fundraising, and cost–benefit analysis. Some of the current concerns of FPS advocates and administrators can provide a useful backdrop for teaching this content in schools of social work.

Financial Management

As with most small nonprofit human service agencies, Homebuilders has struggled with developing an accounting system that incorporates the necessary fiscal safeguards for the agency as well as provides essential information for monitoring and budgetary planning. Contracting arrangements that use a "per client" reimbursement basis and include minimum performance requirements for reimbursement pose particular difficulties for developing and monitoring agency budgets. These challenges lend themselves to the construction of exercises for the variety of spreadsheet software packages available for personal computers such as Lotus 1-2-3 or Symphony.

Fundraising

During these times of resource scarcity, the skills associated with fundraising, including grantsmanship, have taken on new importance. Many public child welfare agencies are currently struggling with identifying federal, state, and local funding mechanisms that will support FPS. Some administrators of FPS programs that are located in private agencies are aggressively pursuing contracts with mental health, juvenile correction, and developmental disability agencies as a way of expanding the market for their services. To support FPS program funding efforts, the Center for Study of Social Policy in Washington, D.C., is conducting a study of what federal, state, and local funding mechanisms are available.

Marketing as a revenue-enhancing mechanism is also becoming increasingly important for certain FPS agencies as they publicize their program with allied professional agencies, educate the public, and compete with other service providers for referrals. In fact, developing a competitive marketing analysis and plan may be a necessity for FPS agencies in certain urban areas with multiple overlapping programs.

The search for funding requires creative approaches and program models adaptable to a variety of client populations and problem areas. The Homebuilders program and other FPS agencies have been very successful in convincing legislators and agency administrators of the benefits associated with supporting these services. They have accomplished this with the help of key board members, use of a professional lobbyist, effective public relations, creative grantsmanship, and a focus upon providing a highly cost-effective service. Thus, instructors of grantsmanship or other administration courses would find current FPS agency activities in these areas to be good examples of the steps necessary to develop a grant proposal or maintain agency funding.

Cost–Benefit Analysis

One of the major driving forces behind the popularity of FPS programs with state legislators and administrators is the perception that this service is more cost-effective than traditional child welfare, juvenile justice, or mental health services. The cost–benefit research conducted thus far for FPS has produced a mixed set of findings.[3] Some evaluations have documented significant cost savings (e.g., Halper and Jones, 1981; Kinney *et al.,* 1977); while other studies have determined that a high quality FPS program may cost as much or more than traditional services (e.g., Hayes and Joseph, 1985; Rosenberg *et al.,* 1982).

The benefits of family preservation programs in terms of quality of life or prevention of future child dysfunction, however, are often not fully measured in these types of analyses.[4] Quantifying the benefits that are produced by FPS beyond comparing the savings in substitute care funds is difficult. For example, how does one begin to quantify the financial value of improvements in parent self-esteem, child school attendance, or cessation of child maltreatment?

Some of these benefits can be assigned market values, while other "intangible" benefits must be estimated using the amount that analysts think people would be willing to pay for that benefit (e.g., the ability to use nonabusive discipline techniques, anger management skills). As one might imagine, there are a host of problems associated with implementing this in practice, including the conflict between personal/societal willingness and the ability to pay (Buxbaum, 1981). The issue of sorting out the relative importance of pecuniary benefits (personal versus societal benefits) needs to be addressed as well.

Tangible costs that form the basis of the analysis include (1) therapist, supervisor, and administrator salaries and fringe benefits along with other agency overhead costs; (2) community service costs incurred while the family is participating in FPS treatment (and possibly for a certain period of time after); and (3) child placement costs involving an analysis of the various types of placements, average cost of care per day, and the average length of stay for various types of clients.

From a more technical perspective, determining a suitable time horizon and discount rate are additional challenges. The time horizon is generally concerned with when the benefits are expected to take effect and the length of time that the various benefits of the service will last. Calculating time horizons for FPS client outcomes is dependent in part upon the availability of research data that specify client outcomes based on rigorous follow-up studies. Most FPS evaluation studies have used follow-up periods of 6 months or less. In addition, because some benefits will occur in the future, the value of these benefits must be discounted because dollars saved later are worth less than dollars spent or saved immediately (i.e., the "net present value" of the funds must be calculated). While the concept of discounting is relatively straightforward, the choice of a discount rate and the implications that it has for the cost–benefit ratio are complex (Buxbaum, 1981; Sherraden, 1986).

For example, let's assume that the provision of one model of FPS for families in Group A prevents immediate foster care placement. Another model of FPS provided to families in Group B prevents child placement and also increases the high school graduation rates of the children. The children in both groups are all under age 10. The prevention of foster care placement can be thought of as an immediate cost savings and the dollar value estimated without much of a discount. However, the benefits and savings associated with the increased high school graduation rates of the children in Group B must be discounted, because these children are all under age 10 and their benefits in this area will not be realized until they would be eligible to begin high school. Depending upon the discount rate used, the present value of the benefits for Group B will be high or low: if the rate is 15% the benefits will be rated lower than if the discount rate is 5%. Thus, in comparison with the FPS model used with Group A, the second model will produce benefits that will vary greatly in value, depending upon the discount rate and time horizons that are employed.

The question of whether family preservation programs, in improving family functioning and preventing child placement, save taxpayer dollars is an important one. Answering this question is, in part, dependent upon the availability of program evaluation data gathered through rigorous research designs, as well as carefully constructed cost-benefit comparisons. Both pose challenges to the most enterprising FPS administrators, social work educators and students.

Homebuilders Case Study

Implementing family preservation programs is a challenging process, especially given the political, financial, organizational and personnel management hurdles that must be overcome. The experience of the Homebuilders administrators and staff members in addressing some of the treatment design and worker caseload challenges is described by Kinney *et al.* (this volume, Chapter 3). The approach and strategies they employ to address the issues of worker screening and supervision are discussed in the case study below.

Screening and Supervising Homebuilder Therapists:
A Case Study

It would be very nice if the characteristics that make an effective Homebuilder thera-pist were easy to spot. In some ways, it seems that the reverse is true. Characteristics such as therapist sex, age, race, marital status, parenthood, educational field or degree have not been strongly associated with job effectiveness. Because of the difficulty in quantifying factors that are important, we have developed a multi-layered screening process to give us a maximum amount of information about job applicants.

In the initial paper screening of resumes, we look for experience with troubled families, crisis intervention, and cognitive behavioral approaches to problem solving. We are also interested in people who have worked in innovative or unusual programs and settings. We screen out candidates who appear to be committed exclusively to more interpretive therapeutic approaches such as family systems therapy or psychoanalysis.

Applicants having the most relevant clinical experience and approach participate in an hour-long discussion with a supervisor. We use part of this time to provide a realistic account of the job. We discuss flex time, being on call, living in the catchment area, and coping with clients who are sometimes dangerous or, at least, unpredictable. We want people to be very aware of the demands the program can make on their private lives, so that they may make the most informed choice possible. We also want them to know that we expect them to follow an already developed model, rather than inventing one as they go. Positive aspects of the job such as the high rate of success with clients, low caseload, clear cut goals, training and support are also discussed.

Two of our favorite initial areas of discussion involve the applicants' descriptions of the most difficult client they ever had and the most difficult supervisor they ever had. We hope to find people who can be compassionate and specific in describing individuals who were problematic for them. We also want to know if they hold personal and professional values compatible with those of the program and program staff. We like people who want to be creative and who value autonomy and independence, but at the same time are able to function as part of a team. We want people who are flexible and can handle ambiguity.

The most qualified applicants, as judged by the individual interviews, are asked to return for role play sessions where experienced Homebuilders staff portray a family in crisis. The applicant is to demonstrate his or her ability to defuse the crisis situation, gain the confidence and cooperation of family members, and clarify the issues.

During the role plays, applicants are rated by staff on their performance in several areas. They get credit if they wait to be invited in, give clients clear messages regarding the purpose of the visit, and listen to family members without blocking or advising. We are looking for people who can remain calm, be supportive of all family members, and respect clients' decisions regarding their own participation in the session.

Applicants are marked down for ordering or commanding clients, ridiculing them, insisting on having all family members together, asking lots of questions, and making lots of inferences about "what's really going on" with family members.

After the role play, applicants and the Homebuilders who played family members debrief. We ask the applicants how well they think they did, and why. We give them feedback regarding their performance and watch how they respond. Often we ask them to try a particular interaction again after hearing our feedback. We want people who will accept constructive feedback, and who can utilize information rapidly to improve their skills. We also continue to evaluate applicants' social behavior. Do they make appropriate light conversation? Smile? Have good eye contact? A sense of humor? Do we like them? Would we like to become friends with them?

If there are any doubts about an applicant, he or she will be called back one more time, usually for a meal with the supervisor and possibly an agency administrator. We like to talk in a less formal setting. We want to express every doubt we have about some applicant's suitability for the job, both to give them a chance to convince us our doubts are inappropriate, and for us to gather further information about how they will behave in a challenging, stressful situation. We are concerned about putting too much pressure on applicants, but we are more concerned that the people we hire will ultimately be facing circumstances where lives may be at stake. We need to know if they can remain calm and think clearly in difficult situations.

Once an applicant is hired, supervision is closely connected to training. New staff usually receive six days of formal classroom training during their first six months on the job. After the first three days they meet with their supervisor to develop an initial plan for individualized on-the-job training. Depending on their initial skill level and the difficulty of the client population they will be serving, they are accompanied by their supervisor or an experienced therapist during their work with the first two to four families. Some new workers only observe the casework process for their first family, gradually taking on more responsibility with new cases.

New therapists usually attend formal case consultation sessions two mornings a week, usually tapering to once a week after the first year. In most sessions, all open cases are discussed, although the amount of time spent and the specificity of the discussion depend upon both the difficulty of the cases and the experience of the worker. These sessions last two to four hours, with three to six members in each group. We want to increase workers' options for helping clients, foster team building, and encourage personal growth by helping workers understand their feelings about clients and their jobs.

Supervisors and administrators are on call 24 hours a day to therapists, in the same way therapists are on-call to clients. Workers are also encouraged to talk with their supervisor to obtain individual case consultation during regular office hours if they don't know if a case is appropriate to take, if they are having problems defusing a case, if they are having difficulty formulating goals, or if no progress is being made on goals. They are also encouraged to contact their supervisor if they don't like the family, if they question the desirability of the family remaining together, or if they are putting in large amounts of overtime and are feeling tired and overwhelmed.

Therapists must call their supervisors immediately whenever they become aware of any concern for the safety of any family members or themselves. If the supervisor is unavailable, the worker must call other agency administrative staff. Any case where clients present a serious threat to themselves or others should be discussed daily with a supervisor or administrator during periods of instability. A therapist should call a supervisor any time he or she is feeling pressured to make a decision, and suspects a better decision could be made with consultation.

Supervisors are also available to accompany therapists whenever the therapists request assistance or whenever supervisors suspect a worker's performance is not as effective as would be desired. In addition, supervisors review records to monitor clarity of goals, client progress, and completion of forms.

Thus the supervisor's role is to help workers complete their initial training plan and reach an acceptable basic skill level, and then to continue to help them increase their skills with clients for as long as they have the job.

Although the worker's supervisor is critical in providing support, other agency procedures, values and rituals are also used for preventing burnout. The training is probably the most important, not only to facilitate workers' success in helping clients, but in teaching them to manage their own feelings.

All agency staff strive to view themselves and others as complicated whole people, rather than roles within an organizational chart. We try to break down the status barriers, get to know each other personally and build a culture of shared values and goals. We make a big deal out of personal milestones. Birthdays are always celebrated in the group. It is common for workers to bring their own families and extended family members to the office. Certain holiday rituals and games have became tradition. New staff get T shirts. If they go through rough times they often are awarded small plastic purple hearts. We have yearly award ceremonies where awards are presented for categories such as "best socks" as well as "most clients served," "highest success rate," and "most supportive." It is not just a supervisor's job to take care of the people he or she supervises, it is everyone's job to take care of each other.

Conclusion

This chapter has presented some of the challenges and issues associated with designing and managing family preservation programs, as they relate to administrative concepts and strategies. There are a variety of curriculum issues that also must be addressed if social work schools are going to be able to respond to the manpower needs of this rapidly growing program. Some of these are listed below:

- To what extent are schools preparing students with the practical skills necessary for designing Family Preservation Programs?
- Does the arrangement or separation of administration and clinical content in the curriculum hamper efforts to educate all students regarding what is necessary to design, implement, and maintain innovative clinical interventions?
- Are administration courses preparing students with practical skills for recruiting, selecting, and supervising human services staff in ways that promote organizational excellence?

- What other strategies exist for using innovative program models such as Homebuilders to teach specific administration-related course content?

Because FPS programs are relatively new, they present excellent opportunities for students to blend their knowledge of clinical intervention strategies, program evaluation methods, and personnel management principles in the analysis and design of these programs. The continued growth of family preservation services will also require an increased number of social work graduates who both understand FPS program components, and have the administrative skills necessary to manage these programs.

Notes

1. For information regarding what worker competencies may be important for effective job performance in FPS programs, see other chapters in this volume, also, Bryce and Lloyd, 1981; Fraser *et al.*, 1988; Goldstein, 1981; Haapala, 1983; Haapala and Kinney, 1979; Kinney *et al.*, 1981; and Maluccio, 1985.

2. See Kadushin (1985) and Munson (1983) for a discussion of the functions and issues of group supervision.

3. Cost–benefit analyses in this area have examined whether the outcomes of a particular FPS program are worth more in pecuniary terms than the costs of the program. Generally, a program is compared to itself, in contrast to cost-effectiveness studies where two or more programs are compared (White, 1988, pp. 430–431).

4. For more information about cost-benefit analysis and studies conducted for human service programs, see Armstrong, 1982; Buxbaum, 1981; Haugard *et al.*, 1983; Kugajevsky, 1979; Levin, 1983; Magura, 1981; Orr and Bell, 1987; Settles *et al.*, 1976; Sherraden, 1986; Young and Allen, 1977.

References

Armstrong, K. A. (1982). Economic analysis of a child abuse and neglect treatment program. *Child Welfare, 62,* 3–13.

Bardach, E. (1977). *The implementation game: What happens after a bill becomes law.* Cambridge, MA: MIT.

Barth, R. P. (1986). *Social and cognitive treatment of children and adolescents.* San Francisco: Jossey-Bass.

Buxbaum, C. B. (1981). Cost-benefit analysis: The mystique versus the reality. *Social Service Review, 55,* 453–471.

Frankel, H. (1988). Family-centered, home-based services in child protection: A review of the research. *Social Service Review, 62,* 137–157.

Fraser, M. W., Pecora, P. J., and Haapala, D. A. (Eds.). (1988). *Families in crisis: Findings from the Family-Based Intensive Treatment Project: Technical report.* Salt Lake City: University of Utah, Graduate School of Social Work, Social Research Institute; and Federal Way, WA: Behavioral Sciences Institute.

Goldstein, H. (1981). Home-based services and the worker. *In* M. Bryce and J. C. Lloyd (Eds.), *Treating families in the home: An alternative to placement.* Springfield, IL: Charles C. Thomas.

Haapala, D. A. (1983). *Perceived helpfulness, attributed critical incident responsibility, and discrimination of home-based family therapy treatment outcomes: Homebuilders model.* Report prepared for the Department of Health and Human Services, Administration for Children, Youth and Families. Federal Way, WA: Behavioral Sciences Institute.

Haapala, D. and Kinney, J. (1979). Homebuilders approach to the training of in-home therapists. *In* S. Maybanks and M. Bryce (Eds.), Home based services for children and families: policy, practice and research (pp. 248-259). Springfield, Ill: Charles C. Thomas.

Hackman, J. R., and Lawler, E. E., III. (1971). Employee reactions to job characteristics. *Journal of Applied Psychology, 55,* 259-286.

Halper, G., and Jones, M. A. (1981). *Serving families at risk of dissolution: Public preventive services in New York City.* New York: Human Resources Administration.

Haugard, J., Hokanson, B., and National Resource Center on Family-Based Services. (1983). *Measuring the cost-effectiveness of family-based services and out-of-home care.* Oakdale, IA: University of Iowa, School of Social Work, National Clearinghouse for Family-centered Programs.

Hayes, J. R., and Joseph, J. A. (1985). *Home based family centered project evaluation.* Columbus, OH: Metropolitan Human Services Commission.

Holder, W., and Corey, M. (1987). *Child protective services risk management: A decision making handbook.* Charlotte, NC: ACTION for Child Protection.

Jones, M. A. (1985). *A second chance for families: Five years later.* New York: Child Welfare League of America.

Kadushin, A. (1985). *Supervision in social work,* 2nd ed. New York: Columbia University.

Kinney, J. M., Haapala, D. A., and Gast, E. (1981). Assessment of families in crisis. *In* M. Bryce and J. Lloyd (Eds.), *Treating families in the home: An alternative to placement.* Springfield, IL: Charles C. Thomas.

Kinney, J. M., Madsen, B., Fleming, T., & Haapala, D. A. (1977). Homebuilders: Keeping families together. *Journal of Consulting and Clinical Psychology, 45,* 667-673.

Kugajevsky, V. (1979). Foster grandparents program. *In* J. G. Abert (Ed.), *Program evaluation at HEW: Research versus reality,* Volume 3, pp. 123-179. New York: Marcel Dekker.

Levin, H. M. (1983). *Cost-effectiveness: A primer.* Newbury Park, CA: Sage.

Magura, S. (1981). Are services to prevent foster care effective? *Children and Youth Services Review, 3*(3), 193-212.

Maluccio, A. N. (1985). Education and training for child welfare practice. *In* J. Laird and A. Hartman (Eds.)., *A handbook of child welfare practice.* New York: Free Press.

Munson, C. E. (1983). *An introduction to clinical social work supervision.* New York: Haworth.

Orr, L. L., and Bell, S. H. (1987). *Valuing the labor market benefits of job training and employment programs: Procedures and findings from the AFDC homemaker-home health aide demonstrations.* Washington, D.C.: ABT Associates.

Patti, R. J. (1983). *Social welfare administration: Managing social programs in a developmental context.* Englewood Cliffs, NJ: Prentice-Hall.

Patti, R. J. (1985). In search of purpose for social welfare administration. *Administration in Social Work, 9*(3), 1–14.

Patti, R. J. (1987). Managing for service effectiveness in social welfare organizations. *Social Work, 32*(5), 377–381.

Patti, R. J., Poertner, J., and Rapp, C. A. (Eds.). (1987). *Managing for service effectiveness in social welfare organizations.* New York: Haworth Press.

Pecora, P. J., and Austin, M. J. (1987). *Managing human services personnel.* Newbury Park, CA: Sage.

Pecora, P. J., and Hunter, J. (1988). Performance appraisal in child welfare: Comparing the MBO and BARS methods. *Administration in Social Work. 12*(1), 55–72.

Pecora, P. J., Fraser, M. W., and Haapala, D. A. (1987). *Defining family preservation services: Three intensive home-based treatment programs.* Salt Lake City: University of Utah, Graduate School of Social Work, Social Research Institute.

Pecora, P. J., Kinney, J. M., Mitchell, L., and Tolley, G. (1989). *Providing intensive home-based family preservation services through public and private agencies: Organizational and service delivery issues.* Research Report No. 2 from the Family-Based Intensive Treatment Project. Salt Lake City: University of Utah, Graduate School of Social Work, Social Research Institute.

Peters, T. J., and Waterman, R. H. (1983). *In search of excellence: Lessons from America's best run companies.* New York: Harper and Row.

Pine, B. A. (1986). Child welfare reform and the political process. *Social Service Review, 60,* 339–359.

Reid, W. J., and Hanrahan, P. (1982). Recent evaluations of social work: Grounds for optimism. *Social Work, 27,* 328–340.

Rosenberg, S. A., McTate, G. A., and Robinson, C. C. (1982). *Intensive services to families-at-risk project.* Omaha: Nebraska Department of Public Welfare.

Rubin, A. (1985). Practice effectiveness: More grounds for optimism. *Social Work, 30,* 469–476.

Schoech, D., and Schkade, L. (1980). Computers helping caseworkers: Decisions support systems. *Child Welfare, 59,* 566–575.

Selznick, P. (1984). *Leadership in administration.* Berkeley: University of California Press.

Settles, B. H., Culley, J. D., and Van Name, J. B. (1976). *How to measure the cost of foster family care.* Washington, D.C.: U.S. Department of Health, Education, and Welfare, Office of Human Development Services (DHEW Publication No. 78-30126).

Sherraden, M. W. (1986). Benefit–cost analysis as a net present value problem. *Administration in Social Work, 10*(3), 85–97.

White, K. R. (1988). Cost analyses in family support programs. *In* H. B. Weiss and F. C. Jacobs (Eds.), *Evaluating family programs,* pp. 429–443. New York: Aldine de Gruyter.

Williams, W. (1980). *The implementation perspective: A guide for managing social service delivery programs.* Berkeley: University of California.

Williams, W., and Elmore, R. F. (1976). *Social program implementation.* New York: Academic.

Wiehe, V. R. (1980). Current practices in performance appraisal. *Administration in Social Work, 4*(3), 1–11.

Young, D. W., and Allen, B. (1977). Benefit–cost analysis in the social services: The example of adoption reimbursement. *Social Service Review, 51,* 249–264.

Chapter 8

Applying Practice Research Methods in Intensive Family Preservation Services

Betty J. Blythe

As our knowledge and understanding of applying research methods in practice is expanding, social workers are fortunate to have available to them a set of practice research tools that facilitate the discovery of better ways to help clients. Rather than requiring sophisticated training in research and statistics, using these tools calls for an open mind and an ability to impose some structure on practice and to systematically follow certain guidelines. As will become apparent, social workers using these tools typically adopt a particular mind set as they think about practice: they are always looking for ways to improve what they do, they frequently experiment with new approaches, and they are willing to learn from clients and other workers. Besides helping the worker do a better job, this open mindedness and continual attempt to improve one's practice methods works against the burnout and frustration that often accompany work with difficult, multi-problem families.

Routine use of these practice research tools benefits the overall program and the individual practitioner as well as the families being served. To begin, applying certain practice research techniques can facilitate regular monitoring of progress toward general program goals. For example, Homebuilders has a program goal of restoring each family to the level of functioning it experienced before the crisis that precipitated the involvement of Homebuilders. Thus, if the targeted level of functioning is routinely specified for each family and then family functioning is continuously assessed until this desired level is reached, workers will have documented support for their decision to continue or to close a case. Viewed across several cases, the program will have some data on effectiveness, as measured by attaining program goals. Workers can use these same basic techniques to monitor progress toward individual client goals. Such monitoring provides feedback to the family members regarding their progress—feedback that can play an important role in encouraging a family whose members may feel defeated or have been "branded" as hopeless by the social service system. Some workers also find the feedback to be reinforcing. At the same time, this feedback helps workers to quickly recognize if interventions aimed at individual client goals are not having the desired effects and to more rapidly institute necessary changes. In being open to such feedback, workers are acknowledging that their interventions are not always effective and can even do harm as well as good. As with the aggregated information regarding overall program goals, data generated through monitoring individual client goals can be compiled to make some statements about overall program effectiveness or success. Obviously, information about overall program effectiveness can be helpful in addressing accountability issues related to clients and to third-party payers.

Practice research techniques also facilitate the standardization of existing components of intensive family preservation services, and the development of new components. This enables practitioners working in these programs to share their knowledge and experience with their colleagues and with professionals in other settings.

Aggregated practitioner-generated data may suggest certain types of families or problems that are more or less likely to benefit from family preservation services. This information can be used to revise screening criteria, or to identify staff training needs and/or intervention areas requiring more development.

To be sure, this approach to practice is challenging. Workers must be willing to evaluate their own work—to be honest about successes and failures and about those instances in which the outcome is less certain. Nonetheless, the benefits of taking such an optimistic and growth-oriented perspective are numerous and have value for the worker, the client, and the larger social work profession.

The Role of "Personal Scientist"

This outlook on practice has been termed a number of things. Perhaps the most appropriate label is that of "personal scientist." A personal scientist is an individual who can engage in both practice and research simultaneously and in an integrated fashion. Personal scientists break down broad goals into smaller, more manageable goals so that they can accomplish desired changes incrementally. As much as is possible, personal scientists are flexible both with logistical concerns such as scheduling visits to families and determining the length of sessions, and with treatment concerns such as type of services delivered—including concrete services—and the exploration of new treatment techniques or adaptations of old ones. Flexibility, however, should not extend to developing or using techniques that might be more fun or make workers feel more creative without necessarily improving services to clients. When developing a treatment plan, researchers and practitioners must choose interventions with the greatest potential for bringing about the most change in the shortest time. Related to flexibility is another characteristic of personal scientists—a willingness to adopt a trial-and-error approach. In order to find techniques that work, personal scientists must be willing to take some risks by trying new ways of solving problems when their usual methods do not appear to be working or are taking too long to have the desired effects. Most personal scientists find the trial-and-error approach to be less frustrating than trying to replicate a standard intervention that is failing to have the desired effect.

In terms of the information used to determine if their interventions are having the desired effects, a personal scientist must have a broad view of what constitutes data. Information might be gathered by the worker, the client, or significant others. Any information that seems relevant to the general tasks of assessment, monitoring treatment implementation, and monitoring treatment effects is a possible source of data. The information must be carefully specified and then systematically collected and analyzed. In turn, these data provide information for case decision making as personal scientists proceed in their efforts to attain goals. If evaluation data consistently indicate that a "tried and true" program component fails to help a particular client, the worker should try a different approach.

An important point regarding the personal scientist role is that the worker expects his or her supervisor and clients to be personal scientists, too. As a result, workers, supervisors, and clients have a more collegial relationship than is typical in most agencies and service programs (Haapala and Kinney, 1979). The personal scientist role typically comes easily to supervisors who were workers at one time and may continue to work with some families. Moreover, the incremental steps toward change, the flexibility, the broad view of data, the trial-and-error approach, and the data-based decision making all facilitate supervisors' efforts to oversee the work of their staff and help them solve difficult practice dilemmas. Having a more collegial relationship with one's supervisor makes it easier for the social worker to determine when consultation is needed. The personal scientist model emphasizes that we all get stuck from time to time and that no one has all the answers. In fact, supervisors are expected to send clear messages encouraging workers to ask for help. Supervisors should communicate the expectation that workers will need help, that they will not always be certain about how to proceed, and that the job of providing intensive in-home services to families is a difficult one.

When clients adopt the role of personal scientists and become more like colleagues, the mutual respect between worker and family members is underscored. This posture removes some of the barriers to change or "resistance" so often reported by professionals working with multiproblem populations. Clients, as personal scientists, can provide information about their life situations, the constraints that may limit what they can accomplish or how they can proceed, and the resources they can call on to help them make necessary changes and maintain these changes.

Assessment

To a personal scientist, assessment typically is an ongoing process that begins as soon as the first client contact is made and continues throughout the work with the family. This reflects the fact that the personal scientist has a broad view of what constitutes data and that practice research principles call for continuous monitoring and follow-up of clients.

Initially, assessment is concerned with gathering general background information and an overview of families' problems. In conducting family assessments, Homebuilders workers translate clients' initial definition of their problems into behaviorally specific terms that elaborate how each particular family experiences its problems. These become goal statements specifying the changes clients want to make. Priorities are established by workers and family members, and the goals to be addressed are selected. After goals are established, the assessment process focuses on monitoring progress toward goal attainment.

Available Tools

In many instances, similar tools can be used both for the initial information gathering phase and for the ongoing monitoring. The most frequently applied and most basic tool is the interview, or more specifically, active listening (Rogers, 1957). Workers use the interview to obtain increasingly specific statements of the presenting problems. For example, parents may initially complain that their daughter does not accept "no" for an answer. Upon further questioning, the worker will learn what types of requests the daughter makes, the manner in which the parents say "no," and the subsequent behavior of the parents and the daughter. If this issue later develops into a treatment goal, the worker may request other information (via the interview), such as family members' thoughts and feelings during these exchanges.

Based on the initial interview, other assessment tools for gathering specific descriptions of the family's problems might be selected. A role play or observation of a "live" family interaction in which the parents turn down a request from their daughter can be a rich source of assessment information (see Hersen and Bellack, 1981 for a discussion of observational assessment tools). The worker can see how the family actually communicates, rather than relying on a second-hand report which is subject to several sources of bias. Because they spend so much time with families in their homes, workers in intensive family preservation programs often are able to collect information with observational tools. Once an intervention to remedy the problem interaction is in place, workers can continue to observe family members to determine if they are using some of the methods suggested by the intervention and if the intervention is having the desired effect when the parents refuse a request from the daughter. To achieve the greatest benefit, the worker should follow some systematic evaluation of family interactions. This evaluation may be a simple, global rating on a five-point scale of the effectiveness of the parents' refusal or of the daughter's calm acceptance of the refusal, or the worker may want to actually count or rate certain behaviors such as the use of "I"-statements, or the expression of feelings in a straightforward manner.

Another assessment tool involves having the clients or significant others monitor the frequency of selected behaviors, cognitions, or feelings. In the above example, one or several family members might be asked to record how often the daughter accepts "no" from her parents, or they might record the parents' use of certain communication skills when expressing their refusal. Supposing that she was trying to modify some of her irrational beliefs about why her parents said "no" to her, the daughter might self-monitor the frequency of these irrational beliefs.

In some instances, standardized paper-and-pencil instruments are available to assess a client problem. These are more likely to produce a general picture of the problem, rather than extremely detailed information. Hudson (1982) has developed a package of brief instruments for assessing a range of common concerns, including depression, marital satisfaction, and attitudes toward family members. Several resources have compiled a large number of standardized instruments to facilitate the process of locating these tools (Corcoran and Fischer, 1987; Edleson, 1985; Levitt and Reid, 1981). With some notable exceptions, many of these instruments are more appropriate for initial assessment purposes than for ongoing monitoring, in part because the time involved in completing and scoring the measure is prohibitive. While they may not be adequately sensitive to increments of client change, standardized measures can be helpful in providing an overview of certain client attitudes, beliefs, knowledge, or behavior.

Workers can develop simple scales, often in collaboration with families, to assess a range of very specific behaviors, moods, or cognitions. Returning to the above example, the parents, the daughter, other family members, and/or the worker all might rate the daughter's ability to accept "no," without an emotional outburst, along a five-point scale. At least the two end-points and the mid-point would be anchored with very specific descriptions of what the daughter's response looked like, using words understood and agreed upon by the rater(s). (See Bloom and Fischer, 1982; Gottman and Leiblum, 1974 for more details on developing these scales.) Such scales are primarily helpful in monitoring client change in relationship to treatment goals. Accordingly, they should be completed on a routine basis, and the results graphed and compared across time.

A variation of these rating scales is the goal attainment scaling used by some intensive family preservation service programs. As depicted in Figure 8.1, Homebuilders' workers complete goal sheets on each client. The statement of the problem is the result of the assessment and provides a behaviorally specific description of the problem. The relevant family members and the worker determine the least and most favorable outcome and what might occur at three points between these two extremes. Each time a goal is scored, the worker and family have a measure of the progress toward goal attainment. Obviously, this has greater utility as the goal and problem statements and the anchors for each level of goal attainment become more specific.

Sometimes an elaborate measurement plan is not necessary to monitor goal attainment. Many client goals involve completion of concrete tasks or obtaining services or resources. For example, a goal might be to clean a kitchen, to obtain homemaker services, or to link a child with a Big Brother program. Such goals represent dichotomous variables that simply indicate if the task was completed or the resource obtained. Nonetheless, the process of specifying exactly what must be accomplished is useful in planning the necessary interventions and determining if the goal has been accomplished. Although they seem quite basic, straightforward indicators of goal attainment such as these should not be ignored because they do offer valid indicators of client progress.

Considerations in Selecting Assessment Tools

Given the range of available tools, workers may need some guidelines to help them in selecting assessment tools. Things to consider in making these selections include: goals of assessment, logistic and pragmatic considerations, reliability and validity, and sensitivity to incremental change. Several authors have addressed these and other issues, so this discussion will be limited to those considerations that seem to have particular relevance for intensive family preservation services (Bloom and Fischer, 1982; Blythe and Tripodi, in press; Tripodi and Epstein, 1980).

As previously indicated, assessment may take the form of initial informa-

Goal 1: Improve Laurie's depression management skills

Family name:	Therapist: Leavitt	Whose goal: Family/Therapist

Rating when goal scaled (−1 or −2): −1   Weight: 9 (9 most impt./
                                                                    1 least impt.)

Statement of problem:

Laurie has been feeling very depressed over the past few months and had talked of wanting to kill herself. Because of the threats she has been placed at Fairfax Hospital two times in the past month.

−2   Laurie is depressed and threatens suicide. Placement at Fairfax is made.

−1   Laurie is often depressed, does not threaten suicide, but placement at Fairfax is considered.

  0   Laurie is sometimes depressed. Placement at Fairfax is not considered and Laurie is beginning to use depression management skills.

+1   Laurie is occasionally depressed and uses the depression management skills.

+2   Laurie is rarely depressed and uses the depression management skills.

Plan

Week 1: From 8/20/84 To: 8/26/84	Rating: 0
1. Contract with Laurie	
2. Introduce RET concepts	
3. Introduce anger mangement	
4. Develop relationship with Laurie	

Week 2: From 8/27/84 To: 9/2/84	Rating: 0
1. Continue as above	
2. Develop crisis card	
3. Begin daily mood rating	
4. Practice RET	

Week 3: From 9/3/84 To: 9/9/84	Rating: +1
1. Continue as above	
2. Monitor progress	
3. Help Laurie become involved in outside activities	

Week 4: From 9/10/84 To: 9/18/84	Rating: +1
1. Continue as above	

Figure 8.1.   Goal Sheet.

tion gathering or a more specific evaluation of a particular problem area. With the former type of assessment, the worker is typically looking for background information about presenting problems. This type of general information may be most helpful in forming hypotheses and suggesting points of intervention. Workers will need to consider assessment tools that are not too narrowly focused but give an overview of the family and/or their presenting problems. Problem inventories, open-ended interviews, and paper-and-pencil measures are likely to yield considerable information about the background of a given family. Once a profile of client problems has been assembled, workers will need more specific information about those particular problems and their resolution. At this point, workers turn to assessment tools that look at narrowly defined problems and can be used repeatedly to assess problem resolution. Observational measures and rating scales are more likely appropriate for this purpose.

Numerous logistic and pragmatic concerns dictate the selection of assessment tools. The concern that most often comes to mind among practitioners is that of time. The assessment tool cannot take up so much time to administer, score, and interpret that the time available for intervention is sacrificed. With a few obvious exceptions, such as the lengthy Minnesota Multiphase Personality Inventory, this rarely is the case. Even so, intensive family preservation services have the advantage of extended client contact in the home, which allows one family member to complete a measure while the social worker is talking to other members. Assessment plans that are too intrusive, such that the client is at risk of public embarrassment when completing the measure or recording information, should be avoided. If reading is involved, the language skill levels must be appropriate for the respondent(s). A seemingly endless list of small details can affect the ease of completion for clients [see Bloom and Fischer (1982) for more information about these potential impediments]. As much as possible, these factors should be taken into account in selecting, and later in establishing procedures for administering the measures.

Because personal scientists are continually responding to information about client progress and revising their interventions as needed, measurement tools should be selected for their sensitivity to incremental change. The brevity of treatment also demands that the measurement tools be able to promptly detect client change, so that workers and clients have timely feedback. In general, measures that distinguish a greater number of levels of the target problem are more sensitive to change. For example, a measure that indicates how often a child is truant from school is more sensitive than a measure that simply indicates whether or not a child has been truant in the past week.

Using Assessment Information to Inform Treatment Planning

Treatment plans are individualized for each family based on the findings from that family's assessment. In one family, for instance, parent–adolescent conflict may be dealt with primarily as a family issue with considerable attention being devoted to negotiation and commnication skills practice. For another family experiencing parent–adolescent conflict, the assessment may suggest that the adolescent and parents need to be seen separately for awhile since there is so much mistrust and bitterness. Information about factors that cue the occurrence of a target problem or help to maintain it can also inform the treatment plan.

In addition to developing the treatment plan, the worker must specify the tools for monitoring the effects of the plan. For the personal scientist, these tasks are often intertwined. In fact, the process of identifying or developing a monitoring system can actually influence the treatment plan. This occurred in the case of a single mother who was in her third trimester of pregnancy. Child protective services staff had serious doubts about whether she could care for the infant and were considering a foster care arrangement. The mother had an 8-year-old child who was being raised by the child's maternal grandmother. All three generations lived together, but the assessment revealed that the grandmother was "burned out" on parenting and reluctant to assume major responsibility for raising another child. Concern about the mother's ability to care for the unborn infant stemmed from her borderline intelligence, a disability that rendered her left arm useless in holding, supporting, or lifting a baby, and the fact that she had continually avoided caring for her son. Yet the mother expressed a high level of interest in caring for this infant and was eager to learn the necessary skills. A treatment goal was immediately identified: to teach the mother basic infant care skills, including feeding, bathing, and ways of interacting with and stimulating the baby. The assessment involved having the mother role play the infant care routines with a doll. Since the worker knew of no readily available measurement tools for assessing infant care skills, one was developed specifically for this client. The worker and her supervisor devised a checklist of the important actions to be taken in feeding, bathing, and diapering. For example, feeding was broken down into these actions: correct preparation of the formula, checking the temperature and flow of the liquid, holding the bottle at the proper angle, supporting the infant's head and back, triggering the baby's sucking reflex, and periodic burping. The process of identifying the items for this checklist also prescribed a set of skills to teach the mother. Thus, development of an assessment tool simultaneously informed the intervention plan. Moreover, the results of the first application of this checklist (while the client role played caring for a doll) revealed that the client already possessed some of the infant care skills, but needed to be taught others. This initial assessment also helped the worker and client identify some environmental modifications that could be made to compensate for her disabled arm. Finally, data from the ongoing assessment of her infant care skills, collected via the checklist, suggested that the client was able to master the physical skills but that she was not making much observable progress in interacting with and stimulating a baby. Both the worker and the client agreed that it was difficult to work on these skills when a doll was being used to represent a baby. The worker modified the intervention plan to allow these skills to be addressed after the birth of the child.

Monitoring Progress Toward General Program Goals via Individual Client Goals

Homebuilders specifies the following three general program goals as operating with each family served by the program: (1) resolve the immediate crisis that precipitated the program's involvement; (2) restore the family to their precrisis level of functioning; and (3) maintain the children in the home. Like most family preservation programs, Homebuilders examines its effectiveness in terms of the third goal—maintaining the children in the home—which is assessed at the termination of the case and at various follow-up intervals. As is appropriate for program evaluations, the primary focus of the effectiveness data is an overall assessment of the program's ability to prevent the breakup of a certain percentage of the families served. While this is the bottom line and therefore a most important measure of success, there is a wealth of additional effectiveness data that workers operating as personal scientists, can and do accumulate. These data can have important implications for the design of individual interventions as well as the overall program, and provide supplemental information about the extent to which the program goals are accomplished. The information generated by workers—because they are looking at case-specific instances of these broad program goals and assessing them accordingly—provides a different, and perhaps more precise, evaluation of program effectiveness. The following sections will give examples of typical family goals falling under each of these general program goals.

Resolve the Immediate Crisis

Each family's immediate crisis that precipitates the involvement of a family preservation services worker is unique but, in almost all instances, this immediate crisis must be resolved if the family is to stay together. For one family, there may have been a general downward spiraling fostered by the father's unemployment, increasing marital distress, and a child's out-of-control behavior becoming more deviant as he gets older. Yet a specific event, such as the mother's decision to separate from the father and his subsequent physical abuse, precipitates the involvement of family preservation services. In another instance, the family may have been functioning adequately for some time, until an institutionalized child returned home. The parents do not feel they can control the child, whose behavior has become increasingly disturbing, and they request foster care, which initiates the involvement of a family preservation worker.

In the first case, a goal for resolving the immediate crisis might state that the mother and their children must be safe from abuse by the father, and the father must refrain from physical violence (directed toward the mother, himself, or others). The assessment of whether this goal was attained would involve the interview, observation, and possibly reports from significant others. The variable representing goal attainment would be dichotomous—yes, the conditions stated in the goal existed, or no, they did not yet exist. In the second case, a goal for resolving the immediate crisis might be to find respite care to give the parents some relief and additional time to prepare for resuming full parenting responsibility for the child. Again, the variable would be dichotomous, indicating whether respite care was or was not attained.

One of the first tasks facing a family preservation worker is to determine what changes must occur to resolve the initial crisis or crises. This should result in a goal statement. As is true in the two examples above and in many cases, goals related to resolving the immediate family crisis frequently involve changing a behavior or an environmental condition. This type of goal is measured by clearly and carefully specifying the conditions that must be present to resolve the initial crisis and then using interviews, backed by some observation, to determine when the goal is accomplished. Obviously, this type of specification is done in the initial assessment and simply reinforces the importance of a thorough and detailed analysis of the family situation. Because the goals often refer to dichotomous variables and because of the crisis nature of the work, monitoring the resolution of the immediate crisis rarely involves elaborate or continuous measurement plans. The crisis situation almost always precludes the possibility of withholding treatment to gather a baseline indication of the level of the problem.

When aggregated across several cases, a minimum amount of information available will be the number or percentage of cases in which the immediate crisis was resolved. Categories also could be developed to distinguish different types of crises. If time were an important factor, family preservation service programs might want to examine the number of days required to resolve the immediate crisis or different types of crises. Care would have to be taken in interpreting these data, however, because some crises, by their nature, require more or less time to reach resolution.

Restore the Family to a Precrisis Level of Functioning

While assessment and goal setting are always important social work tasks, they are particularly important in this stage of intensive family preservation services if the program is to maintain its time-limited nature. Thus, the worker should take great care to identify all major family problems and select for intervention only those problems that must be resolved to allow the family to resume the level of functioning that was present before the crisis occurred.

Once these target problems are identified, the worker must attempt to determine the level of the problem prior to the crisis. This enables the worker and the family to have a clear notion of the degree of problem resolution being sought. The same research principles and techniques that are helpful in assessment and ongoing monitoring can be applied to specify the precrisis level of the problem. Guidelines for developing a reconstructed baseline may be useful in getting family members to supply necessary information (see Bloom and Fischer, 1982). In other situations, the family may desire some improvement over their precrisis level of functioning or actually seek change in a different direction. The worker will have to determine if this is appropriate within the framework of the overall goal of maintaining the children in the home. In any case, research principles and techniques will remain helpful in specifying the goals.

An example of a problem that might fall into this category is that of depression experienced by one of the family members. The goal might be to reduce this individual's level of depression such that she is not suicidal and is able to carry out her daily responsibilities. Attainment of this goal might be assessed by the use of a standardized depression inventory, a rating scale that asks the client to regularly identify her level of depression, a checklist of symptoms of the client's depression which are monitored daily, or simply the client's report regarding the presence of depression and her ability to carry out her responsibilities. Of course, data from any of these tools would be supplemented by the worker's observations and other sources of information that examined suicide potential in the client.

Determining if clients have attained their precrisis level of functioning could rely on any of the assessment strategies reviewed earlier in the chapter, depending on the nature of the goal. Beyond the determination of goal attainment for a particular family, data could be aggregated across all goals in a particular category—for one family, for all families within a particular grouping (such as geographic area, referral source, presence of violence in the home, and so on), or for all families served by the agency. Then each goal could be determined to have been attained or not attained, and the number of goals attained totaled. This box-score approach gives a general idea of the level of success for each set of client goals. Meta-analytic techniques—quantitative procedures for combining the results obtained from monitoring a number of client goals—have been adapted for single-case data and could be applied as well (Gingerich, 1984; Jayaratne et al., 1988).

Maintain Children in the Home

To assess goal attainment in this area, the worker must specify what conditions must exist before it seems likely that the children can be maintained in their parents' home. These conditions would be developed into goal statements for the family. One example of a problem that might be addressed in this category is a child's unwillingness to accept "no." To examine client progress toward overcoming this problem, the worker and the child's parents could develop a goal attainment rating that describes five different levels of the child's response to being told "no," as illustrated in Figure 8.2. This scale could be completed daily to monitor the child's ability to accept "no."

As in the previous category—restoring families to precrisis functioning—any of the full range of assessment tools might be employed to monitor client progress. Similarly, data could be aggregated as described above. In addition, follow-up data on whether children have been maintained in the home, which is typically collected by intensive family preservation programs such as Homebuilders, would offer a more direct measure of attainment of the overall program goal.

Analyzing the Information for Case Decision Making

To allow data from monitoring goal attainment to inform treatment planning and other case decisions, workers must routinely examine the monitoring information. Of the two methods of analyzing information—visual analysis and quasistatistical analysis—the former is probably best-suited to the needs of family preservation workers. In brief, visual analysis involves constructing a graph of the monitoring information plotted across time and then following some straightforward guidelines for "eyeballing" the data patterns to discern if the client is making progress in the desired direction and at an adequate pace. Texts are available that explain the basic steps involved in constructing graphs and visually analyzing data (Bloom and Fischer, 1982; Blythe and Tripodi, in press; Sanders, 1978).

Quasistatistical methods are generally helpful for making determinations about the statistical significance of the observed client progress. They are less likely to be applicable in family preservation services work as most of these analysis techniques require seven to ten baseline data points before intervention is initiated—something that is often not possible in intensive, brief work. Jayaratne (1978) and Bloom and Fischer (1982), among others, describe these quasistatistical procedures, and Bronson and Blythe (1987) present a microcomputer program that graphs the data yielded by case monitoring and completes quasi-statistical analyses.

Insofar as workers are interested in attributing client change (or lack

Goal 2: Improve Laurie's skills for accepting "no"

Family name:	Therapist: Leavitt	Whose goal: Family/Therapist
Rating when goal scaled (−1 or −2): −1		Weight: 9 (9 most impt./ 1 least impt.)

Statement of problem:
When told no, Laurie becomes angry and yells, argues, swears, calls names and threatens to run or to harm herself.

−2   When told no, Laurie yells, argues, threatens to run away or kill herself.

−1   When told no, Laurie yells and argues for over 5 minutes.

  0   When told no, Laurie yells, argues for less than 5 minutes.

+1   When told no, Laurie complains but accepts it and does not yell or become angry.

+2   When told no, Laurie accepts it without yelling, arguing, complaining, or threatening.

Plan

Week 1: From 8/20/84   To: 8/26/84
   1.   Introduce anger management skills
   2.   Introduce alternative way of accepting no
   3.   Develop relationship with Laurie
	Rating: 0

Week 2: From 8/27/84   To: 9/2/84
   1.   Practice anger management skills
   2.   Practice RET
   3.   Practice negotiating
	Rating: =1

Week 3: From 9/3/84   To: 9/9/84
   1.   Continue as above
   2.   Monitor progress
	Rating: +1

Week 4: From 9/10/84 To: 9/18/84 1. Continue as above	Rating: +1

Figure 8.2.   Goal Sheet.

of change) to the intervention, care must be taken in distinguishing implementation failure from treatment failure. In other words, if a client is not progressing as hoped, a worker following the personal scientist model would be inclined to revise the treatment plan and to avoid the future use of the unsuccessful intervention. Before making such a decision, however, workers should be certain that they have implemented the intervention as prescribed. To give a simple but common example, a worker may ask a client to use time-out to reduce a child's aggressive behavior. Unfortunately, clients sometimes do not apply our suggested interventions at all, sometimes apply them inconsistently, or sometimes apply them incorrectly. A worker should explore the possibility that one of these instances of implementation failure is occurring before revising a treatment plan, particularly when an intervention that enjoys strong empirical support for dealing with a given client problem appears to be unsuccessful.

Specifying Components of Intensive Family Preservation Interventions

Given an agency structure that allows and even encourages creative problem-solving in handling cases, workers in intensive family preservation programs often discover some innovative and effective methods of dealing with client problems. When caseloads are small, the duration of treatment is brief, and supervisors are seen as consultants, workers have an optimal situation for trying out new interventions when old ones have not worked or are otherwise contraindicated, or when a client presents an unusual problem. Similarly, viewing clients as personal scientists and bringing them into the problem-solving process often results in creative solutions.

Newly developed interventions rarely consist of radically different sets of procedures, but rather small innovations or adaptations to tried and true methods. For instance, a treatment goal for a young boy called for him to complete his morning routines each day without supervision. To help cue him, the worker had the boy make an audio recording of his daily routines that he could play to himself each morning. This "innovation" was apparently helpful in getting the boy to complete his routines.

Adaptations to tried and true interventions often occur when the monitoring information suggests that the existing intervention is not having the desired effect. The case of an 8-year-old girl and her mother demonstrates the role of both client and worker as personal scientists in their mutual efforts to adapt and test interventions. The young girl, Susan, had refused to attend school for nearly a month after she and a friend reported seeing a man expose himself on the school playground. The first intervention involved enrolling Susan in a different school and then having her mother accompany her to school. In return for attending school, Susan would receive several prizes and a trip to McDonald's with an older sister. This intervention worked on the first trial, but not on the next day, although similar reinforcements were offered. The worker and mother decided to try physically taking Susan to school, but this plan was abandoned as it became apparent that the young girl had strong feelings about attending school. Because the original reinforcement plan had been successful, the worker and Susan's mother decided to set up a chart which allowed Susan to earn stickers and other prizes for attending school. This worked as long as her mother could attend school with her. School personnel, however, expressed their concern about the mother attending school. A meeting with them resulted in a plan to allow Susan's older sister to earn high school credits for working as a teacher's aid in Susan's classroom in the late afternoon, which allowed her mother to leave school and do her work as a housecleaner. Over time, the teacher gave the mother some tasks to complete outside of the classroom, thereby phasing her out of remaining with Susan during the morning and early afternoon.

This case demonstrates that, although a drastically different intervention was not developed, the combined efforts of worker and client devised an effective modification, which carefully detailed how the general intervention plan of reinforcement and support in the school would be put into place. If workers merely try out new methods, but are not vigilant about specifying exactly what these new methods involve and then disseminating this new information to colleagues, the innovation cannot have any impact beyond the present case for which it was tested. Guidelines for specifying the components of new interventions and for disseminating them are available (Fraser and Leavitt, this volume, Chapter 9; Thomas, 1984).

Supports for Being a Personal Scientist

Earlier, the characteristics of a personal scientist were outlined. Hopefully, this chapter has further illustrated some of the ways in which personal scientists apply practice research principles and tools to conduct their practice and expand our knowledge about intensive family preservation services. While these characteristics must be in place for a worker to act as a personal scientist, certain other kinds of supports may need to be present as well. In addition to having supervisors also act as personal scientists, the administrative structure of the larger agency must be one that supports and even facilitates the flexibility that is required. Administrators, then, must understand the importance of the personal scientist model and the potential contribution of practice research findings (Briar and Blythe, 1985).

Although there are no data to support or refute this, it is likely that the very fact that family preservation services are intensive supports the personal scientist orientation. Because they need to get results fast, workers have built-in motivation to try whatever seems likely to work and to make changes rapidly when information suggests that goals are not being met.

Clearly, having peers who also are acting as personal scientists and applying practice research tools is likely to be an important influence. Some combination of peer pressure, expectations, modeling, reinforcement from like-minded colleagues, and readily available peer consultation probably is operating to provide support for this approach. What is unclear is the importance of agency size, particularly in reference to peer support. As agencies become larger, workers' ability to share the results of practice research efforts with one another may be inhibited.

While it is not a requisite, a computerized client information system would enhance the ability of workers in family preservation services to act as personal scientists. Such a system could record information about clients' presenting problems, about goals and means of assessing progress toward goal attainment, and about interventions and outcomes. Thus, workers would have immediate access to information about their own and their co-workers' current cases and past cases. With thoughtful planning, such a computerized system could provide a data bank on effective and ineffective interventions and tools for assessing presenting problems and progress toward goal attainment (Briar and Blythe, 1985). In fact, the system might actually mitigate the potential problem of an agency's increasing size inhibiting communication among workers. The system could also meet some of the agency's needs for program evaluation by aggregating information on clients, services, and outcomes.

Even with a full array of supports to help workers become personal scientists, however, the process of changing one's practice to include routine monitoring of client progress requires an initial expenditure of time and effort. Probably the biggest hurdle to overcome is learning to devise measurement schemes that are specific to client problems and not overly complex. Novices have a tendency to develop elaborate measurement plans that seem quite rigorous but ultimately consume too much of the client's or worker's time to complete. Another necessary step is to personalize the process so that it fits the worker's style. For instance, most workers would want to develop a way of introducing the concept of measuring progress to clients. This must be done in a manner and at a time that fits in with other tasks workers carry out as they help clients. As with most things, practice improves performance. Workers will find that as applying practice research tools becomes a routine part of their practice, the process will become far less time consuming. While using these tools will always take more time than not using them, the benefits of doing so should make them worthwhile.

References

Bloom, M., and Fischer, J. (1982). *Evaluating practice: Guidelines for the accountable professional.* Englewood Cliffs, NJ: Prentice-Hall.

Blythe, B. J., and Tripodi, T. (in press). *Measurement in direct social work practice.* Beverly Hills, CA: Sage.

Briar, S., and Blythe, B. J. (1985). Agency support for the outcomes of social work services. *Administration in Social Work, 9*(2), 25–36.

Bronson, D. E., and Blythe, B. J. (1987). Computer support for single-case evaluation of practice. *Social Work Research & Abstracts, 23*(3), 10–13.

Corcoran, K., and Fischer, J. (1987). *Measures for clinical practice.* New York: Free Press.

Edelson, J. L. (1985). Rapid-assessment instruments for evaluating practice with children and youth. *Journal of Social Service Research, 8,* 17–32.

Gingerich, W. J. (1984). Methodological observations on applied behavioral science. *Journal of Applied Behavioral Science, 20,* 71–79.

Gottman, J. M., and Leiblum, S. R. (1974). *How to do psychotherapy and how to evaluate it: A manual for beginners.* New York: Holt, Rinehart, and Winston.

Haapala, D., and Kinney, J. (1979). Homebuilders' approach to the training of in-home therapists. *In* S. Maybanks and M. Bryce (Eds.), *Home-based services for children and families: Policy, practice, and research.* Springfield, IL: Charles C. Thomas.

Hersen, M., and Bellack, A. S. (1981). *Behavioral assessment: A practical handbook,* 2nd Ed. New York: Pergamon.

Hudson, W. W. (1982). *The clinical measurement package: A field manual.* Homewood, IL: Dorsey.

Jayaratne, S. (1978). Analytic procedures for single-subject designs. *Social Work Research & Abstracts, 14*(3), 30–40.

Jayaratne, S., Tripodi, T., and Talsma, E. (1988). Comparative analysis and aggregation of single-case data. *Journal of Applied Behavioral Science, 24*(1), 119–128.

Levitt, J. L., and Reid, W. J. (1981). Rapid-assessment instruments for practice. *Social Work Research & Abstracts, 17,* 13–20.

Rogers, C. R. (1957). The necessary and sufficient conditions of therapeutic personality change. *Journal of Counseling Psychology, 21,* 95–103.

Sanders, R. M. (1978). *How to plot data: A manual for students, researchers, and teachers of the behavioral sciences.* Lawrence, KS: H & H Enterprises.

Thomas, E. J. (1984). *Designing interventions for the helping professions.* Beverly Hills: Sage.

Tripodi, T., and Epstein, I. (1980). *Research techniques for clinical social workers.* New York: Columbia University.

Chapter 9

Creating Social Change: "Mission"-Oriented Research and Entrepreneurship

Mark Fraser and Shelley Leavitt

Many innovative programs are created and then fail. How is it that Homebuilders came not only to survive but to be widely recognized? The answer lies, in part, in a philosophy of program development that has roots in empirically based practice, entrepreneurial management, and social action.

Most administrators advocate for their programs, but Homebuilders staff did more. In the mid-1970s, they took strong and vocal action on behalf of public policies that might protect children who they felt were victimized by a child welfare system that needlessly separated families. Their advocacy extended beyond efforts to insure adequate program funding. They argued for social reforms.

Homebuilders staff became outspoken social advocates and "entrepreneurs." They were sharply critical of a system that appeared to place more resources into efforts to create substitute families than into efforts to strengthen families. They created an innovative program to meet a need that they believed public policymakers had overlooked. Their insistence on the use of data to refine their services provided them with evidence to argue that the home-based, family preservation model was both a viable and ethically desirable alternative to out-of-home placement. In the context of developing a new program, they contributed to social change.

Using the Homebuilders Program as an example, this chapter will describe agency-level actions that can promote changes in public policies. In particular, the collection of data to serve strategic political purposes or "missions" will be discussed. And finally, given the unique blend of scholarship, administrative skill, and advocacy that has characterized the Homebuilders organization, implications for program development and professional training will be considered.

Forces Affecting Social Change

At any time, a variety of forces operate both to promote and discourage new public policies and, from a broader perspective, social change. It is not clear whether there is an actual science—with underlying principles—or social change or whether social change is merely the propitious blend of time and circumstances, the process of history.[1] This is a point of hot debate between sociologists and historians (e.g., Boudon, 1986). But the balance between forces that promote innovation and those that tend to preserve the status quo contributes to the rate at which public policies change.

Forces that Preserve

In practice, a variety of forces tend to impede innovation, to limit creativity, and to preserve the status quo. These include laws, traditions, and "practice wisdom"—all of which are representations of conventional beliefs about norms for behavior. But forces that promote the status quo also include funding patterns and practices that require new agencies to be bonded, to have operated for 2 to 3 years before receiving funds, to have evaluation data showing that a program has an impact, or to be staffed by "professionals." In a similar sense, professional training and education as well as professional associations tend to promote a narrow band of knowledge that often excludes the innovative, unusual, and risky.

Forces that Produce Change

Countervailing the forces that tend to preserve that status quo are forces that tend to promote change. These include general social trends—e.g., the increasing complexity of bureaucracies, the automation of manufacturing, and the growth of computer technology—and what Thomas Kuhn (1970) called "anomalies," or information that does not conform to existing beliefs. Anomalies create contradictions. They force rethinking and refinement of theory. In large numbers, they can lead to rejection of conventional wisdom.

In social work, conventional wisdom is affected by evaluation findings that show innovative programs to be effective or promising and by social critics who point out the anomalies of educators', policy-makers', and practitioners' beliefs. The status quo is affected also by general social trends toward deprofessionalization—hiring by job function rather than by profession—and by the increasing cultural diversity of the country. The concept of a cultural "melting pot" that once guided American political thinking has given way to the concept of a cultural "salad bowl" in which ethnic and racial diversity are encouraged and are viewed as contributing uniquely to society. In social services, the richness that arises from multicultural practice strengthens the social work profession, while challenging many traditional modes of practice.

Such factors may be considered endogenous or internal change-producing factors, but change can also occur as a result of outside or exogenous factors. Historically, one of clearest examples of an exogenous influence occurred when missionaries inadvertently brought European diseases to the Hawaiian Islands in the 18th century and caused terrible epidemics.

In social welfare, exogenous influences have created changes in both public policies and front-line agency practices. When psychotropic medications were discovered in France in the early 1950s, major changes in the treatment of the mentally ill became possible. Coupled with the endogenous influences of unionization, changes in labor laws, investigative journalism, and advocacy (both law suits and public outcry that focused on the conditions in mental hospitals), the discovery of psychotropic medications contributed to the creation of a nationwide system of community mental health centers. Research and development projects such as the ones that led to the development of psychotropics, as well as specialized training or knowledge dissemination projects, may create change in the status quo.

Finally, law suits may promote change. The sheer weight of case law often leads to administrative decisions and legislation that produce social change in the nation. Both the Education for All Handicapped Children Act (PL 94-142) and the Adoption Assistance and Child Welfare Act (PL 96-272) arose, in part, from years of litigation that promoted the rights of dependent children.

Between forces that tend to preserve the status quo and those that tend to alter it, there is constant friction. These forces differentially affect social policies. Their balance influences the rate of change and, across history, this rate has not been uniform (e.g., Chirot, 1986). Depending on the strength of the leaders and forces promoting change, we have moved in and out of periods of growth when public policies were rapidly reshaped.

Community Leadership and Entrepreneurship

In the sense that they created an innovative program and that they advocated for new public policies, Homebuilders staff were entrepreneurs and community leaders who helped create social change. As indicated above, a wide variety of factors affect social change. It is rare, however, that change occurs without substantial efforts on the part of many people. Community leadership is a critical component of creating change, and it is an important component of the Homebuilders Model.

Three beliefs are often shared by community leaders: (1) a belief that innovation is facilitated by social interaction (and that people will generally do their best in an open, honest climate where differences of opinion are examined rationally): (2) a belief that large-scale change occurs as a result of incremental change; and (3) a belief or bias toward action (Joiner, 1987; Tornatzky, *et al.*, 1980). In 1974 when the Homebuilders program was started, the directors did not believe they had the perfect solution to the problem of out-of-home placements, but they were committed to undertaking an action strategy that might keep families together (Kinney *et al.*, 1977). They focused on opportunities for innovation rather than on the control of existing resources, and took action which they recognized as incremental. It is in this sense that they were both leaders and entrepreneurs.

Corporate Entrepreneurship

Entrepreneurs place value on challenge and action, while administrator-trustees place value on management and control (e.g. Hisrich, 1986). Both perspectives are important and the positions are not opposite, but it is often difficult for an entrepreneur to become an administrator. Homebuilders, a multistate division of the Behavioral Sciences Institute, has been distinguished by its enduring entrepreneurship. Fifteen years after its founding, it is an organization in which staff are encouraged to break tradition with fresh ideas and new ways of working with families in crisis.

Challenge-Focused Management

At the same time, Homebuilders administrators and supervisors are managers who exert control in the context of challenge. They are very precise about the nature of the Homebuilders model, and the process of breaking with tradition is clearly delimited. Therapists are encouraged to accept challenges but to avoid risks (that might endanger children, parents, or staff members). For example, workers who are interested in assisting clients in developing social support networks might create a special project to pilot-test a social support intervention. But such a project would not be undertaken in absence of close monitoring or delivering of the basic Homebuilders services. Within bounds and from the perspective of empirically-based practice, entrepreneurship is encouraged inside the organization. Challenge-focused management and control characterize the organization's leadership.

"Mission"-Oriented Research and the "Personal Scientist"

Commitment to social reform, an entrepreneurial management style, and empirically based practice contribute to an emerging Homebuilders "philosophy of practice." As discussed by Blythe (this volume, Chapter 8), Home-builders staff are encouraged to be "personal scientists." They use data in treatment and their supervisors use data in supervision. In aggregate, they conduct research to advance the "mission" of the agency. That is, they collect data using carefully constructed measures that serve political purposes as well as clinical purposes.

It has been the view of some experts that serving people is essentially a political process (e.g., Withorn, 1984), and although they acknowledge this, Homebuilders staff take a somewhat broader view. From their perspective, data are to be collected to test new clinical ideas as well as to advance the political mission of the agency. Their research is "mission" oriented. They believe in entrepreneurship in practice and leadership in the community. In this sense, Homebuilders staff are both personal and political scientists, for the data they collect are used both to refine the Homebuilders intervention and to support arguments for public policies that focus on family preservation.

The Development Model of Practice: A "Mission" Orientation

Developmental research is one force contributing to social change and innovation. From pilot project to nationally recognized "model" child welfare program, Homebuilders is an example of an applied research model of program development and dissemination.

The goal of developmental research is to generate social technology—the technical means to meet social work goals (Thomas, 1978). Like the research and development model of engineering, developmental research in human services is oriented to the generation of new products—new technology—to address social concerns. The developmental research and utilization model described by Thomas involves five phases: analysis, development, evaluation, diffusion, and adoption. Although all phases were not followed formally as the Homebuilders program developed, activities in each of these areas were pursued.

Analysis—Identifying the Need. The Homebuilders program, like other nationally recognized programs (e.g., Blase *et al*, 1983), began as a response to an identified need in the child welfare field. In the early 1970s, there was growing recognition and concern over the increased number of children in out-of-home placements. The child welfare system and existing community services were not working as planned. In large numbers, children were being removed from their families and drifting from placement to placement. Along with the increase in placements, the cost of substitute care became a public concern. The system was not only potentially damaging to children and families, it was expensive. The need for new social technology—innovative interventions—to address the problem was clear.

Development—Designing the Technology.   Using data and existing technology from the fields of social work, psychology, and counseling, the Homebuilders program took form in response to this need. Research in the field of applied behavior analysis had already documented the effectiveness of teaching parents to be change agents for their own children (Patterson and Reid, 1973); and technology (interventions) developed in other settings (e.g., schools and institutions) was successfully being transferred to the home setting (e.g., Christopherson *et al.,* 1972).

Taking the role of personal scientists, Homebuilders staff "experimented" with interventions, assessed their effectiveness, and used evaluation information to make changes in the design of the program model. As the development continued, the program elements became more clearly defined. The model of in-home services that evolved consisted of specific structural components (e.g., 4-to-6-week time limit, caseload of two families, 24-hour accessibility), specific intervention strategies (e.g., skill-building approach, provision of concrete services), and a specific set of values (e.g., clients viewed as colleagues). The new technology was a combination of innovative program elements (e.g., highly concentrated, intensive in-home services) and well-established and empirically based practice technology (e.g., skills training). Incrementally over the years, the specific skills used by therapists and supervisors, and specific administrative structures and procedures were identified and more precisely defined so that new workers could be trained and the model could be replicated in other locations.

Evaluation—Assessing the Program.   Throughout its development, trial and field implementation of the Homebuilders model occurred. Using behavioral science research methodology, data on outcome (e.g., placement prevention rates, behavior change), process (e.g., service intensity, clinical, and concrete services provided), and client satisfaction were routinely collected. Information on the costs of Homebuilders and the costs of out-of-home placement was gathered and cost comparisons were made. Through these routine evaluation activities, the effectiveness of the model and its costs and benefits were assessed. Comparison group studies conducted in 1976 and 1979 generated detailed information on program effectiveness. These research projects along with ongoing program evaluation allowed not only the continual refinement of the technology, but provided fuel for dissemination and advocacy efforts.

Diffusion—Disseminating Information.   Diffusion of information about the Homebuilders model took, and continues to take, many forms. As the model became more precisely defined, staff training materials were developed and training workshops were designed. As new data were collected and technology refined, existing training materials were revised and new ones produced. An interface, or interdependence, between practice, research, and training was established early on; without it, the diffusion of information and the broad-scale adoption of the model could not have proceeded as they did.

Since 1975, information about Homebuilders has been disseminated through articles in professional journals and books, presentations to professional and public groups, newspaper and magazine articles, and television and radio programs. As a result, more and more requests for information about the program were received and additional dissemination products and materials were produced. Over the past few years, there has been an increased interest in replicating the Homebuilders program in other states, and with it an increased need for more comprehensive training and site development procedures and materials. These have included: (1) informational materials and consultation procedures to help public and private agencies design Homebuilders-like programs, client pathways, and staff hiring and training protocols; (2) the technology for providing ongoing training and technical assistance to line staff, supervisors, and administrators; and (3) a site development package that involved systematic and comprehensive technical assistance and training over a 1-to-2-year period.

Dissemination efforts should not be limited to service providers, and the Homebuilders training programs recognize the many public and private officials who have a "stake" in preserving families. Information on the program, its costs and benefits, and its philosophy of service was disseminated to state and national legislators, judges, policy makers, and advocacy groups. Homebuilders staff testified before U.S. Congressional committees, the Washington State legislature, and legislative committees in three other states.

Adoption—Implementing The Program. State funding for the continued implementation of the Homebuilders program in Washington State was obtained in 1976. Using the data gathered on treatment and cost effectiveness, Homebuilders staff continually sought to obtain additional funding and support for expanding the service. Since 1974 the program has been successfully implemented in 4 counties in Washington, and in 1987 the program was implemented in the Bronx, New York. In 1988, Homebuilders programs were expanded to four additional counties in Washington State. In an exogenous sense, the adoption of the strategies of the Homebuilders model has not been limited to the states of Washington and New York. Between 1978 and 1988, more than 25 states implemented programs based on the Homebuilders model, and comprehensive, large-scale site development activities currently are underway in five states. Helping others to adopt family preservation programs has distinguished Homebuilders from many other programs. It is a manifestation of their belief that social welfare programs have social action as well as clinical missions.

Issues in Creating Social Change in Mission-Oriented Practice

The example of Homebuilders, its development and expansion, and its effects on public policies highlight three factors critical to mission-oriented practice.

Taking Risks.   One salient factor demonstrated in both the mission and the design of the Homebuilders program is the willingness to take on challenges that include both personal and professional risks. Rather than maintaining the status quo, the Homebuilders staff experimented with methods of service delivery that were often very different from traditional services. For example, clients were seen sequentially (caseloads of two at a time) rather than simultaneously (caseloads of 20 to 40). Services were designed to be accessible, intensive, and tailored to the family. Staff training and ongoing evaluation and feedback were considered integral components of the program, allowing continual examination, refinement, and innovation. And, focusing on the family and its ecology instead of the child created a challenge to traditional child welfare services and systems. By taking risks, a new client group—families in which children were at risk of placement—was identified and with it a radically new service approach.

Taking personal and professional risks was also fundamental to the development and implementation of the treatment approach. Homebuilders staff often encountered unpredictable and sometimes dangerous situations, and the definition of what a therapist or counselor does in the name of "treatment" was stretched to the limit—for example, therapists were asked to babysit, advocate, help clean, and provide transportation, and were required to give out their home phone numbers. Professionally, the program cut across disciplines (social work, psychology, and counseling) and human services agencies. The technology used with child welfare clients was often the same as that used with mental health, juvenile justice, and developmentally disabled clients. In the mid-1970s (and to some extent every today), the program involved not only an innovative technology and approach, but it also reflected an unconventional way of thinking about and responding to child and family issues.

Specifying the Model Rigorously.   Another force contributing to change appears to have been the use of a well-defined program model that was grounded in theory and research, rather than in anecdote and tradition. Instead of creating the illusion of "value-free" practice, Homebuilders defined its values and utilized only methods that were congruent with these values (see Blythe, this volume, Chapter 8). The use of a clearly specified practice model allowed systematic training, monitoring, and dissemination, and guarded against the tendency for workers "to do their own thing" with clients.

Mastering the Model Incrementally. The practice of using data to improve technology was a major force affecting service delivery and publid policies. As described earlier, in the Homebuilders program there is close monitoring of both process and outcome; changes in clients are constantly assessed. Characteristic of Homebuilders staff is a fundamental belief that their own learning—i.e., mastery of the skills necessary for family preservation—is an ongoing process based on systematic feedback. Rather than becoming "masters" of the model, Homebuilders staff continue to refine and hone their skills, while discovering new applications for the model.

Program Development and Professional Training

Embedded in the Homebuilders experience are lessons for the directors and staff of all family preservation programs. Perhaps most important is that empirically based practice, an entrepreneurial style of management, and advocacy for public policies can be implemented concurrently in a social agency. At Homebuilders, mission-oriented research, entrepreneurial leadership, and social action appear to have contributed in nearly equal measure to the organization's accomplishments.

Implications for the Development of Family Preservation Programs

It is tempting to explain the success of Homebuilders by describing the leaders and staff as unique and gifted—as having the "right stuff." While this may be true in part or in total, there appear to be underlying principles of practice that contributed to the success of the organization. In this section, we will attempt to distill from the Homebuilders experience those principles that might be applied in other family preservation programs.

Program Staff Must Be Encouraged to Identify and Exploit Opportunities to Enhance Program Resources. Usually family preservation programs are viewed as "nontraditional" and the resources allocated to them are limited, contingent on performance (e.g., showing that out-of-home placements are reduced). Based on the Homebuilders experience, the development of new program resources may be as important as the control of existing resources. At Homebuilders, a spirit of entrepreneurship was combined successfully with administrative control to create an organizational climate in which workers became personally committed to the family preservation model and sought to develop new resources to promote the model. In short, the staff became interested both in developing a model for practice and in changing public policies related to family preservation programs. If one can generalize from the Homebuilders experience, family preservation projects—from directors to line staff—appear to be enlivened by a sense of being on the cutting edge and by commitment to political as well as clinical goals.

Program Staff Must Have an Ecological View.   The clinical and social change perspectives that emerged at Homebuilders were rooted in an ecological view of human behavior (e.g., Bronfenbrenner, 1979). Concrete and clinical services were provided to families in their homes because staff recognized that families embedded in adverse conditions are often so overwhelmed by the sheer necessities of life (providing for physical needs) that learning from treatment is difficult (e.g., Dumas, 1984; Wahler and Dumas, 1986; Whittaker and Garbarino, 1983). In order to optimize treatment conditions, Homebuilders staff made lateral contacts with other organizations to develop resources—day care, income assistance, health care, and transportation—that might be used with families.

An ecological perspective also characterized the administration at Homebuilders. Program directors recognized that they needed to interact with the larger social and political environment of the agency in order to survive. They visited key state officials; they testified at legislative hearings; they spoke in the community; they gave presentations at public schools; they taught university classes; and they recruited faculty members for board and advisory positions. Based on an understanding of the importance of this perspective for their clients and for the project, they were both program advocates and community educators.

Services Must Be Developed with Great Specificity.   The Homebuilders intervention was carefully specified and the guidelines for service were rigorously implemented. Workers were required to work in clients' homes. Service was limited to 4 weeks. Across more than 100 kinds of concrete and clinical services that are part and parcel of the Homebuilders model, treatment was structured to focus primarily on relationship building, strengthening communication in the family, and building parenting or child management skills. (For an in-depth analysis of the elements of service, see Lewis, 1988; and Kinney *et al.*, in preparation.) The attention to detail that characterized the development and implementation of the Homebuilders service permitted the staff to be precise about the treatment model and to strengthen it using an empirical approach. Service specificity appears to be a critical element in developing successful family preservation programs.

Successful hiring, training, and evaluation also depend on careful program conceptualization and implementation. At Homebuilders, the program became a subculture in which staff and directors shared common values, perceptions, and commitments. Such unity facilitated the development of specific criteria for hiring new staff, and it enabled the experienced staff to develop exacting in-service training programs. Because criteria for service provision were highly specific, it was possible to evaluate the implementation of service as well as service outcomes.

Data Must be Collected and Used to Advance the "Mission" of the Program. At Homebuilders, data were collected to advance the clinical and social action missions of the program. Staff actively identified measures of service provision (e.g., service goal attainment) and outcome (e.g., placement rates, length of placement, days in the community after the close of treatment, consumer reports of family problems) that might be used to insure that services were helping families. Their evaluation activities were "mission-oriented" in the sense that they served to refine the treatment model and to generate evidence to be used in advocacy efforts. A mission-oriented data collection strategy appears to arm program directors and staff with information that helps to promote family preservation projects and public policies that support families.

Implications for Social Work Education

The experience of the Homebuilders program also contains lessons for social work and human services educators. At the worker level, the blend of clinical and research skills that are required implies that educators in social work have been right in emphasizing research skills that focus on the evaluation of practice (Council on Social Work Education (CSWE), 1982). But the Homebuilders emphasis on interventive specificity and their use of research to advocate for public policies raise important other issues as well.

Substantive and Interventive Knowledge Must Be Conjoined. The Homebuilders model was developed specifically for families in crisis. Knowledge about the etiology of child abuse, delinquency, spouse abuse, and mental illness was combined with knowledge about crisis intervention, parenting training, communications skills, and relationship-building to create the model.

The development of the Homebuilders model suggests that social work education must focus as much on etiological or substantive knowledge regarding social problems as on interventive knowledge. Interventive methods that "fit" specific social problems can be developed only when workers are both substantively and clinically knowledgeable. Thus, schools of social work should train workers to acquire expertise regarding social problems, as well as teach interventive methods appropriate to a problem-oriented field of practice. A methods focus alone may not be sufficient.

An Understanding of Basic Research Methods and Single-subject Design May Not Adequately Prepare Social Workers to Evaluate Practice. Recent data sug-

gest that many schools of social work have interpreted the CSWE guidelines regarding research training to mean that curriculum content on basic
research methods plus single-subject design adequately prepares students to
evaluate practice (Fraser *et al.*, 1988). The Homebuilders experience suggests
that practice evaluation serves social action as well as clinical purposes, and
it implies that research coursework should cover a broader range of content.

Greater emphasis on clinical measurement and statistics may be needed.
Homebuilders staff selected measures to serve strategic purposes and aggregated data across clients. Moreover, the Homebuilders program used both
quantitative and qualitative methods to advance its mission (e.g., Fraser and
Haapala, 1987).

If the Homebuilders experience were to be used as a guide for creating
research curricula in schools of social work, course content in many schools
would be found deficient. Extrapolating from the Homebuilders approach,
research education should include: (1) study of the developmental research
model; (2) intermediate statistics (analysis of variance, regression analysis,
and nonparametric statistics); and (3) qualitative/quantitative measurement.
Workers must be able to conceptualize and test new social technology, to
analyze data across clients, and to develop clinical measures that will stand
the test of critical legislators, skeptical academics, and concerned community
activists.

*Social Workers Should Be Trained to Disseminate Information About Their
Practice.*   In 1986, the CSWE dropped from its guidelines for research
curricula the goal of preparing students to "contribute to the dissemination
of knowledge for practice." This should be reconsidered.

It may seem unrealistic to expect MSW social workers to write journal
articles; but, as demonstrated by the Homebuilders experience, workers
can be both personal scientists and social change agents who disseminate
knowledge for practice. To be both requires pointing out practices that are
not effective or no longer appropriate, using client data to refine program
services (making them more effective or efficient), and using aggregated data
to advocate for new public policies. The skills necessary to be an effective
trainer or public speaker are similar to those necessary to develop and write
an article or chapter. Students should be able to organize their thoughts in
linear arguments and to present them in writing or speech in a clear fashion.
This is a challenge the profession cannot afford to overlook.

Summary

If a single practice lesson were to be drawn from the development of the
Homebuilders program, it might be that program development and research

are related organically. The collection of client-focused data serves two purposes. First, the careful collection of data provides information useful in incrementally developing and refining the services themselves. Second, the collection of client data provides information useful in altering the social and political environments in which agencies operate. The creative, entrepreneurial characteristics of the Homebuilders program were distinguished, in part, by the strategic use of data to develop and promote services and policies that support families. Mission-oriented research and entrepreneurship appear to be critical ingredients in the development of a culture of challenge and accomplishment in family preservation programs.

Note

1. The following discussion of factors that affect change is not intended to be exhaustive. For that reason, we have included in the text several key references that might prove to be useful starting points for readers interested in the burgeoning literature on social change.

References

Blase, K. B., Fixsen, D. L., and Phillips, E. L. (1983). Residential treatment for troubled children: Developing service delivery systems. *In* S. Paine, T. Bellamy, and B. Wilcox (Eds.), *Human services that work: From innovation to standard practice.* Baltimore: Paul H. Brookes.

Boudon, R. (1986). *Theories of social change: A critical appraisal.* Berkeley: University of California.

Bronfenbrenner, U. (1979). *The ecology of human development: Experiments by nature and design.* Cambridge: Harvard University.

Chirot, D. (1986). *Social change in the modern era.* New York: Harcourt, Brace, Jovanovich.

Christopherson, E. R., Arnold, C. M., Hill, D. W., and Quilitch, H. R. (1972). The home point system: Token reinforcement procedures for application by parents of children with behavior problems. *Journal of Applied Behavior Analysis, 5,* 485–497.

Council on Social Work Education. (1982). *Curriculum policy for the master's degree and baccalaureate degree programs in social work education.* New York: Author.

Dumas, J. E. (1984). Interactional correlates of treatment outcome in behavioral parent training. *Journal of Consulting and Clinical Psychology, 52,* 946–954.

Fraser, M. W., and Haapala, D. A. (1987-88). Home-based family treatment: A quantitative-qualitative assessment. *Journal of Applied Social Sciences, 12,* 1–23.

Fraser, M. W., Lewis, R. E., and Norman, J. (1988). *Teaching research: The state of the art.* Manuscript submitted for publication.

Hisrich, R. D. (1986). *Entrepreneurship, intrapreneurship, and venture capital.* Lexington, MA: Lexington Books.

Joiner, C. W. (1987). *Leadership for change.* Cambridge: Ballinger.

Kinney, J. M., Madsen, B., Fleming, T., and Haapala, D. A. (1977). Homebuilders: Keeping families together. *Journal of Consulting and Clinical Psychology, 45,* 667–673.

Kinney, J. M., Haapala, D. A., Booth, C. L. and Leavitt, S. (in preparation). *Keeping families together.* New York: Aldine de Gruyter.

Kuhn, T. (1970). *The structure of scientific revolutions.* Chicago: University of Chicago.

Lewis, R. E. (1988). The characteristics of home-based services. *In* M. W. Fraser, P. J. Pecora, and D. A. Haapala (Eds.), *Families in crisis: Findings from the Family-Based Intensive Treatment Project.* Salt Lake City: University of Utah, Graduate School of Social Work, Social Research Institute, and Federal Way, WA: Behavioral Science Institute.

Patterson, G. R., and Reid, J. B. (1973). Intervention for families of aggressive boys: A replication study. *Behavioral Research and Therapy, 11,* 383–394.

Thomas, E. J. (1978). Generating innovation in social work: The paradigm of developmental research. *Journal of Social Service Research, 2,* 95–115.

Tornatzky, L. G., Fergus, E. O., Avellar, J. W., Fairweather, G. W., and Fleischer, M. (1980). *Innovation and social process.* New York: Pergamon.

Wahler, R. G., and Dumas, J. E. (1986). Maintenance factors in coercive mother-child interactions: The compliance and predictability hypotheses. *Journal of Applied Behavior Analysis, 19,* 13–22.

Whittaker, J. K., and Garbarino, J. (1983). *Social support networks: Informal helping in the human services.* New York: Aldine.

Withorn, A. (1984). *Serving the people: Social services and social change.* New York: Columbia University.

Chapter 10

Intensive Family Preservation Services: Broadening the Vision for Prevention

J. David Hawkins and Richard F. Catalano

Introduction

In 1984, over 1.5 million children in the United States were reported to be victims of child abuse and neglect, a figure ten times higher than the estimated 150,000 abused and neglected children reported in 1963 (Besharov, 1987). Generally, child protective services across the country have had only two options for responding to this burgeoning social problem: varying periods of home counseling by poorly trained caseworkers with large caseloads, or out-of-home placement of the child. All too often, the former services have failed to change the home environment of abuse or neglect, while out-of-home placement has been inappropriately used in cases that pose no immediate danger of serious or irreparable harm to the child, but rather hold the threat of cumulative effects of inadequate care (See Besharov, 1987). This lack of success has resulted in the current dilemma of child welfare: child protective agencies are under constant threat of legal suits for failure to adequately protect abused and neglected children. They are under pressure to do more, while at the same time, the costs of out-of-home placements are decried as fiscally unsustainable and socially unacceptable for large majorities of youths trapped in foster care limbo. Previous chapters in this volume have explored the Homebuilders model of intensive family preservation services as a promising solution to these problems faced by child welfare agencies across the United States. It appears that when implemented with fidelity, the Homebuilders approach can prevent imminent but unnecessary out-of-home placements of children whose families are in crisis, while increasing parents' skills and supports for raising children without inflicting serious or irreparable harm on them. This chapter examines implications of

179

this model for addressing related social problems beyond child abuse and neglect and explores the implications for human service education.

Research Background

During the 1980s, problems of teenage drug abuse, teen pregnancy, school dropout, academic failure, school misbehavior, delinquency, and teen suicide have emerged as major foci of social concern in the United States. Significant proportions of the next generation of American adults are at risk. While the death rate for most age groups has fallen consistently, the death rate for Americans age 15 to 24 has actually increased in recent years. Those concerned with the future of the society worry about the loss of human capital associated with illiteracy, crime, drug dependence, and suicide among our nation's youths. Attention has been focused increasingly on the small proportion of the youthful population (perhaps 6-10% of each birth cohort) who become chronically engaged in repeated serious problem behaviors (Wolfgang et al., 1972; Blumstein et al., 1985). Concern over chronic adolescent problem behaviors has been heightened by the apparent intractability of such patterns of behavior once established.

These considerations have led to a resurgence of policy interest in the prevention, as distinct from treatment, of adolescent problem behaviors and to serious investigation of promising and empirically supportable strategies by which the prevention of chronic, serious adolescent problem behaviors can be achieved.

The search for promising strategies for preventing adolescent problem behaviors has been informed by important research developments. Research in the past decade has shown that many adolescent problem behaviors, including school dropout and misbehavior, delinquency, problem drinking, drug abuse and precocious teenage sexual activity are linked empirically (Elliott and Morse, 1985; Elliott and Huizinga, 1984; Hawkins et al., 1987a; Jessor and Jessor, 1977; Osgood et al., 1988). Youths who engage in any one of these behaviors are likely to engage in several types of problem behavior during adolescence (Jessor and Jessor, 1984). A certain proportion of the adolescent population appears to be particularly prone to repeated problem behaviors of all types during adolescence. Different problem behaviors appear to be, in part, different behavioral manifestations of a general underlying proneness to problem behavior (Osgood et al., 1988). This is an important finding from a prevention perspective, because it suggests that a goal of prevention could be to reduce this general proneness to problem behavior in high-risk groups.

Risk-Focused Approach to Prevention

This suggestion raises the question: How can proneness to problem behavior be reduced? In public health, a similar question has been answered by adopting a risk-focused approach to prevention. Researchers have, for example, identified factors that increase the risk of heart disease—factors such as a diet high in fats, a family history of heart disease, a stressful lifestyle without adequate stress coping skills, and lack of exercise. They have designed and tested successful interventions to prevent heart disease by addressing those empirically derived risk factors.

This risk-focused approach can be applied to the prevention of adolescent problem behaviors. Interventions that address and reduce risk factors for adolescent problem behaviors should be effective for lowering the incidence and prevalence of these behaviors. An important research development of the last decade has been the identification of precursors or risk factors for adolescent problem behaviors. Research has shown that the same key factors are precursors or risk factors for different problem behaviors (Hawkins *et al.,* 1986, 1987a). These risk factors are summarized in Table 10.1.

Importantly, as shown in Table 10.1, several factors related to the family and its functioning have been found to be shared antecedents of teenage problem behaviors. Among these family risk factors for adolescent problem behavior are poor family management practices, as indicated by unclear and/or inconsistent expectations for children's behaviors, poor parental monitoring of children, and negligent or excessively severe and inconsistent discipline; high levels of conflict within the family; and extreme family disorganization as indicated by simultaneous entrapment in conditions of extreme poverty, poor housing, single parenthood, and low parental education, occupational, and social skills.

It is noteworthy that these family risk factors for delinquency and drug abuse are, in essence, the kinds of parental practices and family characteristics that characterize abusive and neglectful families. They are the specific family problems that appear to be at the core of family dysfunction which produces both out-of-home placement and children who are prone to antisocial behavior. The interrelationship of these factors is underscored by the results of recent analyses of the longitudinal data of the Cambridge Study in Delinquent Development, which revealed that separation from parents prior to the age of 10 is predictive of both an early onset of delinquent behavior and persistence in crime during early adulthood among delinquent males (Hawkins and Farrington, 1988). Family risk factors for removal from the family, delinquency, and other forms of antisocial behavior are clearly interrelated.

This knowledge suggests that interventions that successfully strengthen high-risk families—by improving parents' family management skills, reduc-

Table 10.1.   Risk Factors for High Rate Offending and Drug Abuse[a]

Risk factor	High rate delinquency	Drug abuse
Early variety and frequency of antisocial behavior (grades K–3)	X	X
Parent and sibling criminal and antisocial behavior	X	
Family history of alcoholism		X
Poor and inconsistent family management practices	X	X
Family conflict	X	X
Low bonding to family	X	X
Extreme family social and economic deprivation	X	X
School failure	X	X
Truancy	X	X
Low school bonding	X	X
Association with drug using and delinquent peers	X	X
Favorable attitudes toward antisocial behavior	X	X
Attitudes favorable to drug use		X
Alienation, rebelliousness, high tolerance of deviance	X	X
Low religious involvement	X	X
Frequent mobility	X	X
Neighborhood disorganization	X	
Constitutional and personality factors		
Low autonomic and central nervous system arousal	X	
Attention deficit disorder	X	
Cognitive deficits	X	
Sensation-seeking orientation		X
Early initiation of delinquent/drug using behavior	X	X

[a]Source: Hawkins et al. (1987a).

ing family conflict, and empowering multiply entrapped parents to overcome extreme family disorganization—hold promise for preventing teenage delinquency, drug abuse, and school misbehavior.

Intervention Strategies

Knowledge of the risk factors for adolescent problem behaviors provides clear definition of the goals that programs seeking to prevent those behaviors should address, but it does not identify the means by which those goals can be most effectively achieved. Two questions must be considered in assessing the promise of strategies for strengthening families in these ways. First is the obvious question of the efficacy of the strategy in actually improving parents' family management skills, in reducing family conflict, and/or in empowering parents to overcome or escape disorganized or entrapped circumstances. Second, and equally important, is the question of how those at highest risk can be reached with the intervention strategy.

In the fields of delinquency and drug abuse prevention, several strategies focused on the goal of strengthening families have been advocated and tested. The major interventions tested have been family counseling, parent training, and social casework. Social casework and insight-oriented family counseling approaches have generally failed to prevent delinquency (McCord, 1978; Robins, 1981). In contrast, interventions that have used social learning approaches to teach parents to use specific behavior management skills with their children have shown some short-term positive effects on children's behavior and on parent–child interactions (Baum and Forehand, 1981; Patterson *et al.*, 1982; Wahler and Dumas, 1987). In addition, behaviorally oriented family interventions that have taught parents specific skills in communication, social reinforcement, and contingency contracting have shown positive effects in reducing the delinquent behavior of children referred for minor offenses (Alexander and Parsons, 1973; Parsons and Alexander, 1973) and of their younger siblings (Klein *et al.*, 1977), when compared with controls.

Unfortunately, while showing some effectiveness in reducing childhood conduct problems, parent training programs have often encountered serious implementation problems. There is some evidence that parent training programs are disproportionately available to white rather than minority families nationwide (Hawkins and Salisbury, 1983) and that white, middle class, two parent families participate in parent training more readily than do minority low income single parents (Hawkins *et al.*, 1987b). Parent training strategies have typically required parents to attend group training sessions in a central location and have been plagued by problems of recruitment and attrition of participants (Fraser *et al.*, 1988). High dropout rates from parent training are common, and it appears that families experiencing disruption and disorganization are particularly difficult to enlist and maintain in parent training (Patterson, 1982; Wahler *et al.*, 1979). In short, group training in parenting skills may be most appropriate and successful with parents who are basically functionally adequate.

While the content of parent skills training may be particularly appropriate for families experiencing high levels of the family risk factors outlined above, parent training classes appear to have difficulty reaching, as well as changing, high-risk families. Effective techniques for reducing family risk factors for adolescent problem behaviors are becoming available, but effective strategies for making those techniques available to families at highest risk are needed. It is in this context that intensive family preservation services of the Homebuilders type are of interest for their potential for the prevention of adolescent problem behaviors.

Intensive Family Preservation Services: Characteristics and Potential for Problem Behavior Prevention

The combined characteristics of these services suggest their potential as an effective and implementable intervention with families whose children are at greatest risk for serious and persistent adolescent problem behaviors.

Providing Services in the Home

Perhaps the most striking characteristic of the intensive family preservation intervention is the provision of services in the natural environment of the family, usually the home. It is clear from previous studies that simply providing services in the home is not enough to prevent adolescent problem behaviors. In-home services were included in several previous delinquency prevention experiments—including the Cambridge-Somerville Youth Study (McCord, 1978) and the New York City Youth Board's validation study of the Glueck prediction table (Glueck and Glueck, 1950; Berleman, 1980)—which failed to prevent delinquency. Nevertheless, in-home service may be important in several specific ways to the success of interventions targeting identified family risk factors for adolescent antisocial behavior.

The first benefit of providing services in the home is that this facilitates accurate assessment both of the child and his or her potential for serious problem behavior, and of the nature and extent of risk factors in the family. Research has shown that the greater the variety, seriousness, and frequency of problem behaviors in early childhood, the greater the risk of serious persistent adolescent antisocial behavior (Loeber, 1982). In-home observation allows the therapist to adequately gauge the extent and seriousness of child misbehavior. Equally importantly, it allows in vivo assessment of family interaction, child management practices, degree of conflict in the family, and the extent of disorganization and entrapment.

Improved assessment is often aversive for client families when it requires them to complete forms or long structured interviews. The in-home assessment process of Homebuilders intensive family preservation services is designed to have the opposite effect. Visiting clients in crisis in their homes with the explicit message "I am here as a friend to help you get through this," makes it possible both to quickly access important diagnostic information and to strongly motivate clients to participate in the intervention. In-home services obviate the problems of recruitment and retention of high risk parents, which plague programs that seek to train parents in groups outside the home.

Finally, providing services in the home increases the probability of successfully teaching and learning specific family management skills when such skills are lacking in the family. By being present in the daily lives of clients for extended periods over the course of a month, Homebuilders therapists have the opportunity to take advantage of "teachable moments"—for example, when parents have expressed frustration with a child's behavior and willingness to learn a new technique for controlling it. Moreover, in-home training in the presence of the therapist provides an opportunity for supervised practice and corrective feedback for naturally occurring behavior. The ability to take advantage of teachable moments and in vivo training, practice, and feedback may enhance generalization of learning so that skills learned can be more easily applied in a variety of situations. It is possible that in vivo training in child management practices with corrective feedback in the home may result in rather rapid skills acquisition, especially where efforts to learn skills are followed quickly by desired changes in children's behaviors. However, studies have shown that skills training of longer duration is desirable for skills acquisition (Snow *et al.,* 1985), and decay of skills occurs rapidly in the absence of training or booster sessions (Hawkins *et al.,* 1988). While the Homebuilders program seems to be ideally suited to skill improvements in a short time frame, investigation of skills acquisition, generalization, and maintenance following intensive family preservation services is warranted.

Comprehensive Approach

The second characteristic that suggests the promise of intensive family preservation services for preventing adolescent antisocial behaviors is the comprehensive or noncategorical approach to the presenting problems of families. As noted by Nelson (this volume, Chapter 2), "family preservation workers are deliberately charged with a responsibility for recognizing and responding to a range of presenting needs." Families differ in the extent to which various risk factors for adolescent antisocial behavior are present. In some families, conflict between parents may be the major issue; in others, skills for parenting may be lacking; still other families may be struggling with extreme poverty and disorganization. Unfortunately, many families served by family preservation therapists experience multiple problems, though the combinations differ from family to family. Because the services of intensive family preservation are not categorically limited, therapists can tailor the intervention to address those risk factors most salient in each family. Concrete

services are provided to families in disorganized circumstances, while conflict reduction skills are taught to families where conflict is a major problem.

In seeking to provide what is missing, regardless of what it is, intensive family preservation services are conceptually quite similar to the traditional model of social casework. What appears to set the Homebuilders
model apart from social casework—as practiced in delinquency prevention
experiments such as the unsuccessful Cambridge–Somerville Youth Study
(Berleman, 1980; McCord, 1978)—is the application of specific, goal-driven
technologies to specific diagnosed problems identified collaboratively by the
family and therapist. In the Cambridge–Somerville model, delinquency was
to be prevented by a warm friendly adult serving as a role model and sticking
with a boy for a prolonged period of time (Berleman, 1980). In the Homebuilders model, therapists are expected to be warm and friendly, but this
simply provides the interpersonal foundation for the selection and application of specific technologies to address identified problems. Success requires
a high level of therapist skill both in assessment and in a whole battery of
intervention technologies that may need to be applied in different families.

This difference between intensive family preservation services and traditional social casework must be underscored. There is a risk that a noncategorical approach to family intervention will degenerate into empathetic
counseling or be taken as a warrant to apply the therapist's personally preferred theory or approach to the family. In a very time-limited intervention,
intensive family preservation services require the use of specific technologies
in response to specific identified problems. The Homebuilders group provides
line staff with training in 21 specific training modules, including "defusing,
engaging, and confronting clients; teaching skills to families; teaching families behavior management skills; teaching assertive skills to families; anger
management with families; teaching families problem solving skills; termination issues" and more (Kinney et al., this volume, Chapter 3). Each training
module includes instruction and supervised practice in a specific set of intervention skills identified as potentially useful in helping to address the
problems likely to be encountered in some dysfunctional families. This for-
malization and routinization of the intervention—not by applying a single
intervention technology to all families, but rather by training therapists to
assess what specific intervention modules may be of most immediate use
and teaching them the necessary skills to apply those interventions—is one
of the most important achievements of the Homebuilders group.

Brief Duration of Intervention

The brief intervention at a crisis point may hold promise for producing rapid
change in family relations. Families in crisis are often motivated to use the

service to avoid an out-of-home placement. Beyond that, the fact that the service will be available for only 30 days creates its own urgency. The implications of this time limit are clear: (1) the time to make change is now; (2) the success of the change will depend on the family's active involvement; and (3) long-term dependence on the therapist is simply not possible.

Again, a comparison to the Cambridge–Somerville Youth Study is instructive. In that delinquency prevention experiment, counselors visited families two to three times a month for an average of 5 years. Thirty years after the intervention, treated subjects actually fared worse than their randomly assigned control counterparts on several objective measures. Higher proportions of the treated children evidenced signs of alcoholism, serious mental illness, stress related disease, lower occupational prestige, and lower job satisfaction. These undesired and unanticipated outcomes may have resulted, in part, because the prolonged intervention created harmful dependence on the counselors. In discussing these findings, McCord (1978, pp. 288–289) cautions:

> Agency intervention may create dependency upon outside assistance. When this assistance is no longer available, the individual may experience symptoms of dependency and resentment. The treatment program may have generated such high expectations that subsequent experiences tended to produce symptoms of deprivation.

These two intervention approaches—Cambridge–Somerville Youth Study and Homebuilders—represent the ends of a continuum of length of service delivery. There are advantages of a 30-day provision of intensive services, and some clear disadvantages of providing less intensive services for a 5-year period. However, the literature on family services with high-risk families suggests that to be effective in reducing child conduct problems, skills training interventions need to be intensive but also of longer duration (Patterson and Fleischman, 1979; Patterson and Reid, 1973; Wahler, 1980). Experimentation with the length of intensive family preservation services for particularly high-risk families may yield important information on the relationship between length of service delivery and outcomes.

In summary, it appears that the Homebuilders group, in seeking to find an effective strategy for preventing out-of-home placements, has developed an intervention technology that holds promise for successfully preventing a variety of adolescent problem behaviors. From the perspective of risk-focused prevention, Homebuilders interventions address specific risk factors for adolescent antisocial behaviors and use principles of social learning to teach parents skills to more effectively manage their families. Although other parent training approaches have shown positive effects in reducing children's problem behaviors, problems of recruitment and retention of high risk parents in the training have been encountered. From an implementation perspective, the Homebuilders approach shows promise for reaching and retaining high risk families in an intensive intervention without creating long-term dependence.

Implications for Prevention, Policy, and Social Work Education

Three implications can be drawn. First, the Homebuilders model of intensive family preservation services is a strategy worth testing for its effect on preventing child and adolescent problem behaviors. To date, the model has not been subjected to experimental investigation which would allow its effectiveness in this regard to be assessed. While some evidence of the model's effectiveness in reducing out-of-home placements is available, the model should be evaluated for its broader effects on parents and children.

Evaluation studies should measure family risk factors for adolescent problem behaviors; assess parents' and children's baseline skills, behavior, and attitudes; and after the intervention is completed, assess parents' skills in key areas, such as family management and conflict containment, for evidence of skill acquisition, generalization, and maintenance. This would help demonstrate the efficacy of short-term intensive services in changing parents' skills and family risk factors. Finally, such an investigation should examine the efficacy of service in reducing the antisocial behaviors of children from families at different levels of risk.

Consideration of the promise of intensive family preservation services for preventing adolescent problem behaviors also suggests the importance of broadening the focus of policies and programs seeking to assist youth and families. In the same way that Homebuilders looks at the family as a whole, seeking to identify the specific needs and problems which should be addressed in order to avoid out-of-home placement, policy makers need to consider the problems of child welfare, delinquency, drug abuse, teenage parenthood, and teenage suicide as related phenomena. Although social programs continue to categorize individuals and families according to the particular problem the program has been funded to address, there is increasing evidence that the problems and characteristics of these individuals and families are similar across categories of service. A comprehensive family policy is needed to integrate the pieces of social programs and interventions into a coherent whole. The empirical base for such a policy exists in the emerging evidence regarding shared risk factors for adolescent problem behaviors. The policy's goal should be to reduce and eliminate these common risk factors while promoting the healthy social, cognitive, and personal development of children in families.

Finally, there are implications for the field of social work and for the education of human service workers. Over the past decade the goals of child welfare policy have been broadened. The emphasis has shifted from protecting children from inadequate parents by removing them from their families to protecting children in families at risk by assisting parents to adequately care for them. This shift signifies a major change in assumptions made about the family and in the conceptualization of social work services. In a model that emphasizes protection of children by removing them from inadequate families, children are the clients. Families are assumed to be adequate until proved otherwise. Social work is a residual service that protects children from inadequate families. In contrast, in a family preservation model, families are assumed to be doing the best they can under the circumstances they face. Social work services are focused on helping families to develop additional skills and to obtain the needed resources to meet basic standards of child care. Social work is no longer an intervention of last resort, but rather performs a mission of habilitation and education for parents. Social workers become educators and skill trainers—collaborators in a problem solving team rather than child therapists.

In this society we provide at public expense a basic education for all children in the skills required to function in the adult world of employment. We do not expect children to become functional employed adults until they have received a certain number of years of schooling. In contrast, we expect children to become functional parents without providing them any basic education in the skills required. The shift in child welfare policy toward an emphasis on family preservation and provision of the services needed to accomplish that goal indicates a change in this expectation. The shift implies that, for some parents, remedial education in family management, child rearing, and family conflict management is needed. Just as schools of education have trained the teachers who provide basic education, schools of social work must now train the human service workers who will provide remedial education to parents in family management and other skills needed to successfully rear their children. Part of this training must include instruction in the skills necessary to effectively intervene with high-risk families without creating dependence.

The growing emphasis on the prevention of child and adolescent problem behaviors which parallels the emphasis on prevention of out-of-home placement in child welfare services will also push social work in the directions outlined above. The curricula of schools of social work will be broadened to include training in prevention services for social workers. To the extent that this prevention training is based on a model of risk reduction, it will require that social workers learn to address the risk factors for adolescent problem behaviors including poor family management practices, high levels of family conflict, and extreme family disorganization. Social workers will need to be prepared to teach basic family management skills and basic conflict resolution skills to families in crisis. They will need to be prepared to assess and work with families in their homes if the highest risk families are to be reached, and they will need to learn to take advantage of strategic opportunities for teaching new skills without creating long-term dependence. The practice wisdom of those involved in intensive family preservation services provides a rich resource for those in schools of social work seeking to design human service education programs that prepare social workers for their expanding roles in prevention.

References

Alexander, J. F., and Parsons, B. V. (1973). Short-term behavioral intervention with delinquent families: Impact on family process and recidivism. *Journal of Abnormal Psychology, 81,* 219–225.

Baum, C., and Forehand, R. (1981). Long term follow-up assessment of parent training by use of multiple outcome measures. *Behavior Therapy, 12,* 643–652.

Berleman, W. C. (1980). *Juvenile delinquency prevention experiments: A review and analysis.* Washington, DC: U. S. Department of Justice, Office of Juvenile Justice and Delinquency Prevention, U. S. Government Printing Office.

Besharov, D. J. (1987). Giving the juvenile court a preschool education. In J. Q. Wilson and G. C. Loury (Eds.), *From children to citizens: Families, schools and delinquency prevention,* vol. 3, pp. 207–238. New York: Springer-Verlag.

Blumstein, A., Farrington, D. P., and Moitra, S. (1985). Delinquency careers: Innocents, desisters, and persisters. *In* M. Tonry and N. Morris (Eds.), *Crime and justice: An annual review of research,* Vol. 6, pp. 187–219. Chicago: University of Chicago.

Elliott, D. S., and Huizinga, D. (1984, April). *The relationship between delinquent behavior and ADM problems.* Paper presented at the ADAMHA/OJJDP State-of-the Art Research Conference on Juvenile Offenders with Serious Drug, Alcohol, and Mental Health Problems, Rockville, MD.

Elliott, D. S., and Morse, B. J. (1985). *Drug use, delinquency and sexual activity.* Paper presented at the NIDA Conference on Drug Abuse and Adolescent Sexual Activity, Pregnancy and Parenting, March. Bethesda, MD.

Fraser, M. W., Hawkins, J. D., and Howard, M. O. (1988). Parent training for delinquency prevention: A review. *Child and Youth Services.* 11(1), 93–125.

Glueck, S., and Glueck, E. (1950). *Unraveling juvenile delinquency.* Cambridge, MA: Harvard University.

Hawkins, J. D., and Farrington, D. P. (1988). *Prediction of participation, early and late onset, and desistance of officially recorded offending: The relevance of the social development model.* Unpublished manuscript, Cambridge University, Institute of Criminology, Cambridge, England.

Hawkins, J. D., and Salisbury, B. R. (1983). Delinquency prevention programs for minorities of color. *Social Work Research and Abstracts, 19,* 5–12.

Hawkins, J. D., Lishner, D. M., Catalano, R. F., and Howard, M. O. (1986). Childhood predictors of adolescent substance abuse: Toward an empirically grounded theory. *Journal of Children in Contemporary Society, 8,* 11–48.

Hawkins, J. D., Lishner, D. M., Jenson, J. M., and Catalano, R. F. (1987a). Delinquents and drugs: What the evidence suggests about prevention and treatment programming. *In* B. S. Brown and A. R. Mills (Eds.), *Youth at high risk for substance abuse.* Washington, DC: National Institute on Drug Abuse (ADM 87-1537).

Hawkins, J. D., Catalano, R. F., Jones, G., and Fine, D. N. (1987b). Delinquency prevention through parent training: Results and issues from work in progress. *In* J. Q. Wilson and G. C. Loury (Eds.), *From children to citizens: Families, schools and delinquency prevention,* vol. 3, pp. 186–204. New York: Springer-Verlag.

Hawkins, J. D., Catalano, R. F., Gillmore, M. R., and Wells, E. A. (1988). *Skills training for drug abusers: Generalization, maintenance, and effects on drug use.* Unpublished manuscript, University of Washington, School of Social Work, Seattle.

Jessor, R., and Jessor, S. L. (1977). *Problem behavior and psychosocial development: A longitudinal study of youth.* New York: Academic.

Jessor, R., and Jessor, S. L. (1984). Adolescence to young adulthood: A 12-year prospective study of problem behavior and psychosocial development. In S. A. Mednick, M. Harway, and K. M. Finello (Eds.), *Handbook of longitudinal research: Teenage and adult cohorts,* Vol. 2, pp. 34–61. New York: Praeger.

Klein, N. C., Alexander, J. F., and Parsons, B. V. (1977). Impact of family systems intervention on recidivism and sibling delinquency: A model of primary prevention and program evaluation. *Journal of Consulting and Clinical Psychology, 45,* 469–474.

Loeber, R. (1982). The stability of antisocial and delinquent child behavior: A review. *Child Development, 53,* 1431–1446.

McCord, Joan. (1978). A thirty-year follow-up of treatment effects. *American Psychologist, March,* 284–289.

Osgood, D. W., Johnston, L. D., O'Malley, P. M., and Bachman, J. G. (1988). The generality of deviance in late adolescence and early adulthood. *American Sociological Review, 53,* 81–93.

Parsons, B. V., and Alexander, J. F. (1973). Short-term family intervention: A therapy outcome study. *Journal of Consulting and Clinical Psychology, 41,* 195–201.

Patterson, G. R. (1982). *Coercive family process.* Eugene, OR: Castalia.

Patterson, G. R., and Fleischman, M. S. (1979). Maintenance of treatment effects: Some considerations concerning family systems and follow-up data. *Behavior Therapy, 10,* 168–183.

Patterson, G. R., and Reid, J. B. (1973). Intervention for families of aggressive boys: A replication study. *Behavior Research and Therapy, 11,* 383–394.

Patterson, G. R., Chamberlain, P., and Reid, J. B. (1982). A comparative evaluation of a parent training program. *Behavior Therapy, 13,* 638–650.

Robins, L. N. (1981). Epidemiological approaches to natural history research: Antisocial disorders in children. *Journal of the American Academy of Child Psychiatry, 20,* 566–580.

Snow, W. H., Gilchrist, L. D., and Schinke, S. P. (1985). A critique of progress in adolescent smoking prevention. *Children and Youth Services Review, 7,* 1–19.

Wahler, R. G. (1980). The insular mother: Her problems in parent-child treatment. *Journal of Applied Behavior Analysis, 13,* 207–219.

Wahler, R. G., and Dumas, J. E. (1987). Stimulus class determinants of mother-child coercive interchanges in multi-distressed families: Assessment and intervention. *In* J. D. Burchard and S. N. Burchard (Eds.), *Prevention of delinquent behavior,* Vol. X. Newbury Park, CA: Sage.

Wahler, R. G., Afton, A. D., and Fox, J. J. (1979). The multiply entrapped parent: Some new problems in parent training. *Education and Treatment of Children, 2,* 279–286.

Wolfgang, M., Figlio, R. M., and Sellin, T. (1972). *Delinquency in a birth cohort.* Chicago: University of Chicago.

Afterword

Elizabeth S. Cole

Now that you have finished this book, I hope you will conclude, that with all its limitations and complexities, barriers to implementation, and unresolved policy issues, Family Preservation Services must become an indispensable component of communities' aid to fracturing families. You may also believe as I do that, because of its clear conceptualization and accomplishment, the Homebuilders model will continue to be widely replicated and should be taught in human services education. This book should help in that instruction.

I find myself wanting to turn up the decibel level on certain points made by Brenda McGowan and implied in a number of other chapters. She reminds us to see as equally important the need to reduce the toxicity of the environment our families live in as well as to eliminate destructive interpersonal relationships. She also warns us not to allow a successful treatment of families' troubles to be passed off as an effective attack on the societal causes of these problems.

A perennial dilemma for social work professionals is how to discharge their obligation, outlined in the Code of Ethics, to assist the individual and family, while at the same time addressing negative environmental factors which bear on them. The need to be an advocate for social change, to link with advocates, or to otherwise see that advocacy is done is frequently ignored by practitioners, administrators, and boards. Their time and energy are given to the survival of their client families and of the agencies themselves.

There are warnings being voiced now that our poorest communities are becoming more depleted. Professionals and business people—positive role models—have left the ghettos. So have employers and industry. The concentration of crime, drug traders and users, and the inexorable rise in AIDS is isolating these communities farther from the mainstream of our society. It will take much more than a powerful therapeutic intervention to preserve the fragile, mostly minority families and children who live there.

The educator of current and future "family preservationists" will also need to imbue professionals with a commitment to participate in social change. They will need to give them practical examples of how a harried professional and administrator can discharge this obligation.

Therapists, practitioners, and administrators help strengthen families and thereby conserve our society. Advocates help make the quality of that society's life worth the effort to save it.

193

Author Index

Subject Index